LOST TRADITION
BOOK ONE

Sudden Dawn

FOLASADE FASORANTI

Dedication

This book is dedicated to the memory of my
grandmother Beatrice Atanyemi, who first told the story.
She was an intelligent and brilliant person who was
denied Western education because she was a woman.

ॐ

Acknowledgements

Great power of Almighty God

With gratitude to my family, Sola, Bamidele, Bolaji, and Kayode and to my friends Sarah, Diana, and Philip for their support over the years.

Prologue

Rolake stretched out both hands to pull Omotola off the mat. Reluctantly, Omotola gave her mother one hand and picked up her sleeping wrapper with the other. She stood up and snatched away her hand. She wrapped the sheet around her body like a shield.

Rolake smiled. "You don't need to take that along."

"I need to, Mama, just in case," Omotola hissed. "I hate Papa and his stupid parlor. I have to cover my body in case he descends on me with a *koboko* whip. At least, it will make it less painful."

"It is not about flogging, Sunshine. He just wants to talk to you."

"How do you know?" Omotola asked, looking edgy.

Rolake smiled. "As you wish, love," she said. "But hurry up."

Omotola wanted to cry. She was in undisclosed trouble. She noticed her mother's pleasant expression, though, as she tried to make light of her predicament. Rolake's smile meant nothing. They both knew that when Paul, her father, grew enraged and engulfed with insanity, five solid men could not stand in his way. He just turned into a manic beast.

One of two fates awaited Olorunfemi family members of who were summoned to Paul's parlor unexpectedly, that Omotola knew of. The two fates were never terrific: a thorough scolding, or a thorough flogging with a koboko whip. Paul specialized in tattooing an offender's body from neck to leg. Those marks she had seen on her mother's body a few days after she was reinstated back in primary school. Omotola avoided situations that would conjure her to Paul's parlor, to Paul's face.

In truth, this was Omotola's first summons to Paul's parlor, to face him one on one. She avoided trouble as much as she could, especially since she knew her schooling was folly to Paul; he could use any little mistake as an excuse to stop her. Despite sharing the same roof, apart from occasionally crossing each other's path once in a while, they were total strangers. Their weekday schedules were totally different. And on weekends, Paul was rarely at home, except to discipline offenders, a category Omotola had never fallen into.

Why would her mother be urging her to go to the revolting, terrorizing, hunting parlor of Paul? And worst of all, on Sunday at dawn. The ambient noises confirmed it was still morn, as the Muslims were chanting, urging people to come to the mosque for the morning prayers, and the Catholic bell was ringing endlessly for early mass. Not just any day, but Sunday morning, a resting, holy day!

Even though the day was breaking with brightness already, she would be dull and sad in a moment, Omotola concluded. She would have still had a long way to go with sleep that had just been terminated by Paul. She was terrified. Her head hammered big time, searching for the root of the problem....

Part One

$\mathcal{LR}$

Chapter One

Nigeria, Ibata-Itan, 1940, All Saints Primary School

Kola's heart filled with apprehension and fear as he stood waiting to register his sister Omotola in elementary school in Ibata-Itan. The school sat on the outskirts of town. Ibata-Itan lay between Ireti-Itan and Ajoni-Itan—within walking distance, for people with an aptitude for promenade. The town was one of the treasures of Itan Land, from its plump cocoa trees to the palm trees that produced the best palm wine in the world.

Kola was Omotola's half-brother. He knew the registration would bring a ton of issues, with a long time of pain for both of them and their mothers. But he had to do it. Otherwise, Omotola would be married off as soon as possible, since their father, Paul, gave not a hoot about education. The primitive jerk of a man would want to marry her out at a young age, just as he'd done with Kola's elder sisters. Kola hated the thought of Omotola meeting that fate, especially when she was so intelligent. She was just like him.

Kola knew that, out of all of Paul's children, Omotola was special. She could express herself well and mimic him like a parrot, compared to the other young ones who littered the house and surroundings. And it started a bond between the two of them. Omotola had always been happy to carry some of Kola's books as soon as he came back from school. She would sit as long as Kola could afford the time, asking questions about what he was learning. She sometimes pretended to read Kola's books. Her unexpected, acute curiosity about what went on within the four walls of the school, never getting bored, made Kola willing to teach her from an early age.

He encouraged and guided Omotola toward reading and learning. And it was paying off. Omotola could already recognize the entire alphabet. In a short time, not only could she recite all the letters and count to a hundred, but she could do arithmetic. She was more than a fast learner. She was a chameleon—she grabbed it all and blended it into her life. She had a photographic brain. She absorbed, "cloned," all that she was taught, from A to Z.

It takes one genius to know another! Kola could see that Omotola was a gifted girl. He was determined to do everything within his power to preserve her potential. Kola admired Omotola. He wanted her to follow in his footsteps despite knowing that home and school would be a tug-of-war for her. The nightmare rich kids from Hades in the school might dampen and dent her courage, but Kola was prepared for all of this. His greatest worry was Rolake, Omotola's mother. Would she be willing, like his mother, to sacrifice a lot for her daughter? He balled his fists, not knowing whether he could count on Rolake's courage.

He'd had his own issues in pursuing his education, almost beheading Paul before being left alone to attend school. At a tender age, he would have committed murder over the right to do so. Indeed, he would have killed Paul without hesitation. And that would have caused an uprising in the family, perhaps leading to more killing.… The scenario replayed in Kola's head, making him more uneasy as he stood with Omotola.

It was Kola's sixth week in elementary school, and the last thing he was expecting after several hours in school—six miles of trekking to and fro, a truckload of books painfully balanced on his head with both hands, home at seven p.m.—was Paul's rage. As Kola approached the house, he could see Paul pacing up and down in front of it like a lunatic. Concealed beneath his dashiki was a *koboko*. The whip peeked out from the garment, and Kola instinctively dodged beside the wall of their bungalow. "This is bad," he murmured to himself.

He knew Paul was waiting for him; he had always been the last one back home since starting school. If he had come home with the others, Paul would've been gone by now since they all shared the same earlier schedule. Normally, Paul came back from the farm at five p.m. He would turn up at his palm wine joint at six, not returning home until midnight or later. They never saw each other, not since Kola had started school. And it was seven p.m.

Paul was hanging around the entrance of the house, the coast of the front porch was as clear as a desert, and he ranted alone! Surely, all other family members were in hiding. Hell would break loose around him in a minute. This Kola could foresee.

Paul is about to go crazy. The indications—the usual signs the boy had known since he was small—were all there. He couldn't help but wonder: what is this all about?

His best guess was school. What else could it be?

Kola and so many other children heard about the school from the "come and go" reverends, fathers, and catechists who came to Ibata-Itan to convince parents of the importance of education. That had been four months earlier. He couldn't resist the advantages that Father George had enumerated: that if he chose to go to school and finished elementary school, he'd get a white-collar job. If he could go as far as finishing secondary school, he could obtain a scholarship to study a course of his choice abroad, and could come back to work in a high place in a company, or in what he called "government parastatals," in any town of his choice. Kola's mind had flown to Ladden then. It was a new beginning, a reimagining, a relief.

He was tired of tilling the ground from morning to evening. He was tired of cracking palms and handling hoes and cutlasses all day long. Instead of this routine occupation, he wanted to make headway toward another arena. He wanted to try something challenging, something new, and something that could better his life. He'd decided enough was enough with the farm. And he was among the few kids present from his background to start elementary school at All Saints Primary. Even though it was far away, at the edge of town, he loved school for what it promised him—well, he loved the activities in school, but he did not love the bullying from some of the students.

Kola's guess was accurate. He could hear his father's angry monologue while Paul paced back and forth as he cowered beside the house wall, peeping at him from time to time. He wanted to run, unsure where to go. But his greatest fear—the consequences for his mother, Adewumi, paralyzed him. If he ran, something might happen to her. Paul had a nasty habit of extending the punishment of a child to his mother. Kola knew he had to stay. He prayed that whatever came his way wouldn't involve her.

When would Paul leave him alone to follow his bliss? Kola wondered.

Twice, he'd had discussions about school with Paul. Both of those times, Kola had insisted on his decision. It was at dusk, the second week after school started, that he had his first talk with Paul. The rat bastards (his two half-brothers) had busted him, revealing his whereabouts to their father since he had failed to show up twice for the cultivation of yams. Paul had called Kola over to address the rumors that he had walked six miles to register at a school.

"What am I hearing, Kola?" Paul said angrily. "You want to forgo the farm for school?"

"Not like that, Papa," Kola had replied. "I went to see what school is all about and decided to try it out. But, I promise, I'll help out on weekends."

"You don't decide for yourself. I do," Paul said, tightly. "I want you to stop playing truant and do the work that was allocated to you at the farm tomorrow." His tone went soft. "Son, school is to enslave…"

Paul went on to relate why he hated school. His "once upon a time" sounded like a century ago to Kola. Paul had attended school, and so had his younger sister Sarah. Only, Sarah had had the nerve to stomach all that was inedible to Paul. And she had pursued what he called crap and what she called education until she had a certificate and "became their slave." But Sarah was a dunce, Paul elaborated. He wasn't.

The words Paul spat out were erratic; the school routines, values, regulations, doctrines, and ideology had been "irritating and bothersome." And, worst of all, they had wanted him to stay still for hours in noiseless classrooms that bored him to death. They had wanted him to imbibe and emulate the jargon preached, like a "Dumbo," Paul had said. At the end of all the dirt absorbed in school, he would have had to use his certificate to work for them as a servant. He added it all up, deciding that an African man was better on his own—free, not confined to jail, with handed-down rules.

Enumerating further, Paul had said that on the farm, he was a man of his own devising, with so many activities to dabble in. He could, as he said, "busy-body" with other boys of his age without anyone questioning his authority. In the afternoons, he could dictate what he had for lunch and when he wanted to eat it. He could smoke out rodents, sometimes go fishing. That, he said, was what makes a man: the power to choose for himself. Paul went on and on about the out-of-school advantages.

And at the second discussion about school that nearly ended in fiasco, Paul had added his father's point of view to buttress his own. Kola knew from Paul that his grandfather, Gbadamosi, a man Kola barely knew, had also had issues with school, and all that goes on within the four walls of what he called "jail." Paul had broadcast what Gbadamosi thought about it: that every Oyinbo man was really Simon Legree, even though they all pretended to be upright, proclaiming themselves righteous and bringers of good tidings. Their so-called colonization was meant to establish slavery, to steal the locals' labor and rule forever—thereby relegating African culture into the background. Africans were privately portrayed as dummies with dullard culture. And they praised their ranks as superior while turning African men into plants, watering them with their bullshit. To crown it, Gbadamosi said they were "whitewashed hooligan rogues."

"My father was right," Paul had said. "He was a man with integrity and culture, not a puppet. I left the godforsaken hole, and since then, Son, I've vowed that not a single member of this house will ever be a pauper. Kola, you are my son." Paul had pleading in his eyes. "I know what is best for you. Education is just a means to turn you into a slave. I allowed you to drift away to school as my father allowed me at first. I thought you'd see the light, be bored to death with the fatiguing routines, that you'd see the end result would turn you into a slave."

Paul drummed his own view and that of Gbadamosi into Kola, to try to reduce the boy's urge to go to school. But his words and cajoling had made no difference to Kola.

"Papa, I love school. I promise to help out at the farm on weekends and holidays," Kola had said firmly.

"No, Son!" Paul had shouted. "Foreign culture will never prevail in my house. Your schooling stops now."

"No, I'm going to school." Kola had folded his arms around his chest, telling his father that he had made his decision, and it was final.

"Well, Kola, since you've made up your mind to follow your doom without my knowledge," Paul had threatened angrily, "you'll have to cater for your schooling on your own. And life will be unbearable for you. Not a single penny of mine will help your lust."

That was the end of the conversation with Paul.

Afterward, Kola approached Adewumi, his mother, with his wishes. She'd promised to stand fast, in solidarity with Kola. She had been doing that since Paul first set forth his threats. So, what was new?

What was new was that even though Paul had refused to provide the essentials, that had made Adewumi run from pillar to post, draining herself to support Kola. Paul hated that they were, as he called it, "sailing without a hitch."

"Woman! You should support me and tell Kola to stop all his nonsense," Paul had yapped Adewumi. "Because if you don't convince him to want what I want, you'll see my wrath."

Adewumi didn't tell Kola about Paul's confrontations. She was Paul's second wife, a striking beauty whose pet name before her marriage had been *"Egbin."* She was elegant with an aura of gentleness. And it was understood that all she ever wanted was for peace to reign. She was ready to do anything, to sacrifice everything, to make her only son with Paul attain his aim in life.

Kola knew and understood there would be more pain to follow. But he would not let it bother him. He loved education. And so far, so good. He was okay with Paul not participating in it at all. He was okay with Paul's endless grumbling, backward and forward, about needing more macho hands on the farm. He tuned out the refrain that Oyinbo men brainwashed people like them—to erase their culture, blah, blah, blah…

"Needing more macho hands on the farm" ignited the new fire, making Paul rant like a lunatic while waiting for Kola. Apart from the fact that Paul hated everything about Oyinbo, Kola knew his father had another problem. Paul had mistakenly talked about it during one of his "lunatic parades," as Kola called the displays. He'd said that losing him to school meant a shortage of manpower on the farm, a risk he wasn't prepared to take. There would be serious consequences.

The problem was, Paul had few male children. He had six children by his first wife, Moji: four boys and two girls. His second wife, Adewumi, had given him four children: three girls and Kola. Paul's third wife, Rolake, had produced one child: Omotola. Rolake had had so many miscarriages. Yet, the last thing Kola would ever do was to compromise his own desire to satisfy Paul.

Paul had been ranting under the odan tree for longer than Kola imagined he was. He had been back from the farm since three o'clock, since Kola's two half-brothers had jointly complained (again) that they needed Kola's manpower on the farm if all the clearing and planting was to be done on time.

Paul had hung up his hoe and cutlass without washing the two, as he usually did, in Ara water, and without changing from his work clothes. He had come home, restlessly muttering like a loco until the rest of the family arrived at five p.m. Since then, everyone had been holed up in their rooms in fear.

Adewumi was crying her head off as if Kola were dead. Even John, Paul's drinking buddy, was surprised as Paul shouted like a hawker on the street, after he made him answer questions over and over again: Why wasn't the pain and stress working on Kola? Where did he go wrong? Why was it taking so long to break him?

"Probably time will do the trick," John said.

"I don't have the luxury of time," said Paul. "Today, he stops going to school."

John gave up and left.

For four hours, Paul had been pacing, ranting, and occasionally glaring at the small path that Kola trekked back home from school, becoming more and more agitated.

At last, Kola decided to come into view. He stood a few paces away from Paul, uncertain of what to do. Paul spotted him and charged toward him like a bull.

"Well, well, well!" Paul shouted, his voice ominously musical. "Look who's finally showing up at the house. *Mister Truant*, if you don't stop the nonsense of going to school, you're looking for my wrath. And I'll enjoy giving it to you and your mother unless you're at your allocated plot of land tomorrow."

"N-n-n-n-ooooooo, Papa," Kola cut in, stammering, showing how angry he himself now was.

Paul's tone became baleful. "No, Son; Adewumi has to talk sense to you or else—"

Kola cut in again. "No, there is nothing to talk about. I don't want to go to the farm. I love school." He gasped, and then controlled his breathing. "Leave my mother out of this. She has nothing to do with my going to school."

Kola refused to be scared. It was now or never. How much worse could it get?

Paul's mean face as he approached didn't deter Kola. He put both hands firmly on his head to steady the books and keep them from falling off, in case he had to escape. In fact, he was ready to leave Paul standing there, counting him as nonexistent, and enter the house. But he feared for his mother. Paul had mentioned her name already. For peace to reign, Kola bowed his head to avoid eye contact. Silently, he prayed to God for mercy, for the matter to slip away without him and Adewumi—getting thoroughly beaten.

"Kneel down!" roared Paul.

Kola did as he was told. Paul bent forward, shaking a finger in his face.

"Listen," Paul shouted. "I'm not going to repeat myself again. None of my household will ever be a slave to Oyinbo man. Get that into your brain, and be punctual on the farm tomorrow. You understand?"

"Papa," said Kola calmly, "as I've told you several times since we've been having this conversation, I'm not going back to farming. I want to attend school. I promise to help during the weekends and holidays. Please, Papa, please…"

"Never," Paul said, outraged. "If you insist on going to school, I will make life hell for you and for your mother. Adewumi, come out! Talk to your son!"

Adewumi rushed out of the house, looking frightened.

"Kneel down," Paul commanded.

She bent down on her knee like it was a log of wood, with a crack from her joints that could be heard in neighboring houses.

Kola was in fear of what he knew would follow. He was mad and lost the spirit of meekness. He stood up, backing off from Paul. He soccer-headed his books away from what was about to be a crime scene, yelling, "My mother has nothing to do with my going to school! Leave her out of this, Papa."

"She has a lot to do with your craziness," Paul said, enraged. "She'll share your punishment. She is your mother—she's supposed to have talked sense into your head, and since she hasn't done her job, she will share your pain."

Kola saw Paul remove the koboko whip from his armpit and saw the horror in his mother's face. He knew in seconds that Paul would whip her until she was paralyzed for the sin she hadn't committed.

"She never aids or abets!" shouted Kola. "It was my decision to run away from tedious work from dawn to dusk with a minimum profit in return. Not hers."

Kola ran into the house. He took one of the machetes Paul kept at the back of the main entrance door and ran out. He rushed to Paul's side as he bent towards Adewumi, reproaching and scolding her like a child. He held the machete with both hands, raising the blade up with the aim of bringing it down on Paul's neck. He was willing to cut Paul into pieces—send him to hell where he belonged. But he gave a final warning: "If you don't leave her alone, I swear I'll kill you."

Paul saw the machete above his neck. He shrank and retreated into a corner like a coward.

"You bastard, you want to kill me because of your lame mother? You'll both pay for this!" Paul roared. "When you find it hard to eat, you'll both stop your nonsense. As from today onward, Adewumi, I don't want you to step on your farmland. Find another means to support your dimwit son. I will make life hell for you and your dummy son."

Kola closed his eyes as the reality hit his brain that he was about to open yet another Pandora's box. *Registering Omotola in school is insane. Paul would go crazy,* Kola thought, regretfully. He needed to ask the secretary of the school what options were available to her.

* * *

Omotola was happy to stand next to Kola in the entrance of the building that helped him speak a foreign language—English—and learn new things. She was full of enthusiasm. Soon she'd be like Kola!

She looked through the pool of children getting ready for registration and saw a familiar face: Dupe Akindele. Omotola had seen her at the palace with her father, a man Kola described as very affluent. Kola had demonstrated his riches with his hands forming a globe, which made Omotola believe he was the wealthiest man in the whole world. She was dying to be Dupe's friend, to go to Dupe's house, since she'd first said hello to her in the palace, to which Dupe had replied with friendliness. Dupe's brother, Akin Akindele, had been at the palace the same day—another reason to want Dupe as a friend.

Omotola tugged one of Kola's sleeves to bring his attention to her. "Kola, Dupe is over there. I want to go and say hello."

"Go," Kola said, skeptical of her reception with the upper-class girl. "But be quick; we might be called in next."

She gave Kola an understanding nod and hurried over to Dupe.

"Dupe, I didn't know you were going to be registered in this school. Are you?" Omotola demanded in a bubbly voice. "Can we be friends, because I like you and…"

"Who are you, and where did you come from?" Dupe cut in, with a drop-dead look.

"We live in the same town, and…" Omotola said,

confused about the lack of recognition and the attitude.

"I don't know you. We can't be friends," Dupe said brusquely. "Get lost before other girls see you with me. Stinky-Shabby. That's right, that's your new name."

That's not true! I don't stink. Omotola knew for sure she didn't stink because she had taken her bath with a full pail of water in the bamboo bathroom at the back of her house. She had washed her mouth with a *pako* chewing stick. She had made Rolake plait her jet-black hair into a lovely all-back style the day before, and she wore the latest handmade gown. So, where did "stink and shabby" come from? She was confused about it all.

Omotola was speechless as her eyes dashed here and there, and she wondered what to do next since Kola was not in view. He had gone inside the building. She was on the brink of crying as she looked around the field. She felt envy. Most kids were beside their parents in what she called "splendor outfits."

Hers was a "degraded gown" compared to the other kids', despite it being the latest gown Rolake had made. It was handmade, woven cotton: *Kirijipa.* It was specifically for the forthcoming masquerade festival. She might get a rebuke if Rolake knew the dress was being worn before that day. Yet, Omotola had no shoes nor school bag like other children who were dressed smartly in well-tailored outfits plus trendy Cortina sandals from Bata. Omotola got more and more depressed as the parents and pupils stared at her, and as Dupe's voice sky-rocketed to shoo her away.

In the open field of All Saints Primary School, just Omotola and two other girls wore "shabby" dresses, compared to the rest of the girls' attire. They had the same local appearance, just like her—seeming lost, just like her—their eyes dashing here and there, waiting. To some external observer, it looked as if the school was carved out for the rich kids, but that wasn't so. Most of the illiterate parents didn't see the importance of education, while the more well-to-do viewed the future, not wanting their children to be left behind. Still, too many parents, like Paul, saw education as a *"threat to culture,"* and therefore not welcome.

In all respects, Omotola was a child with great potential to bloom into an A-1 woman later in life, even though she didn't grasp it. And, although she had no shoes, no school bag, and no posh adults next to her like most kids, she was a mouths-agape, upcoming black beauty: tall and slender, with a flawless face and body that gleamed to perfection.

Having fallen into a pit of insults from Dupe, Omotola regretted ever going over there. She should've stayed with Kola, like the other girls had, with their companions.

"That's rude," Dupe's nanny reprimanded her charge.

"Well, that's her problem. I didn't ask her to come over, anyway," Dupe shouted back at the woman.

Omotola stood in pain, unsure what to do. Some girls joined Dupe, and they started to chat about her.

"Who is that girl you were talking to, Dupe? And what is she wearing?" one of them called Ibukun, a longtime friend of Dupe, asked.

"A rice bag, perhaps? Her name is Stinky-Shabby," replied Dupe, smiling. "Oh, she is from my town. Her parents are as poor as church rats. By the way, she wants us to be friends. Can you believe that? "

"Friends? Is she crazy?" Ibukun asked, frowning at Omotola.

"Yes, she is. Stinky-Shabby-Crazy," Dupe said in a singsong voice. "That's better."

Her friends giggled.

"What is she doing here? Aren't the poor supposed to stay at home or go to a farm?" Dupe joked again.

Her friends giggled and repeated the awful nickname.

"I thought you said you didn't know her," Dupe's nanny said reproachfully. "You are one rude girl. I'm telling your father!"

Dupe ignored her comment and continued to laugh with her friends.

A rush of shame washed over Omotola's body completely, like that of smallpox, as the girls laughed uncontrollably and the people in the field stared.

Kola came out of the school secretary's office. One of the teachers called Omotola's name. It was their turn to go in for registration. Kola scanned the crowd for Omotola. Spotting her, he broke into a run as intensive laughter rolled out from the girls. He understood what was going on—that Omotola was their object of scorn as she stood there, unhappy. He had witnessed and experienced the same bullying when he had started school. He shot the girls a dirty look, fixed his eyes on Omotola's mortified gaze.

"C'mon, Sis. Let's go to the headmaster's office," Kola said loudly. "They're a bunch of stuffy kids with no brains. Pay no attention to them because soon, Sis, you'll make them cry!"

"I will?" Omotola asked, unconvinced.

"Yes, Omotola," Kola said earnestly. "You'll be better

than them in academics because all they'll think about will be fashion and stupid things. Trust me! I know what they are. I've confidence in you."

Slowly, Omotola walked beside Kola to the headmistress's office. They entered a classroom where four nuns sat, looking friendly. Omotola relaxed a bit as Sister Anne, the headmistress, introduced herself. Kola introduced Omotola to them.

"Omotola, please touch your left ear with your right hand as I demonstrate."

Sister Anne stretched her right hand to touch her left ear. It was the first measuring tool to start elementary school. It had to be, since only a few of the children the nuns had met since starting the registration in the school had birth certificates. The minimum age to start elementary school was six. Omotola had a problem with that exercise, as her right hand couldn't reach her left ear.

"Little girl," said Sister Anne, smiling. "I'm grateful you've come this year, but you're too young to start Primary One unless you have a birth certificate to prove your age. Kola, do you have that?"

"No, I don't," Kola said pensively. "I'm sure I can't get it, either. Our father didn't go to the local council to register Omotola and get the certificate. Please… I'm sure she is up to the age of schooling. Please register her."

"I wish I could, Kola, but she doesn't meet the requirement," Sister Anne replied. "I'm afraid she has to try next year. I'm sure by then she'll be able to reach her left ear with her right hand."

"Please, Sister Anne, my sister is old enough to start school!" Kola sobbed, and Omotola joined in. "You don't understand. Please, Sister, I beg you in the name of God."

"Kola, you don't have to do that," the Sister said, baffled. "Look, your sister is upset, too. The reason we have to make the children perform this simple task is to be sure they are old enough. Toilet trained. Then they won't soil themselves in school, since they have to sit in the classroom for hours. We don't want children who need to go to the bathroom and can't wait to soil themselves instead. Please understand, she'll be welcome next year."

"I promise, she is toilet trained and very intelligent," Kola said, nodding at his sister, "Omotola, recite the alphabet for Sister Anne to convince her you're mature enough to handle Primary One."

Like a waterfall gushing nonstop, Omotola started to recite the alphabet. She finished, jumping into numbers until she had almost counted to a thousand.

Astonished, Sister Anne gently tapped her on the shoulder. "You can stop now, little girl," she said, impressed. "Blessed be the almighty God. You have God's blessing to start Primary One, even though you might be underage. Go over there with Sister Teresa and register."

Sister Anne beamed, as did Sister Teresa, who sat at the table next to her with a long, flat booklet.

"Thank you, *ma*," Omotola replied. Kola had taught her to say *ma,* which stands for "madam" in Yoruba land.

The nuns and the teacher in All Saints Primary School were proud of the young child's accomplishment, so, gallantly, she enrolled.

"I can do some arithmetic exercises if you want, Sisters," Omotola said.

Sister Teresa abandoned her post to the woman next to her. She walked Omotola to a corner and gave her some equations to figure. The nun watched closely as Omotola answered the addition exercise correctly within a snap of the fingers.

"Omotola," she said, "you're one of the most gifted little girls I've seen in my career, here and in Britain! I'm glad you are going to attend school."

She gave Omotola a complimentary slate board and a set of colored chalk. At that moment, Omotola could have died a happy girl, as she tingled throughout her body.

As the day finally came to an end, the scary part began—going home. Kola and Omotola were in torment. Both sat on the path, a few yards away from the house. They could see its roof, debating, rehearsing how to go about breaking the news to Rolake, who was standing on the front porch as if waiting for them.

Omotola reflected—it was one thing to shine like a star in school, loved by all the teachers. And they wanted you to start school in a jiffy. But it would be another thing when the house they were about to enter might strip off all the sparkles. They were both depressed. Eventually, after minutes of deliberation, they decided Kola would be the one to explain their expedition in detail to Rolake.

Chapter Two

Christopher Akinrinola Akindele ("Akin"), heir to the Akdrend group of companies worldwide, was also a student of All Saints Primary School. He came from his class to join his sister Dupe for a ride home to Ibata-Itan. It was Dupe's first school day. Their ride was ready and waiting for them—a Mercedes Benz. The driver held the door open for them near the exit of the school. Akin was as happy as Dupe, who bubbled toward him with a friend tagging behind.

"How was your first day, Dupe?"

"It was good. You were right. I didn't need to panic that I won't make friends. Ibukun chose my school too." Dupe smiled, making introductions. "This is my brother Akin, and this is my best friend in the whole world, Ibukun."

"It's nice to meet you, Ibukun," Akin said, happy that Dupe's anxiety had gone with the wind.

"My sister is in the same class as you," Ibukun said. "Her name is Bola Rawa."

Akin knew Bola. They were in the same class in Elementary Three. He knew, as well, that her parents from Itan Land aristocrat families, from which his father also came. But Akin hated girls whose parents were members of the club. They had the kind of attitude that pissed him off. Even though Bola was honestly a beauty, with a European-influenced sophistication inside and out, she meant nothing to Akin, like many of her kind.

Christopher Akinrinola Akindele had the world at his feet. He could afford to make grievous mistakes that wouldn't make a difference to his life. Simon, his father, was the richest man in West Africa, a raw material exporter who could make any difficulty go away. Simon appeared in newspapers all over Nigeria, which had nicknamed him "King Solomon of Africa" for his wealth and his collection of women.

Akin was a cute boy who made the hearts of girls skip a beat at any given time, but he was a snob. The son of Simon's first wife, Joyce, Akin was tall with a toned body. His eyes were a hazelnut color, his expression determined in a sexy, scrutinizing scan when giving anybody an audience. He was a reserved boy who rarely laughed or got close to people. That made starting a conversation with him an uneasy task. To most people, Akin seemed pompous and self-centered. He had no friends, unlike his half-brother Olu, the first son of the second wife, Arinola. Olu was not bad-looking at all, but the opposite of Akin in his behavior. Olu was charming, popular, and had lots of girlfriends, even though both boys' voices had not yet broken. Olu displayed a lot of father-son tendencies. He would take after their father in his lifestyle. Indulging in girls, however, was not Akin's style. All he ever wanted was to be a great brother to Dupe since their mother had run away, and to create, build, be somebody out of his own sweat.

"Oh, Bola!" Akin said, irked. "She is your sister. I didn't know that."

Bola was within earshot. "Hey, Akin," Bola said, giddily skipping toward them to seize the chance to talk to him. She rushed over to Akin's side, rolling her eyes seductively. "It's great to see you here. I didn't know your sister was starting primary school in our school. I'm happy they are friends and we—"

"It's good talking to you, Bola," Akin cut in. "But we have to go."

Dupe waved to Ibukun and Bola as Akin took her other hand, and he walked her quickly toward their ride.

Dupe cast a second glance at the two girls, still staring after them. "I think Ibukun's sister likes you," she told her brother.

"Well, I don't like her," Akin said firmly.

Chapter Three

Rolake sighed aloud. She was burning with anger as she spotted Kola and Omotola dragging their feet coming home. She'd searched for more than two hours for her only daughter, Omotola, until a woman told her that she had seen her with Kola near her farm, going toward the outskirts of the town. Worried and distressed, Rolake came back home and stood in front of the bungalow, the Olorunfemi's den, and waited—folding her arms over her chest most of the time, eyeballs zooming around, consumed with the pain of losing track of her only child.

"Where in the name of God did she go with Kola?" she'd asked herself over and over. And hot streams of tears had dripped while Kola and Omotola were hiding, scared of going home to tell about their escapade at the school. They had sat, hiding in a bush path, just a few yards away from their house, feeling miserable—until it started getting dark, and they had no choice but to go home.

The bungalow of the Olorunfemi family was built with red clay bricks. Its exterior had never seen the smoothness of cement. The eight crappy rooms inside the bungalow had such wide splits in their cheap, fuzzy plaster walls that the lizards and larger animals could crawl through to say, "Hello!" or, "Catch me if you can, I'm biting your ass! It was not an easy place to live.

Rolake could have been pretty if circumstances in her life hadn't weighed her down, showing on her features. Her average height and impressive body were promising, but they were spoiled by a rag face that looked like a well-used cloth. Rolake had been forced to marry a man she didn't love, and she'd endured successive stillbirths and miscarriages until Omotola came along and the vessels sealed again. She still had nightmares that she might be childless, and as a result, Omotola was always tied to her apron strings. In all senses of the word, Rolake over-protected her only child. Until today—Rolake was still sleeping when Omotola got herself dressed for school and left with Kola. It was Kola's master plan. He knew Rolake would object.

"Follow me, Tola. Kola, you can go," Rolake said, her expression marred with worry.

"Yes, Mama. I'm in trouble, Mama?" Omotola asked with a puppy face.

"Yes, you are in big trouble." Rolake's voice softened a bit, even though she had promised herself she would shout at the top of her lungs to make Omotola understand how upset she had been since the morning. "But how did you know already?"

"Mama, you only call me "Tola," not "Sunshine," when I've done something wrong. And I'm sorry if I've done something wrong, Mama."

Omotola followed Rolake inside the bedroom, with the gifts given to her hidden with one hand behind her back. Kola walked alongside, ignoring his dismissal.

"Where have you been, Omotola?" asked Rolake, staring at the girl, searching for answers.

Omotola stared at the ground, while Kola's eyes ran around the room, avoiding Rolake's scrutiny.

"Omotola, I asked where you have been!" Rolake shouted.

Omotola's voice trembled. "Mama, I was with Kola."

"Doing what?" Rolake demanded in confusion. "Kola is supposed to be in school, not strolling to another town with you." Slowly and deliberately, she added, "You know, Tola, your disappearances will one day give me a stroke, and I might die prematurely."

At this, Omotola was horrified. She looked at Kola, who had promised to lead, standing speechless.

"Do I tell her, or do you do the telling now, Kola?" she said.

"Tell me what? Speak, or I'm reporting both of you to your father." Rolake threatened.

But it was a bluff. She wouldn't go so far as to report her only child to a man who disciplined without common sense. Paul would tattoo her with a whip if her mother dared tell him. It worked, though.

Omotola squawked, looking as terrified as ever. "Tell her now, Kola!" she ordered.

"I registered Omotola at my school to start Primary One," Kola said, scared of Rolake's reaction.

"Mama, I'm starting school. I was tested by the teachers, and they were impressed, even though I couldn't touch my left ear with my right hand. And a teacher gave me all these."

Omotola showed the slate board and the chalk she had been hiding behind her back to Rolake. She was excited, expecting her mother to take a look at her gifts, but Rolake was nervous, close to tears. She flipped both hands to cover her mouth. Omotola watched her curiously.

"She has been practicing all the exercises for Primary One at home with me. She is way ahead of her class when tested. And as a compliment, a teacher gave her some presents."

"Omotola," Rolake said dejectedly. "I don't know what to say about your excellent performance in school, but I know this much for a fact: I mustn't encourage your schooling, even though I stay in wonderment of your … articulation and intelligence at your age! Sunshine, I'm not surprised they want you to start school, but schooling is off-limits for you. You'll never be allowed; your father will refuse." Rolake turned to Kola. "I know you mean well for your sister, but your father is the issue. He'll be insane. You know what that means, Kola. You do know what he did to your mother?"

"I know, ma," Kola replied, but continued, full of hope. "I was a victim. But I have a perfect solution to keep Papa in the dark until it's too late for him to stop Omotola. Elementary school is tuition-free, except for uniform and lunch. Since the sisters like her, they will do everything it takes to keep her in school until she is old enough to choose what she likes. And if Papa does anything stupid, tries to stop her, he can be jailed. I think that's why he's left me alone. I've asked the secretary of the school about all of this before I enrolled her." Kola smiled, happy that he had spoken to the secretary today while Omotola met Dupe on the field. "She can apply for a scholarship in secondary school. And all will be taken care of by the government. Please let her go to school. She is a bright girl, and I promise to take good care of her."

Omotola and Kola both stared at Rolake with puppy faces.

"All right, I'll agree," Rolake said reluctantly. "But let's keep it a secret between us. Thanks a lot, Kola. You've been the best brother to Omotola."

"It's my pleasure, ma," Kola replied with glee.

* * *

A few years back, it had been Omotola's seventh day on earth, her christening. Rolake had observed Jacob, a friend of Paul—the same age, the same crappy lifestyle up the hill—helping with the preparations for the christening. He was performing the role of a groom, a suitor. Rolake had felt sick in her guts. As the day drew to a close, when all the visitors were gone, she had felt a sharp pain down her abdomen, probably because of what she was about to find out from Paul. She had gently knocked at Paul's bedroom door. He hadn't answered the knock, but she knew he was inside. She knew that his other wife might be inside with him, and she knew she could be in a lot of trouble if she entered without his consent. But she had damned all consequences and had entered. Paul was on a mattress, eyes fixed on the ceiling.

"I'm sorry, *Aba*, to interrupt you." Rolake had said, her voice shaking. "I knocked, but you didn't answer, and that's why I came in."

"When you knocked and I didn't answer, what does that tell you?" Paul said rudely as he sat up. "I don't need you tonight. This is Moji's night. I'll call you when I want you."

"I'm not here for that," Rolake said. "I just want to know why Aba Jacob is playing a suitor role at my daughter's naming ceremony."

"Don't ask me questions, woman," Paul roared. "Go back to your room."

"You sold her, didn't you?" Rolake snapped, irritated. "How could you? How? The daughter you scorned immediately when she took her first breaths. I was there, Paul. I saw the hatred in your face as you poked your head inside my room. *Another female child, you women are a disgrace!*" Those were your words to your newborn child. You never acknowledged her, and now you've sold her to the highest bidder. How could you?"

Rolake was hysterical.

"It's none of your business who I marry my daughters to! Get out before you see my wrath."

"Show me your wrath, because I'm ready to die."

Paul stood up, perhaps intent on hitting Rolake until tender, because that was usually the case with him when a wife dared run her mouth off, as Rolake had just done. But, instead, he lifted Rolake from the ground in a rush, threw her into the corridor, then closed his door.

The action was strange. It may have been due to Rolake's condition, having just given birth, or because he refused to harm the mother of his profitable child. He still needed men to come forward to marry two more of his daughters and may not have wanted to scare any off. Who knew what was up with crazy Paul?

"It's not over. You can't sell my child to a man who is crazy like you…" Rolake ranted as she crawled back into her room in extreme abdominal pain. Half passed out, half alive, she managed to grab one of the *oke* baskets in the corner of her room and eat *agunje,* a medicine. She wobbled over to her daughter, who was sleeping like an angel. Rolake wept. "I'm sorry to bring you into this world...."

$\mathcal{P}$

Chapter Four

"Where is Omotola?" Paul exploded.

A few days had passed since Omotola had started primary school. That day, the sun was at its best, and Rolake was doing chores in her bedroom when Paul came back.

Paul had gone early to the farm with some of the family and was due back around five. With his sudden appearance in her room, Rolake knew straightaway that trouble was hovering in a corner. She knew that whatever had brought him back home when he should have reached his farm must be critical. She was so frightened that the calabash cup full of water in her hands dropped to the floor, shattering into pieces. It left the bare floor drenched and muddy. She started to pray in her head for God to help her, to restrain Paul from beating the hell out of her. Dejectedly, she followed Paul into his parlor as he demanded.

"I sent her on an errand … to my mother's house … due back any … now…" Rolake's words were incoherent.

"What is the rubbish I heard about Omotola attending school?" Paul glared.

Rolake shook her head to say, "No."

"It better be "no," or else," Paul said, giving a hard stare. "She is engaged to my friend Jacob. And of what importance is education going to be for her in the long run?" Without waiting for Rolake to reply, he roared on like a wounded lion. "This nonsense must stop right away, or else both of you will get my wrath. Get your daughter to know the culture, what is expected of her in her husband's house, or else she'll face the consequence of an untrained child who becomes a wife. You know what that is? Booted out of matrimonial home. And, get this—if it happens, she is not coming back here. Instruct your daughter, woman!"

After a few months of her existence in the hell hole of living with Paul, Rolake had understood not to speak when Paul talked in a rage and glared like a beast. If she interrupted, he would simply let the rage fall on her, and he would beat the crap out of her. That had happened a lot before. Instead, she fixed her gaze on the old calendar, battered from years of hanging on the wall. She knew she had one solution—stop Omotola's schooling right away and never confirm the obvious to Paul.

As she looked at the calendar, she concentrated inwardly on how to break the news to her daughter without destroying her hope in life. She felt like crying, felt her own hope burst out like a gourd full of water suddenly dropping on the floor. But what was the good of education anyway? How would it help? It could never help, but it could provoke a deadly beating by Paul. She knew that, as she knew she couldn't run away. Rolake's frustration mounted; she had no options. No place would harbor her and her daughter. Her parents wouldn't take her back. Paul held all the cards, and for crying out aloud,

Omotola didn't belong to her; she belonged to Paul. He could do as he wanted with her. He owned her. Rolake had grasped that as well, a long time ago.

A weakness spread through her body as she got lost in her own thoughts, while Paul threatened consequences. His ranting went on for what seemed a lifetime, and finally, he stormed out and slammed the door shut.

Rolake's legs wobbled and unexpectedly gave way underneath her body. Her butt slammed to the floor, and she lost consciousness. She was out cold for a long time, and finally woke up feeling dizzy. After a few minutes, everything that had happened came back to her. Not a single shred was left out. She lost herself in weeping in the cold, dark parlor until the stream of tears dried in her head. She knew for certain that Omotola must stop school immediately, or else. Rolake pulled her hair tight as the reality of what would happen to her only child hit her. "Omotola will be among the long-faced women of the town soon."

She hated the crazy local laws—that mothers should be irrelevant, always in the dark, especially when it came to making decisions about their children, despite hours in painful labor, bringing them into the world and nurturing them. For merely a break of sweat and a shed of sperm, in under five minutes, a father gained the power of God, whether a mother liked it or not. And he had the heavenly power to choose a partner for their children, whether they liked it or not. Women were just vessels to convey children into the world, and all the power and law over children belonged to the father. How was that fair? Rolake felt devastated.

She knew she had no choice but to sort out the future

of her only child herself. She decided she needed to walk half a mile away to have a tête-à-tête with her daughter, in case Omotola threw a tantrum. She wanted them to be far from the snooping, prying eyes in Paul's household, those who might arrive soon, one after another, from the farm. Far away, especially, from Moji—Paul's first wife—and her battalion of good-for-nothings. With two of her sons as crazy as Paul, Rolake avoided the lot of them like the plague. She bet ten to one that one of them was the architect of her present headache.

She picked herself up slowly from the ground, still feeling dizzy, and dusted off her work clothes instead of changing into something fresh. She didn't have the stamina. She felt it, deep down, and knew she was supposed to take a break and rest. Wildly afraid, though, she thought Paul might not go away and then find Omotola. The problem was that Omotola couldn't lie, and that would put her at a rotten disadvantage.

Rolake staggered down the road to the school, waiting in hiding for one hour in the bush, in the full blaze of the sun, listening to the noises of the animals. She was bitten once in a while by who knew what. She made no effort to defend herself. Her personal fear was so great that she had none left for the wild animals that roared from time to time, that might wander from the forest and devour her in an instant. That had happened to others before. Rolake was in more pain than anybody could imagine. In fact, being poisoned or killed would be a blessing in disguise, she thought. At least she would leave the world. She would meet her maker and shout, *"Why did you create me to suffer?"* That was one of the things she thought about as she waited.

She moved closer to the path she knew Kola and Omotola would use—a route they would walk on alone because others would use it much later as the sun was setting, as dusk arrived, as they finished the day's work at the farm and came back to town to rest—except for the faint-hearted, the lazy, and the idle.

Rolake kept her vigil, sitting on shrubs, with her head in both hands as if in mourning, massive amounts of sweat running like a river over her body, until she heard voices she recognized just a few steps away. She lifted her head and caught sight of Omotola and Kola walking side by side. Omotola held her slate and chalk box firmly with her left hand, while Kola held all his books on his left arm. Rolake could see that even though they weren't born to the same mother, they had a lot more in common than most children in Paul's household.

She wanted to stand up and be visible, but their discussion restrained her, so she eavesdropped.

"Omotola, at a point close to home," Kola said, "you have to walk faster than me, and as soon as you get home, hide your school materials. It seems the rats are sniffing around."

Omotola stopped walking, and Kola did the same. She looked up at Kola with all the innocence a child's face could possess.

"Why can't we walk home as we used to do? And what do you mean by 'sniff around,' Kola?"

"Never mind that," Kola said forlornly. "Just understand that, at a particular place, I'll tell you okay: then run or walk as fast as you can, far away from me. And as soon as you get home, do what I told you. If anyone asks where you've been, just tell them that you've been to your grandparents' house. I don't want Papa to find out that you've been to school yet. And as for me, if anyone asks if you've been with me, I'll say no."

"But that's lying!"

"Do as I told you, okay?" Kola snapped. "Until I can figure out something else."

Rolake could see her daughter was confused, because Omotola hated to lie. Sadness was written all over Kola's face. It didn't matter anymore—the coaching, the lies. Rolake closed her eyes from seeing so much pain between the two of them. She knew it was going to get worse in minutes, and she opened them as Omotola screamed.

"Mama! What are you doing in the bushes?"

"Where is she?"

"There!"

Omotola pointed and ran toward Rolake. Kola followed with his books jiggling about on his left arm, desperately trying to stabilize them with his right hand.

Rolake wrapped her hands around Omotola and managed to beam at Kola.

"Thank you for walking her home," she said.

"It's my pleasure, ma."

"I'd like you to go home, Kola. There is a place I would like to show Omotola."

Rolake could see fatigue and reluctance on Kola's face, and it seemed that he wanted to ask a question.

He appeared to change his mind and said, "See both of you later at home."

She had to take Omotola away from Kola with a lie. They would join him and fill in the details later. She wouldn't be able to cope with the two of them throwing a fit at the same time, she'd concluded.

Rolake continued to hold tight to Omotola as she watched Kola disappear toward home. *A remarkable young man* was the thought that crossed her mind. She knew he was noble and gracious, just like his mother—different from all of Paul's other ill-fitting, good-for-nothing sons and daughters, who lived and breathed their father's craziness. It was like a curse, behaving in the same repugnant manner as Paul. Even his newly wedded son's wife had been terrified and full of complaints since the day of the wedding, not even one year ago.

"Mama, why do people sniff around like rats?"

Gently, Rolake released Omotola from her embrace, even though she would have preferred hugging her until the end of the world, until the end of time. It would save both of them from the inevitable talk—and the need to protect her little girl from the crazy world.

"Well, Omotola, it's an expression that means people are trying desperately to know something."

"Oh!" Omotola gasped, face wider. "Kola must be talking about yesterday when we came back from school, then. The second daughter of Mama Moji coughed under the odan tree where she was sitting. It seemed deliberate, as we were about to climb the stairs to the house. And we both whirled round in surprise to face her."

Omotola, panting, swallowed some saliva and continued. "Kola asked me to run inside the house, and I did. You know, Mama, Auntie was shouting at Kola. I could hear them as I was hiding behind the door. Auntie said, in a rage, *Where did you take Omotola to—school?*" And Kola said, *"No, I met her on her way back from her grandparents' house."* Auntie said, *"Omotola's grandparents' house wasn't on the way to the farm; you're a liar."* Kola said,

"Fine, think I'm a liar then. It's none of your business anyway." Auntie said: *"It will soon be, liar!"* Kola walked away and just ignored her, but she wouldn't stop. Mama … she sounded really crazy."

Omotola looked sad.

"It's okay, Omotola, nobody will insult anybody over going to school anymore. It's over. And the reason is…" Rolake's voice trailed off.

Rolake wasn't surprised her assumption had been right, but such is life in a polygamous house. "Someone is always out there to stir up trouble in your life, even though you've done nothing wrong. It's because they're miserable, and they want company."

"Mama, where are we going?" Omotola brightened up a bit.

"That will be later, honey. But first, I have something to tell you."

Rolake motioned Omotola to sit on the grass. Calmly, she did so and placed her slate and chalks next to herself. Rolake sat opposite her. The little girl was all ears, with steady eyes fixed on her mother. Her attentiveness, without a yawn of tiredness, with her eyes vivid and intense, made Rolake feel guilty to the core. These observations burned all the courage in her. She turned her face away in a hurry, making a great effort not to cry.

There was a long silence until Omotola broke it.

"Mama, why do you want to talk to me in the bush rather than in the house?" Omotola asked, concern on her face. Since Rolake had fallen silent, she added, "Is it because of where we're going?"

Rolake stared at her, confused about where to start. She admired her daughter's fortitude—the willpower to commute for hours from home to school, five days a week, come sun, come rain, all because she wanted to learn.

She dropped her head with that realization echoing in her brain. *You are about to disrupt that determination, that dream. In minutes, you'll make her as vulnerable as you are and give her a pathetic life, like yours. You are about to crush her aspirations and throw her into a dungeon where she won't be able to think for herself anymore. You are as worthless as Paul, probably worse than Paul....*

Rolake couldn't talk. She continued to look at the ground like a coward, fidgeting with the cuffs of her *buba*. The echoes were a hundred percent right. She knew the culture as well as she knew her name. She understood the absurd truth of their culture, the other side of midnight that might eventually follow the illogical wedding. Once again, she wished the bank of heaven would open up, envelop her in it. She wished the ground would open up, swallow her, to cover her agony before she had to relate the distorted news from hell to her daughter that would state:

"Daughter, your insane father wants you to give up your dream. Daughter, soon you'll be given to the highest bidder as a wife, irrespective of your age difference, irrespective of whether you're not in love with the dirty ball, irrespective of whether he has a number of wives, irrespective of whether you're too young to understand the world around you, or what marriage means. And daughter, as young as you are, you must understand that you must suppress all your desires and do everything to please your husband. If you refuse to do his bidding, he can beat the life out of you. Or, if you give in, he will shape and mold you into what he wants...."

She felt like a destroyer, a murderer, and a killer. She

gasped aloud. Omotola touched her on one knee. Seeing the strain in her innocent eyes made Rolake fidget harder with her sleeves. Within a few moments, both sleeves were as wrinkled as the face of the witch of Endor.

"Are you okay, Mama? You've started to play with the sleeves of your buba. You only do that when you're nervous or angry with me. Are you upset, Mama?"

Rolake wasn't surprised that her daughter asked those questions. She was a great observer. She had the brain of a sharp twelve-year-old who figures things out fast. Rolake still wasn't ready to talk yet. The words to reduce her daughter's pain stuck in her brain—her brain full of guilt and soreness, unable to process a good starting point. Abruptly, she turned her face to one side.

"Am I in trouble, Mama? Did I do something to upset you? Is Papa angry?" Omotola's voice was tinged with angst.

As Omotola asked question upon question, in agony, with a shaky voice, until Rolake couldn't take it anymore. As amiable as Rolake could afford to be, she said, "Yes, nervous a little, but I'm not angry with you, Sunshine. It's because I had a discussion with your father this morning about your going to school." Rolake sighed before she added, "He wants you to stop going to school. He said school is not good for you—it's just money down the drain."

Rolake continued to look away in shame, avoiding her daughter's face that was surely full of confusion and pain. At the same time, she strove hard to control the urge to break into tears and go bananas.

"Mama, please look at me!" Omotola demanded. "Why does Papa want me out of school? I love school.

Look, Mama, this is what I did today."

Omotola picked up her slate and handed it over to Rolake, as she usually did since starting elementary school. Rolake took it and admired what she had written in white, all ticked correct with red chalk. Everything was still intact, not yet rubbed off. This only made her feel worse.

"Please, Mama, don't make me quit school. Sister Teresa told me I'm extremely bright. Please. I'm begging you." Omotola rolled forward, onto both knees, and reached for her mother. "Please, please, and please, Mama, talk to Papa to allow me to stay in school. And I promise to bring good marks home every time. Mama, I love school. Please, please…"

Rolake glanced up from the slate and looked straight past Omotola's head. "You are a girl, Omotola," she said. "And soon you'll be getting married. I should be teaching you…" She stopped.

Omotola stiffened. Rolake felt it, and something muttered in her brain. "That was a bad start, deranged mother. What about the rest? The rest you should add. Coward."

All of a sudden Rolake shouted, "Haaaaa!" as if on fire.

Omotola was scared and edged away.

"Are you okay, Mama?" she asked with an unsteady voice.

"No, Sunshine," Rolake said honestly. "I'm not okay. I'm sick, and I'm a coward. Sunshine, I need to start talking things through with you, as a mother should to her daughter before marriage, even though it makes me sick. I have to. That must start now. Sunshine, you've a groom and…"

She stopped again. She couldn't add the rest; her tongue seemed to cling to the roof of her mouth. It seemed that all her spit had dried out. She coughed to release her tongue, but the effort proved hopeless. As she flicked a glance at her daughter, she realized she was scared, perplexed, and probably frozen by the two eyes shimmering directly at her without a movement. Rolake felt uneasy and stared at the ground, as if afraid Omotola would see through her eyes to the dirt in her guts and feel disgusted. There was silence.

She was supposed to have started preparing Omotola for the future, as Paul had mentioned since the day Omotola started to walk, long before she started primary school. She had always known that Omotola was going to end up in Jacob's den, whether she liked it or not. She was supposed to teach her the aspects of marriage—the actual marriage and its causality. She was supposed to let her know beforehand that she could start the cycle of childbearing at a young age, that she must concentrate on bringing babies into the world, be submissive. And at all times, she must search for the means to make her husband happy so that he would want her most out of all his wives. If she refused to search for her husband's favor, she would probably be left redundant, like old cloth, when he finished having kids with her.

He might marry another wife in the same month as she became his bride, or later. It had never been considered a crime. Sex with him could be when he wanted, when he was in a good mood, just like her father. The rota could be changed at any time. She couldn't dictate when or be offended by it. She couldn't object to his decision. He paid her *idana,* the bride price. And if she did object, she could get the beating of a lifetime. Men were the lords of the ring, period!

She was supposed to teach Omotola all these things, to pass them down to her as early as when she was a toddler. It was as a gift from mother to daughter—the same fate, doom, bedlam, and horror awaited her. She knew as well that, even bringing Omotola up with knowledge of the reality and causality, their details…sometimes it was never enough.

Rolake's mother had taught her a lot since she could walk, but nothing had prepared her for what she had seen, what she had undergone in Paul's house. Her mother's lectures were like a drop in the ocean. She knew she was supposed to do better than her mother, to pass much down with elaborate explanation, and not a single cover-up. That, at least, might make her transition to married life easier. Would it? Her brain buzzed again. No, it wouldn't. She knew it.

No, she couldn't be a teacher of doom—she couldn't relay that the weirdo Omotola was to marry might never be happy with her. He might be a sadist like Paul. She wasn't demented enough to tell her only child that their culture dictated that a girl must stomach all the dirty deeds a freaky marriage would bring to her lap, whether she liked it or not. No, she couldn't make it simpler—by saying that life can be unfair and that the world she lived in dictated the tune of her life. Sometimes she would have to abide by its hellish crap. She couldn't foist this on an innocent girl. Paul would have to do the dirty job. She burst into tears.

"Mama, please don't. Please stop crying."

Omotola started to cry too. She stood up again and

wrapped her hand around Rolake's shoulder. This seemed to give Rolake the strength to say what she needed to say. In a raspy voice, she whispered, "Sunshine, you'll marry soon. I hate it, but there is nothing I can do about it. Your father wants me to tell you that." She brushed away her tears, and then reached over and did the same for Omotola's. "Sunshine, you must understand it is not my will. I have always wished that your lot would be better than mine, but the choice is not mine to make. All authority belongs to your father. Please understand. I don't have a hand in stopping you from going to school. Your father wants it. He's said schooling is wrong for a girl. You're getting married soon, and starting from tomorrow, you'll be staying at home with me."

Omotola pulled away from her mother in anger. "Mama, what are you talking about? I can't be at home with you tomorrow. I've got to go to school. Mama, I'm not the only girl going to school from our town. Dupe Akindele is a girl, and she is in my class."

"Because Dupe is from a rich family, and…" Rolake plunged into stammering. "You will marry Aba Jacob soon. He made an arrangement when you were born. All the education you've gained will be useless. Right now, you should be learning from me how…" Rolake trailed off.

"No, Mama, I can't marry Papa Jacob. He is an old man. I must speak to my Papa at once and let him know I would prefer to go to school rather than get married."

It sounded strange to hear the endearment coming from her daughter's lips. *Papa* and *Aba* mean the same thing in Itan Land. Both are words used by wives to respect their husband and elderly men. And children use both for their father and to respect older men.

"Sunshine, you will," said her mother, as Omotola frowned.

"Mama, Papa Jacob is my father's friend, and he is an old man. How is it possible for him to want to marry me? I see him as a second father. You're not making sense. I'll tell Papa I want school, not marriage."

"You can't tell your father you've been to school. You know it was our little secret. I told him you were away to my mom's place."

"You lied to him instead of telling him the truth?" Omotola was upset.

"I'm sorry. You know how your father is when he's angry."

"I hate you. I hate you, I hate you!"

Omotola ran home, and once there, she sat sulking in a corner of their bedroom.

Omotola woke up exactly at the time she was used to getting up for school. She tiptoed gently into Kola's bedroom, bidding him goodbye before he went to school. She did not forget to remind Kola to talk to Sister Teresa, her teacher.

"Please, Kola, don't forget to tell Sister Teresa I love school and that she must come and help me. My Mama cannot help. Please, please, I'm begging you. Don't forget to tell her to talk to my Papa soon."

When Kola left for school, Omotola retreated to a corner of the room to sit, putting one hand up to support her cheek, staring into space, lost in thought. Sometimes she would lie on the mat and hit the heels of her legs on the ground as long as she could. And she cried. Sometimes she would take her slate and rewrite what she had learned in school.

The only time Omotola's mood was better was when Kola arrived back from school to play with her. He always promised that Sister Teresa would come around to talk to their father soon, that Omotola must go back to school. That promise seemed vaguer to Omotola each day. Almost two weeks passed, and still there was no visit from Sister Teresa.

Rolake watched her only child gasping for air, struggling to breathe in a drowning pool of insanity created by her father. Paul was sucking the life out of her only child. The town saw nothing wrong with the crazy tradition that incapacitates a mother's wish to do the right thing for her children. She shook her head in disbelief, feeling powerless.

Omotola rarely had an appetite to eat, and when she did eat, she only ate a bit. She was dying.

Chapter Five

Paul knew that most women wanted him to look their way, even just once. He was absolutely gorgeous, with sexy eyes that scrutinized and picked out the best-looking ladies. Moreover, Paul seemed better educated than his peers. He had only the defect of stammering, which had almost faded away with time.

He had not learned about Omotola going to school from anybody in his household, as Rolake had thought, but by accident that same morning. He found out from Yemisi, one of his secret concubines and the best, most recent wife of John, a man who had been devoted to Paul since childhood.

Paul had turned up at a corner nearby John's house and watched him leave for the farm with the rest of his family. Paul entered Yemisi's room after checking that the den was empty by repeating John's name several times. Silence answered each time.

He appeared to Yemisi, who was still wrapped up on the mat. He cleared his throat as he stood by the doorframe. Yemisi shifted her face toward the entrance and smiled. Paul knew it as a sign to come in. He did so without delay.

Yemisi was one of the women he had sex with anywhere he could on the farm—under the orange tree, near the river, in her husband's house. Both were married to other people, so it was dangerous and exciting.

Until Yemisi got pregnant and gave birth to a baby boy, who almost one year old, she was number one on Paul's chart. She was kind of pretty, kind of sexy, kind of ready to run anytime. And the baby boy—Paul was sure it was his. He would have loved to claim him as his own. He needed male children, but it would have caused a clash of the clans, bloodshed, the loss of his best friend, and the stoning to death of an unfaithful woman. "Well, we'll have to go with the affair," he told himself irritably.

Paul was angry with God, who was against him all the time. While he fathered male children from his concubines, the women in his own backyard produced useless female children. Paul knew God was unfair. He had real issues with Him.

He looked at his sleeping "supposed to be" son next to Yemisi for a second before he dismissed the idea of claiming him once more. The cost would be more than it was worth. He glanced at Yemisi, whose facial expression saying "I want you now" hadn't changed a bit.

Paul knew he lived on the edge. That's what made such hush-hush sex more fascinating. Well, John wasn't a saint either. He had made a habit of banging Jacob's second wife—and Jacob was a friend of them both—until recently, but now he'd stopped. The reason he pinpointed was that gravity had taken its toll on her. Old age and sagginess were to blame. Paul had caught them in tight spots in the past, and that would be his blackmailing shotgun if the need arose.

None of Paul's affairs were his fault. The women wanted him. Like others before her, Yemisi had shown up at his farm looking for—it didn't matter. The excuse was irrelevant, the real reason plain. And what was he supposed to do? Paul had convinced himself several times that he should give them what they wanted.

Paul assessed and rated his women for their freshness. Since Yemisi headed the chart, he frequented her, just as he had frequented her predecessors, until she was replaced with a new, younger woman. If still in luck, like just a few that he kept going, he would visit her once in a blue moon, until his two firm favorite places, "breasts and cave," started to become jelly-like, and that would stop the whole deal. If she decided to be a nuisance, he would gently recite the custom in her ears—the cost of her adultery. Usually, it worked like a charm. They would go into a depression in their husbands' houses without any more hassling. To Paul, that was the way it had been, was going to be, and would continue to be, because women were stupid. Even the educated ones that should have known to stay away from married men weren't any better. Simon Akindele's compound showed that. Most of the aspects of Simon Akindele's life Paul adored to the letter, even though he actually hated him as he hated his own present life. He would never forgive him for literally killing his father over Sarah.

In the beginning, Sarah was without a suitor, which had made their father hate her and ignore her. Gbadamosi couldn't care less, as their mother supported her schooling. After her secondary school, when Simon Akindele, the rich and famous, had come forward, wanting to marry her, it was like a miracle. But instead of settling down and embracing married life with the man who paid her nursing school tuition and a lump sum bride price, Sarah had absconded from Ibata-Itan. She ran away, leaving their father to pay every penny back, plus a fine because she had put it in writing, calling Simon "a bully stark illiterate."

All of Paul's family would have to work for Simon until the debt was paid back. That had caused Gbadamosi's depression and death, but Paul liked Simon's power. Simon was able to marry the most beautiful, educated, desirable women and extract their juice in his bedroom for a long time before giving birth. Then, when done, he threw them in the back of his house once their first child was born. Paul wanted that.

"Women are stupid, including the beautiful and exposed ones. If they are not, why would the best of their race follow the same direction, marrying men who already have wives? Stupid gender," Paul often muttered in his head.

Out of Paul's wives, the only woman who pleased Paul, whom he might have faintly loved at first glance, was the mouth-watering Adewumi, his second wife. He married her in the nick of time. He had been lucky, since suitors queued up for her. Out of all of them, Adewumi liked him best. He almost worked his body to the bone to pay her bride price.

He could've stopped at her and only had flings if she hadn't decided to produce "females" to mock him, Paul had complained. He still had two females—ripe or nearly overripe, from his first wife—whom he was currently trying to get rid of since no suitor came to pay their bride price. He wanted them out of his house as soon as possible. If no man came to ask their hand in marriage, pay their bride price, he would have to just give them away as a gift to anybody wanting any old wife. Paul hated women who produced girls. They were stupid, with weak ovaries.

Paul strode toward Yemisi, released the string of his *sooro*, and the trousers dropped down onto his heels, revealing his manhood, as pointed as a unicorn horn. He knelt down behind her heels, opening her wrapper as one opens a delicate gift wrap and teased her where he knew he could send women out of their minds, from her breast down to her "cave." She was hot and wet, with legs wide apart, just as Paul wanted, in a blink.

"Yeah, yeah," she moaned. "I was almost out of my mind yesterday, longing for you, longing for this. God! Yes, like that!" Yemisi said, moaning profoundly. "I almost said to your children, Kola and Omotola, who were going to school, that you must visit this morning. I'm glad you are here; I want this so much."

Paul pulled away, both hands dropping to his side. "You saw who?" he asked.

"That's not important. I'm glad you are here. Do me now, or else I'll explode."

"You saw Omotola going to school?"

"Yes, Paul, come on…"

Paul stood up, picking up his sooro, wearing the trousers in a fury. Yemisi snapped to her feet, naked and pleading. "Paul, please, don't go. Don't leave me like this."

When Paul didn't respond and fled out the door instead, Yemisi was enraged. She yelled, cried, and cursed, un-bothered by the baby, the passersby, or her husband who might come back.…

Out of his female children, Omotola got a suitor a few hours after she opened her eyes in the world. Jacob didn't wait until he saw her grown up to decide whether she was beautiful or not. He said he would pay whatever was demanded for her, and more. She should be untouched by any other man. Jacob did more for Paul than any suitor he knew. A few weeks earlier, Paul had complained that he needed able bodies on his farm to help clear up the ground for the season's planting. When he got to his farm the day after, more than ten men were working there. He would never be able to repay Jacob in cash or in kind.

Paul walked back home like a wounded lion, seriously ranting. "Omotola going to school is a death penalty. Rolake, if it's true, you have a death wish," he swore, continuing. "Marriage was easy before these British missionaries nuzzled their noses where they don't belong and criticized the customary law to marry out their daughters. That is ordained, the right of the father. Those idiots have taken everything. Where is the dignity of a man?" Paul kept talking to himself without stopping.

Before the missionaries showed up with a decree that marrying a girl out must not occur before the age of sixteen, the simple rule had been waiting until after a girl reached puberty. Girls could be married out after a few months of menstruating, especially if they already had a suitor. Those without suitors could be tossed in a pool of insults, in fear of being left on the shelf.

Even though the decree came, read at the king's palace and everywhere in Itan Land, nobody observed the rule. The missionaries couldn't prove the age of a child because children were born at home. As Omotola frequently saw them, Paul knew that they would enforce the law to the letter, and he would be dead meat.

❦

Chapter Six

Reverend Matthew waited pensively in Ajoni-Itan Diocese for others to join him, to proceed to Ibata-Itan and meet Mr. Paul Olorunfemi. Again, he opened the report cards placed on his desk yesterday for his assessment by Sister Anne, the headmistress of All Saints Primary School. He felt a sharp pain of injustice, just like the pain he had felt the first time he read it—a girl, academically sound, a whiz kid—was being refused education. What the teachers had said so far about her was that she showed rare genius but was now deprived of education because of being a girl.

"Omotola, as long as I live, you will never be in bondage," he murmured.

He would mobilize all that was available to bring her back to school before she was damaged for life. Dedicated nuns, money—everything. He would have to involve the British Council if Paul proved unreasonable. He would seek a court order to remove Omotola from her home. Reverend Matthew wished it wouldn't come to that.

He tapped his desk with one finger, thinking to what extent he should go as he waited for the first help to arrive, in the form of two nuns. Sister Teresa was a missionary from Britain as well as being Omotola's teacher. She had been without sleep for almost three weeks. And Sister Rebecca had once been in Omotola's shoes. A devoted nun from Ajoni-Itan, Sister Rebecca had given her life to Christ. She went about her work, joyous in whatever effort would bring humanity to her people.

The reverend father himself had arrived from Great Britain to Africa more than three decades earlier, and for the past ten years, he had been the head of Itan Land's Catholic churches, the headquarters of which was in Ajoni-Itan. At the top of his agenda was education.

He wanted to know Africa and to help, as other reverend fathers and nuns had done when they visited its shores. They all lamented that so many kids were deprived of education and that women were discriminated against, in particular. Reverend Matthew wanted to make a difference. Having lived in many African territories, he realized that the same adverse facts that had met him thirty years before were still important topics to deal with. Just like his counterparts, he had achieved little despite all his efforts to promote education and Christianity.

Of course, Great Britain wasn't without its flaws. In the beginning, women were battered, and kids were neglected. There was an époque in which ridiculously enacted laws actually supported spousal abuse. These were upheld by judges like Francis Buller, nicknamed "Judge Thumb," who had specified that a man had the legal right to beat, or "correct," his spouse with a stick—as long as it was no thicker than a thumb. But education and Christianity had worked hand in hand to bring civilization that eroded the gates of such victimization. Such gates were demolished by upstanding people who lived their lives to make a difference. Matthew had become a reverend father to do so, and that measurable difference would always be his anchor.

He could relate to the kids of Africa. In his neighborhood in Glasgow, people knew when his father, Sean, and some of his friends were paid at the factory. Once the day's work was finished, they spent hours in their regular bar consuming beers and would come back with half their salary gone, wasted on alcohol. Sean would sing and whistle until he got home, then bang on the door like a loco for it to be opened by Matthew's mom. She had to sleep near the door so she could open it quickly, so as not to get punched, but also because the one-room parlor was congested. She could trip on a child if far from the door. Matthew was the third of ten children—seven boys and three girls, who slept like sardines in a can.

Sean had been arrested more than twice for assaulting his mother. In the end, depression killed her at an early age, in her prime. The last baby was only two when they all became motherless. As soon as Matthew made it out of secondary school, paid for by an uncle, he had entered the ministry. Most other siblings never recovered from their childhood trauma. In fact, two of his brothers were chronic alcoholics, following the doomed path their father had paved. He had tried his best to help and make them see reason, but in the end, he realized he couldn't save them.

But he could save Omotola.

He had studied African society and had known how the grass grew in Itan Land since arriving about ten years ago. And just like other places he had visited, he had been upset about the darkness that enclosed the vulnerable kids and women. Sometimes, he sat in the dark and felt the pain of innocent girls dragged into the bondage of marriage. He knew why school was a no-go area for girls, especially from backgrounds like Omotola's. Girls didn't count. Sending girls to school was money down the drain. They could, and did, get pregnant halfway through and abandon school, so it was almost better to marry them off at a tender age before they got promiscuous and started having unwanted babies.

However, on rare occasions, parents from Omotola's background might allow boys to attend school. Girls from such families were few, except for those spared by the church's strongly enforced decree that stated: "no marriage before sixteen." The church had induced the recent British government to enforce the law, to make their intervention easy. Such children always had the backing of the church in everything, but they had to step into school first, just as Omotola had done. Omotola would have all the support she needed, Reverend Matthew vowed, as he closed the report card.

He would never relent in bringing Omotola back to school, even if Mr. Paul chased him out as most fathers did—it had happened several times in the past. Father Matthew and his group had been the victims of so much retaliation, including the drawing of weapons. They'd had to get out of many towns in a hurry, as the angry mobs swore to kill them if they ever come back to preach Christianity or promote education. Their preaching and promotion of Western education conflicted with the norms and culture of the Itan people. To them, such indoctrination was modern-day slavery. Oyinbo, the white man, could not be trusted. White men were the evil of the world; hence, they were not welcome.

It was a difficult task, and Matthew knew it. He wasn't ignorant of the causes of hatred, of the drawing of weapons, either. He could understand the mob, sometimes, and their pain. How could he automatically convince the family and friends about the good news when their people were shackled like slaves by his very own counterparts? How could he easily convince the populace to welcome education and Christianity with all their hearts, when the people were forcefully colonized, hegemony imposed on them, ruled for their own selfish ends?

He understood perfectly that some of these little undisclosed reasons stuck everything in the shadows and made progress move at the speed of a millipede. Despite all of this, he was determined not to be discouraged. He understood that he mustn't give up trying to liberate kids like Omotola. The more educated people were, the easier his job would be. The educated ones would lighten his burden, just like Sister Rebecca had been doing—promoting and portraying to her people the importance of education, the peace and joy Christianity could bring to them. Omotola's case was personal; she had all the potential to make a difference with her people, and the people of Itan Land at large.

Sister Teresa and Sister Rebecca entered and interrupted his ruminations.

"You ready to go, Father?" Sister Rebecca asked.

"Yes, I'm ready. Bless you two for coming this early."

Chapter Seven

Paul drew water from one of the earthenware pots into a silver iron pail at the back of the house, observing that the place was totally empty, as he thought it would be. He knew his family had all disappeared because he had slept in late. They were afraid, thinking it was a deliberate act, to punish the offender. Paul smiled. That was how it should be. A man should be feared. Gbadamosi would be happy that he had all it took to be a man—an *arole* with a strong voice.

"Listen to me, Son. As you make your bed, so you lie on it," Gbadamosi had said. "Women are not to be given any consensus when making decisions, or else you'll compromise your own interest, and in the process, lose your God-given right as a man. Remember, Son, you pay their bride price with your sweat. You must, therefore, make them obey and make them submissive to your will."

This was the advice given by his father the day after he handed over to Paul his first female toy—his first wife, Moji, the woman who Paul never adored because she lacked beauty. Marrying her was, however, a way of helping Gbadamosi.

Paul Olorunfemi wasn't born a maniac—far from

it—but he had been trained by one. Gbadamosi explained and demonstrated in detail to his son how to tame the household with an iron hand as arole, firstborn, and *olori-ebi*, leader of his clan, much later. That included flogging them all like animals until submissive. Gbadamosi elaborated further that to be a man and arole with a strong voice, he must rule his women, his wives, and concubines, without empathy or warmth.

"Women are not worthy of men's hangovers," Gbadamosi had said. "A man is the lord. And what makes a man a lord, Son, is to be without outward 'amore' to anyone. 'Amore' weakens a man."

When Paul was small, his father had been skeptical if he would ever be a lion in his den, an arole with authority in his clan. Paul hung around Reverend Rolland a lot during his childhood. At that younger age, in the palace, Paul interpreted the church's intentions for Reverend Rolland. Lots of parents raised eyebrows, as did Gbadamosi, as he hated the boy's interaction with the church and was scared. With constant training, bullying, and manipulating, Paul became the man his father wanted him to be—strong, with a lion's roar.

Crazy parents produce crazy children. Paul soon understood his role as a man, which was to marry as many women as he could put a roof over. It was to have a fleet of concubines as his heart desired, to marry daughters out before they constituted a nuisance by sleeping around and ending up with unwanted children, which was a taboo and a disgrace. And most importantly of all, it was to train male children to rule their households with a tight rein. These roles Paul Olorunfemi had been performing to the letter.

He carried the pail to the front porch with an awesome feeling of fulfillment of his role as arole. He bent down to wash his feet under the odan tree and took the liberty to hum the latest composed song of the masquerade. As he was enjoying the breeze from the tree's leaves, he felt something. Something strong was flashing reflections of his decaying life in his brain. He stopped humming, looking disturbed.

Almost immediately, he put his brooding aside and rode his heart to the best moment to come, thrills about to happen in an hour. He decided to assume that life was going to be good soon. He was going to a wedding. The wedding was for a friend, which would give him the opportunity to meet the newly available *eleyinju ege omidan*, the mouth-watering spinsters, who were friends of the wife-to-be. He smiled. His attire was in place, a brand new *agbada* that he had purchased with part of the proceeds from his farm, a *boubou* that had promised to make him look his best when he had tried it on. His figure in the mirror had been superb.

Subconsciously again, his mind strolled back to his decaying life, even though he didn't want it to. He knew why it was bothering him—money would be tight soon. It was because he put in his mouth more than he could chew at a time. He needed money for lots of things, but instead, he had wasted it on gambling, plus spending the rest on "want-to-stand-out" rich clothes that really promised sorrow.

He tried to console himself again with good thoughts: getting another (brand new) wife, trim and firm in all his favorite places, that would bring pleasure. It would be better than having to spend money on the wives he had already, their children, or his about-to-be run-down house. For an increase in revenue, he could always vigorously tap the only goldmine in sight—Jacob.

He could make Jacob pay more for Omotola, to increase his income, since he wanted to marry her off as soon as possible. The moment she reached puberty seemed a good idea, as Jacob had suggested. He would make that possible after squeezing a lot of money from him. He had the balls in his court. He knew Jacob had been obsessed with Omotola since the *Ifa* oracle predicted she would make him rich. A desperate man, Jacob would do anything to get ahead, and that anything would include paying out a lump sum of money. He would make sure that Jacob forked over before sampling the cow. He would agree to Jacob's wishes. Omotola had to get married as soon as possible, before the unfortunate happened and she went astray, like Kola, that incorrigible son he had always hated.

Paul would have preferred the wedding to happen when she was much older so he could suck Jacob to the bone marrow, but it must be soon. Huff! He was lucky to have stopped Omotola from going to school when he did. It would have been catastrophic. Jacob would have wanted his money back, the money long gone on gambling. And that would have resulted in a clash of clans, enmities, perhaps bloodshed. Paul was enraged. Rolake was on his blacklist. She had allowed and encouraged Omotola to do a wrong that could have earned him depression and destruction, as it had earned Gbadamosi. Rolake needed discipline. She would serve as a deterrent to others who wanted to be just like her in his compound. He vowed that she would pay for her stupidity.

Again, Paul decided to shed all these worries since it was all water long gone under the bridge. Omotola would marry Jacob as soon as evidence of puberty showed. He had been paying close attention to that, since he would have to send her quickly to Jacob. With all the money that would come from her bride price and with all his economizing, he concluded that he could fill in all the cracks in his life. The conclusion made him laugh. He knew it was easier said than done, as something always cropped up to take all the money he made, something strong, like a whirlwind....

Paul raised his head. He was startled. His mouth opened in shock as he stared at a reverend father and two nuns who seemed to have been blown into his sight from Hades by a tornado. Straightaway, he remembered redemption and the end-of-the-world message he had heard, which had made him totally hate Oyinbo and everything about them. The reverend father had emphasized that the Ten Commandments were a sure pass to Heaven, if observed. Unobserved was a sure pass to hell.

He had heard it on one of those days when he had wandered into church for a purpose he now couldn't really remember. It was the time he was in mourning for Reverend Rolland. He had been grieving. That day, in particular, the reverend father had threatened hellfire for people without redemption at the end of the world. He had said that on the last day, angels would appear without warning in a whirlpool, so suddenly, there would be no place to run or to hide. And since then, he had never gone near a church again. He hated disturbing sermons.

As Paul looked at the invaders, he was convinced it was the end. They all wore grave faces like those of funeral conductors, and their body language from head to toe indicated death's presence, death's watchful stare. *Very well,* Paul thought, *this is the end—the end of the world. It will happen all of a sudden. The world will be destroyed in fire,* he remembered the preacher saying. *Damn Armageddon!*

Surely, it must be hell. This was a bad omen. He hadn't gone to them—they had come to him, violating his space, so silent, so sudden. He hadn't done all that the reverend said he should do so that he could be granted a pass to Heaven. In fact, as he grew older, in his adult world, he did the things that would grant entry to hell. They suited him well, because the reverend's sermon was complicated. It was impossible to do the things he asked.

"There should be no discrimination, men and women were equal"—but how? No adultery? No fornication? No, no—what was the fun in all that? He might as well dig a hole and live in it to avoid the wrong contact, to avoid his "no's." There were too many *no's* in the reverend's preaching. In the end, it left Paul with tons of unanswerable questions. This led to fear, which led to migraines, since there was nobody to whom he could go for an explanation. Paul avoided church. He was safe in his culture.

The only time in his life he had seen a Catholic priest and nuns all together in their regalia, like penguins, was the day of multiple baptisms in the church in Ajoni-Itan. He was a little boy then, on the final lap of Primary Three. Reverend Rolland, the overseer of Itan Land Diocese, the only priest he had ever liked—who treated him like a son, who caught him when he dropped out of school in confusion, who placed him back in school—was conducting the ceremony with some nuns. Right there, he gave him the name Paul, along with the calendar he hung up in his living room, which was still there. He missed the reverend in his life for a lot of things—to start with, shedding light on the misery of the end of the world.

Reverend Rolland went back to England shortly after the baptism, as he was sick with terminal brain cancer. Paul was devastated when his replacement handed him the letter of farewell. It was the darkest moment of his life, but nobody knew this. He was crushed, without the will to live, until Gbadamosi metaphorically scooped him off the ground. It changed everything, and that was the moment Paul lost his soul to the devil.

He couldn't wait to start the new life Gbadamosi prepared for him. Within two months of the holidays, he was converted to his father's beliefs. He lost the desire to go back to school and start Primary Four, the intention of staying in school, as the late reverend had wanted, as he had emphasized in his last letter to him. He embraced the idea of farming.

At a tender age, Paul drank palm wine with his father in the midst of his friends. Also at a tender age, his father shoved him toward a female—a playmate of his youth, who had married his father's friend and wanted him so badly. There, he lost his virginity and became a man. At a young age, he had married. To Paul, he was saved by his father from the doom that would have come if he had insisted on going to school and listening to bullshit. He loved the new life his father had created. In a short amount of time, he had forgotten about Reverend Rolland and his associates in regalia—until now.

He looked at them like he was a trapped animal. His

brain was stuffy with the issues of recent days. He wondered, why now? No warning of their arrival. It was so unexpected. He blamed his brooding over his personal problems for not having the chance to escape. If he had seen the whirlwind that brought them, as the reverend father had said, and he could have run. It was unfortunate that he would have to face them now. As Paul stared, a question came into his head. "Paul, what have you done to yourself? They would like to know."

Paul was a drama queen, a pretender, and many more things when it came to uncertain issues. Since his mind had gone blank, he decided to remain aloof. Maybe, if he pretended he hadn't seen them, the carriers of Armageddon would go away and revisit another time, when he was less busy or in bad enough shape to voluntarily do their will. But not now. Because soon, he would be a happy man as he gazed at the spinsters, one of whom he could whisk home in a matter of moments. The priest and nuns would have to go and revisit another time, he concluded. Out of fear, Paul decided to lower his head, continue with the task at hand, and wait for what was to come—the strong wind and fire that would envelop him.

"*O ju ire mo yin alagba, se a le ba yin soro,* sir?" Sister Rebecca asked.

The voice sounded impatient. Paul hesitated. Finally, when he stood upright, he was curious. There was no wind or fire around them yet. Maybe his assumption was wrong. If his assumption was right, he could still probably make his way out of the whole mess or simply scare them away with physical intimidation. He liked the idea of scaring better.

Inches from the intruders, he managed to shoot a

dirty "get lost!" look at the group, but instead of them getting the hint and clearing off, the group remained adamant, wearing a look on their faces worth a million words. It said, "Oh, we're going nowhere until we talk to you." Paul was mystified.

"Ejowo alagba, oro pataki la fe ba yin so."

It occurred to Paul that angels of death wouldn't say, "Please, may we talk to you on important issues." They wouldn't be that polite. Now he feared nothing, but he was infuriated. A black nun was speaking for them. An abomination! Rudeness! Paul glared at them. He would have loved to be violent at that instant, as his thoughts wandered to what the world around him was turning into. Here was a black woman as a speaker right under his nose… a stout, black nun traitor. He wished to take the woman by the shoulder and shake her until the Oyinbo influences snapped out of her brain, and she realized she was just an object, never meant to speak in front of a man like him. And the other two, staring—he would have loved to chase them away with a dagger for trespassing.

"E soro ni kiakia. Mi o de fe gbo nipa ogun Amageddani' tabi oro inu Bibeli," Paul snarled.

"Alagba, a ba oro ihin rere inu Bibeli tabi ogun Amageddani wa," Sister Rebecca replied quickly as Paul scrutinized them all with eyes of hatred.

She proceeded to introduce the members of the group. "Reverend Father Matthew, Sister Teresa, and my name is Rebecca."

Rebecca paused for Paul to digest the introduction. *"Awa ni alamojuto sukuru All Saints Primary School. Fun igba die, a wo ye pe Omotola ko wa sukuru. A si fe mo idi abajo,"* Sister Rebecca said.

The ugly scenario of Paul's youngest sister jumped into his head. She had wrecked their family and killed their father prematurely because she was educated. Her education was a curse, not a blessing.

Gbadamosi had died in debt, in depression, and the same fate awaited Paul. His mother still had to strive to cope with this devastation each day. Gbadamosi was a dodo to have ignored Sarah and to have ignored their mother, who sponsored her schooling before it was taken over by her suitor.

Well, Gbadamosi was an example to other fathers, namely that a man should never show a nonchalant attitude toward the wives in his own backyard. When they went astray, it should be nipped in the bud before it got out of hand. And without reversing his decision, that's what he would do in Omotola's case.

Paul gave the group another of his drop-dead glares, hissing as he bent over to pour water on his feet.

"*Omotola mo iwe. Ati pe...*" Reverend Matthew said, even though he was not given an audience.

"Rev, you can speak English. I'll translate." Sister Rebecca interceded.

"Thanks, Sister. I think I can mumble my way through in Yoruba language. *Omotola jafafa ...*"

Paul would have laughed at Matthew there and then, assembling Yoruba words as if they were farm firewood, if he hadn't been enraged beyond words. He felt disturbed at their "not going away" attitude. In Yoruba culture, when a host looks at you with disdainful eyes, hissing, it means "not welcome; clear out immediately, there might be danger..."

"Speak English. I understand perfectly well. I was

once in your institution of crap, but understand this about Omotola," Paul sneered, standing erect again. "Omotola is getting married soon. So, if that's all you are here to talk about, leave! I'd like to get myself ready for an outing."

"What I was trying to say is that your daughter is a brilliant girl, and I believe her education can benefit the whole town of Ibata-Itan and the world. Sir, forcing her into marriage when she can barely understand the world around her is sad and barbaric." "It's sad and barbaric, eh?" Paul said, reproaching him right away. "Do you have a death wish, Reverend?"

"I don't mean to insult you," said Reverend Matthew with a face full of apology. "If I did, I'm sorry. I'm just—"

"You already did—barbaric and sad," Paul cut him short, "But going to school is joy, eh? You've got a nerve, Rev, to come into my compound, challenge my authority, and call my culture barbaric." Paul continued rudely, "Why would you say that? Because in your head, just like the rest of you folks out there, you think that your culture is very fabulous. And you love trashing other people's traditions and culture, believing you're superior. Supreme blood runs in your veins. Blacks are brainless apes with barbaric culture, and as a superior race, you have the power to train us and impose your authority. Am I not correct, Rev?"

Paul asked the question but didn't give Matthew the chance to talk, speeding to bring out everything in him against the Oyinbo.

"But get this into each of your heads: your culture is not perfect or supreme to mine. As a matter of fact, you people are rogues, wolves in sheep's clothing. You hide behind Christianity and education to invade our land and take our riches. You infiltrate our towns and forcefully trash our traditional way of life with Christianity and education. Your coming here is a curse that should've been rectified a long time ago. It's a pity nobody is doing anything. But get this into your brain. Omotola is my daughter, and as a father, I know what is best for her. I'm not going to allow you to destroy her life with your crazy ideology and theology. So, please show yourself out of my premises, or I will." Paul hissed again.

"I'm sorry we started off on the wrong foot. I'm truly sorry." Reverend Matthew picked his words carefully. "Like you said, and I quite agree with you, no culture is perfect or superior to another in the eyes of God. We're all equal. On the other hand, about your daughter—we can't just leave it like that, sir. Your daughter is a genius. My wish in life is to give an opportunity to children who want to learn. As I said earlier on, her education will be a blessing to the world in the long run. Later in life, she'll be able to show the world we are all the same in the eyes of God."

Paul was so mad—to the extent that he would have loved to shoot or probably smother Kola in his sleep since he was about to make him depressed and bankrupt. He was the one who had brought schooling into Paul's house and taken Omotola to school. The boy had created illusions in Omotola's mind. For sure, he had sent for these reinforcements, who looked unbeatable. Paul had one choice, he concluded. He must send them all out immediately and discipline the incorrigible boy ASAP. He also decided that "Clever" should be his last name.

"I'm glad we both agree that there is no flawless culture. Thanks for taking an interest in my daughter, but her future is already in place," Paul said politely, for the first time, deciding to dish out the reasons. "Father, going to school for a girl is a waste of time, a bad investment. So, as a result, she'll get married soon."

"Please, sir, try and understand. It is for her own good," Reverend Matthew pleaded.

Paul hated smooth words, so he said sarcastically, "Not yours, father? Not that you wanted her to be *ode*—a plant—like that indoctrinated one over there?" Paul pointed to Sister Rebecca. "Father, we both know you want her to sell her own people as slaves to the white man's ideology and theology. Who are you kidding, Father? Obviously, not me. Please go and look for a dumb father somewhere else to convince. My decision stands."

"Your daughter…"

Sister Teresa spoke up for the first time, since Reverend Matthew seemed lost.

"It's not like that, sir," she addressed Paul. "Omotola has every chance to choose for herself later in life. She can be whatever she wants to be; that is, to choose the profession she likes. It's all in her hands, sir."

"Sister Teresa is right." Reverend Matthew got his voice back and wanted to list further advantages.

"Will you shut up, sir?" Paul said. "Shut up, Reverend." The little respect left for the group in front of him finally flew out of the window. He shouted as if his butt were on fire. "My daughter is engaged! Of what good is school going to be to her? She'll soon settle down at her husband's home. Let's just say I allowed her to continue schooling—what would the end result be? Definitely, she'll finish school, abandon her husband, and fly away like a bird to unknown places, like my sister before her.

She'll leave me to pay back her bride price. And don't forget, she might get pregnant before finishing school, so then it's money down the drain. People! Besides all the facts, plans have been in progress since Omotola was born—to marry a husband and settle down for good. So please leave!"

Paul pointed to the track leading away from the house.

"Please, sir; we implore you to think it through. It's cruel to marry a girl out without loving the man and without her consent. It's the only part of your culture that I feel should be eradicated. Please, sir, give her a chance and a choice in life," Sister Teresa said, placating Paul, who looked as if he might draw a weapon.

"Please, sir," Reverend Matthew said, "give her a chance."

As a matter of fact, Paul would've loved to take out one of his machetes and show the group in front of him what cruelty meant. But he would just be hanged or killed brutally. The British government protected their kind, like hens protect their chicks to the last. He knew this. He now restrained himself, concluding, *Why cry over spilled milk?* The root of the evil was in his own backyard. He would have to deal with this diligently. Because, for sure, the missionaries would keep on coming. Kola would not relent until Omotola was reinstated onto the path of doom, with a fixed future. Omotola could disappear. His sister had done so. She just disappeared into thin air. But at sixteen, as British law stipulated, Omotola would be married out and would move into her marital home. If the missionaries were not satisfied, they could go to hell and hang themselves there.

"Even if I want to send Omotola to school," Paul said in a cajoling way, "I have no money to support her financially. And it will be bad for her to leave school halfway through, right?"

"I'm happy the objection is because of money," sighed the reverend. "Mr. Paul, it has happened in the past, but I can assure you that will never today be a terminal factor for a gifted child such as Omotola, since I am aware. The church is unwilling to let Omotola's potential fade away. Prosperity for a child such as Omotola is prosperity for the church and for Nigeria as a country. Omotola will be provided for financially."

"Thanks for the help, Father," Paul snapped cynically. "I would have loved to provide for her, but I'm not rich."

Paul watched as the group lightened up for the first time since their arrival. The nuns were on the brink of shouting "Hallelujah!" and Reverend Matthew's face broke into a grin. They believed him. What next? With great effort, Paul suppressed the laughter rising up within his throat to mock them. He folded his arms and pretended to listen.

"Sir, it is a great pleasure for the church to be of help. My colleagues and I are happy. I promise you that Omotola will never be a disgrace. We, all of us here—" Reverend Matthew made a gesture that intimated group support "—we will help Omotola to fulfill her dream and her heart's desire."

Paul watched the faces of the two nuns, glittering as if they had won the lottery as Reverend Matthew included them. Paul smiled along with them, hiding his intentions to come. "That's good to know. She can go back to school.

I'm more than glad to hear that. I'm happy I am not obliged to pay a dime for her schooling."

"Not a dime is requested of you. The church will shoulder her school finances," Reverend Matthew said.

"All right, sir, Omotola can go back to school."

"Omotola can be anything she wants to be. The sky is the limit for her," the reverend said triumphantly. "Parents should know that education gives choices. She is a delightful little girl with a promising future. She can be a doctor, a lawyer, or an interpreter like our sister Rebecca here, who speaks many languages perfectly. She can even be the president of Nigeria."

"She can be a president of our country, really?" Paul couldn't control a guffaw, and the group watched silently. As soon as he stopped laughing, he added, "You're just a ninny buried in illusions, sir." He stared and continued casually to taunt them. "Well, probably when the flow of black gold in our land changes from gush-out to run-out. That will take an eternity. Dream on, Reverend Matthew. Your people will never leave Nigeria alone as long as all flows and Nigeria's minerals are embedded intact in its soil."

Reverend Matthew was embarrassed and seemed annoyed. Paul saw it. He could see blood draining from the reverend's face. The two nuns stood there like statues with wan expressions. He shrugged. He didn't care if they were upset. They were not on their own territory, and if they didn't want the truth, they should have stayed away. He would not apologize, he decided, smiling.

"Sir," Reverend Matthew said after an interlude. "I know it's hard to believe, but, yes, she can be whatever she likes to be. The sky is the limit for her—even to be president of Nigeria. Mr. Paul, there are ongoing conferences run by the erudite of Nigeria who are agitating and demanding that the British relinquish power to the indigenous population. Sooner, rather than later, Nigeria will earn its independence. So, it will be the literate who will rule Nigeria. The way it should have been. The transition of power to the indigenous population will make our work easier. We're in Nigeria to promote peace and joy, not the other way around."

The reverend's statements hit Paul like a punch in the face, and his smile disappeared. He now echoed the nuns' previously wan faces. It seemed that there was a truth to the saying of one of Simon's truck drivers, who transported cocoa from Ibata-Itan to Ladden. He had heard it said at a palm wine bar that there were endless ongoing conferences in Ladden, that the Nigerian youth movement under its founder, Professor Eyo Ita, was mandating that the British government to make changes and be prepared to hand over power to the indigenous people.

Paul had sleepless nights over his statements. For the first time in many years, and for days, Paul had cursed himself for not being educated. He could have stayed in school. He could have honored Reverend Rolland's last wishes and got educated. He had wondered what his life would have been if he had refused to listen and put his father's interests first. He could have been a teacher, a doctor, or aspire to be president…

Sure, he wouldn't have married his first wife, Moji, a woman he had never loved. Maybe he could have found a woman and fallen in love with her, could have married a woman his heart wanted, and never indulged in marrying endless wives to prove his wealth—a wealth he never really had. Apart from inherited land from his father, he had nothing. Nothing at all. Maybe he would have had a life that brought income, rather than relying and praying for a suitor to pay a bride price for his daughters in order to live. He eventually concluded it was a lie—gossip spread from a drunkard—but hearing it from British kinfolk meant it was true.

Paul fell mute as he regretted his past. Sister Rebecca spoke of self-merit.

"The greatest gift parents can give to a child is education. With my education, I was able to travel out of Nigeria and understand humanity and its context. Since I came back from abroad, I've been promoting love, kindness, and all the good that education and Christianity bring to life. A bird like Omotola can fly high and far."

Wearily Paul's mind returned to the discussion with Reverend Matthew, who said, "Sister Rebecca is right, and that's why the church will do everything possible, including enforcing the law if…" He stopped and added. "But I'm happy it won't come to that. You're a reasonable father. I know you'll allow Omotola to choose her life after her secondary education. She has that right as an adult. The law is on her side, then. Thanks again, sir."

The threat sounded clear in Reverend Matthew's voice, and his facial expression hardened when he mentioned "enforcement of law." Paul noticed it all. He was back to being angry and afraid as his mind wandered onto the Omotola and Jacob issue.

What was going to happen if Jacob couldn't marry Omotola? It was obvious that the Reverend Father was no fool and would carry out his threat to the letter of the law, which meant ten years in jail for child abuse. Where did that leave him? Broke, depressed, jailed?

Paul had had enough, and tears were about to pour down his cheeks. Paul untied his tongue, and with shivering lips, he said, "Thanks a lot, sir, and sisters. I really appreciate the church's effort to cater for her schooling, but I've things to do now."

"Sir, it has been a pleasure," Reverend Matthew said.

Hastily, Paul stretched out his right hand to clasp Reverend Matthew's right hand. He nodded to the sisters, and they all left.

Paul was in too much shit to think of the task of washing his feet. He sat on one of the tree trunks that was placed there to serve as a chair and reflected on what to do about Omotola. Without any solution in his war-clouded brain, he burst into tears and wept.

Chapter Eight

The party was full to the brim. It was one of many recent lavish celebrations, only this time, it was strictly for Akin and Olu's age groups in Simon Akindele's compound, held in one of the spacious halls in the two-story building that sat on ten acres of land. Simon had recently started to throw children's parties, with a guest list drawn from the "who's who" of the upper class, thinking Akin would find the girl of his dreams among them. Akin wasn't blind to his father's wishes because, after each party, Simon would call him in to ascertain which girls he had talked to. As a matter of fact, he hated talking to the girls, and most of the boys. The kids around were not his friends. The only person he could have counted on before was his half-brother, Olu, who was fast drifting away.

Olu gave Simon less panic when it came to what boys do. Olu was a charmer; Akin was not. Simon worried that Akin might join the priesthood, so he used the parties as a way to intervene. Akin hated hosting them, while Olu reveled in the social opportunity. Olu was becoming like their father, Simon. Akin felt concerned and decided he would have to talk to his brother, knock some sense into him. After all, he was the eldest and needed to take care of him.

The last thing on Akin's mind was girls. For a long time, he had been nursing an ambition to create a standard club, well recognized all over the country. He had even come up with a name for it already. "Lion Club" would be the best. He liked the idea. Along with other things, he wanted to talk about the details with Olu.

Akin managed to wave a hello to the girls and boys, screaming, "Great party!" as he went around looking for Olu in the gigantic meat market called a "party." He stopped by a fellow named Collins, who was wrapping his hands around a girl Akin hadn't seen before.

"Have you seen Olu?" Akin yelled above the blasting music.

Akin was bemused at how their generation went at girls like dogs, and how the girls were submissive without a struggle. Collins was engaged. The girl should have known if her parents came from an aristocrat background or Highlife Circle of friends of Simon—a club for bigwigs and enormously rich Nigerians. The core of the club had been friendship, but it had evolved into a support group for ostentatious, extravagant lifestyles that included parties where anything could happen.

"Olu? He just left for his apartment." Collins yelled back and laughed.

"Alone?" Akin was skeptical.

"You know your brother. That's impossible."

"Great party," the captive girl giggled as Collins firmly placed both hands on her butt and pressed her in front of his groin.

"Would you like to dance with me, Akin?" she asked, perkily.

Akin gave the girl his Akin Akindele Drop-Dead

Signature Look. The girl, ashamed, pulled away from Collins' grip as Akin left.

* * *

Bola, Solape, Cecilia, and Kemi were bitching about the party at the Akindele mansion, to which they had not been invited. The young people had gathered in Solape's posh sitting room in Tunde Ogunlade's mansion, at Ajoni-Itan.

Tunde Ogunlade, father of Solape, was a timber exporter, a tycoon with deep pockets, and the best friend of Simon Akindele. While Simon was a magnate, rated as the richest in West Africa, Tunde was in the tenth position. Simon and Tunde were friends from childhood, both from rich backgrounds. When Joyce disappeared with the mailman, it was the epic scandal of the time in the aristocrat world of the western region, and in Nigeria. Most people in Simon's circle did not spare him from trashing and backbiting, but Tunde stood with him as a good friend. They were both polygamous, with the same attitude towards women.

"How can Akin's father give a party that excludes me?" Solape said, frowning. "His father is my father's best friend."

"That Akin is just too full of himself," Cecilia said.

"You will be when you are as damn elaborate in beauty and wealth," Kemi replied, giggling.

"God, you are right, Kemi," Cecilia said earnestly. "To be honest, I pray he chooses me as his bride."

"Why would he choose you?" Solape said angrily. "He doesn't even know you exist. If it has to be anybody, it should be me. My father and his father go back a long way. And his mother was my mother's best friend when she was still around, so zip it up. It can't be you. I'll be the one when the time comes."

"Give it a rest," Bola shrilled. "All the girls wish to be 'the one,' but sometimes you have to let it go because it's crazy to kill each other for someone who doesn't give a damn. Look for other boys."

Both girls calmed down.

"I've got my head wound around a boy. I just wish he liked me," Bola said.

"Who is the boy you want, apart from Akin, Bola?" Cecilia asked.

Bola gave a sly smile. "You'll never know until I'm ready."

While Solape and the rest attended primary school at Ajoni-Itan, Bola was in All Saints Primary School. Bola secretly liked Kola a lot, and wanted him so badly, but the fortress Kola had built around his existence in the school was just like that of Akin in his personal life. No climbing over. Bola hated it.

"I know. It's Femi. He likes you a lot too," Solape said.

"No, not him," Bola said, disgusted. "I don't like your cousin; he is too juvenile."

"But I like your cousin, as a matter of fact, I told you to introduce me to him," Cecilia said, shooting accusing eyes at Solape.

"He doesn't like you. Femi said you are too ugly," Solape said derisively.

Kemi burst out laughing. Cecilia looked dejected.

"That's not nice, Solape," Bola butted in. "Kemi, will you stop laughing? It could be your turn next."

Kemi wound down the laughter.

One of Solape's many nasty habits, apart from being

full to the brim about herself, was to trash people with words without any hesitation. She hated Cecilia for praying to God for Akin to choose her as his bride. Solape was trying to annoy Cecilia for yearning for the boy she wanted for herself. And Cecilia mentioned her desire for Femi, Solape's cousin, was an opportunity for Solape to thrash Cecilia to the core. Solape'd talked with Oyinkan, her mother, about matchmaking her with Akin a number of times. And Oyinkan had a plan to tell her husband to get the ball rolling, to nudge Simon towards engaging Akin to Solape. To stop the gossip and competition, the announcement of the engagement should be made officially, nationwide.

"I'm not lying. Femi said it. It's the truth. And I don't care if the truth is bitter," Solape said smugly, with a face that said she was better than everybody. Bola glared at her as if to say, "Bring it on."

"Solape, is it true Akin's mom ran away with a postmaster?" Kemi asked to cool the air.

"Can't say, Kemi," Solape said lamely. "There are so many rumors about her disappearances. Some said she was a siren, a goddess of water who got angry with her husband and went back to the bottom of the sea."

"She was one hell of a beauty, according to my mother," Cecilia said.

"Probably too beautiful for any man to handle," said Bola and Solape at the same time, and they all laughed.

* * *

Tunde rolled off Oyinkan, looking satisfied. Oyinkan turned her body toward him and gently started stroking his tummy. Tunde had met Oyinkan at a party in Ladden.

She was beautiful, with seductive moves that made Tunde like her immediately. He'd asked his driver to drop the girl he'd brought to the party back at her house and bring Oyinkan to him at one of his mansions in Ladden. By the time Oyinkan finished with him that night, he was overexcited. He married her as his fourth wife the same month. And since, no woman had meant anything to him.

Oyinkan, a riveting woman, a Laddencian, had had one hell of a spinster life. She'd traveled abroad a lot before ending up in Tunde Ogunlade's lap. She knew a lot about what modern, sophisticated women do—the kind of women who knew about kinky stuff that would thrill their husbands, make them jump like a puppy. And Oyinkan was over the top, performing what most women might consider despicable—*oral sex*, which meant that since she'd married Tunde, he'd rarely leaped after other women. This had made the three first wives before her, including Bola's aunty, suffer sex deprivation.

Before Tunde had rolled off Oyinkan, satisfied with the marathon sex, she'd gone beyond the call of duty and given him some kinky foreplay. With that, she knew she could ask for half of his empire. He would give it up, but she wanted better than that.

"I'm thinking you should talk to your friend, Simon, to match-make Solape with Akin," Oyinkan said, slowly sending a hand down to his genitals.

"Consider it done," Tunde said instantly, with an appeased face. "Akin is the son I'd have loved to have, and being my son in-law, he will do. Thanks for bringing it up, Oyinkan; I'll see him in the morning. I've got to before others get the idea."

She smiled and continued to seal the deal.

Chapter Nine

At his farm, Jacob examined and selected the best yam tubers from a pile of some that had just been harvested. There were twenty. He called two of his sons to put them into two large baskets and follow him.

The masquerade festival would take place in a week. This was a time when a man must honor his father-in-law to be, because he is king until the man takes his daughter as the damn bride and owns her. The best, most robust, yams were for Paul. Jacob had been doing this, and many other things, each year, as a prospective son-in-law should.

He was Omotola's suitor. He was a bulky man from the warrior family of the town. Just like the majority of males in his family, he had a giant frame and was incredibly gruesome and beastly in looks, with a face full of pimples. He preferred to introduce his intent of marrying any female child immediately after asking Ifa oracle about their *isedaye,* their destiny. Doing so soon after they were born would help him avoid paying too much when they were grown up, when many competitors arose. That was how he was able to marry five women. He'd asked Ifa about Omotola right after she was born.

And luckily, Ifa had predicted that Omotola would not only be a most beautiful woman, but she would make him rich beyond his imagination. Ifa had spoken well. Even though Omotola hadn't made him rich materially yet, mentally, she had made him rich, as he chanced to glimpse her once in a while. He noted that her beauty was opening up like a bud yearning to develop into a beautiful flower.

Jacob was totally crazy about Omotola, even though he already had five wives. The little girl captured his imagination. He considered himself a great investor, to have made his move when he did. He heard whisperings that many men were rushing after his beautiful bud. Moji, his lover, the first wife of Paul, had told him these things.

* * *

Moji, Paul's first wife, was a pipeline and a canary. She made sure Jacob was aware of everything going on in Paul's house. When Jacob married Omotola, she would compete, put it in Jacob's head that he should treat her as Paul treated his women. Omotola's unhappiness would eventually kill her mother. That had been Moji's primary aim recently.

She loved to torment, rain pain on Omotola and all of Paul's offspring, male or female, from other mothers. She would keep her ears to the ground to know when Omotola started her period. And she would be the one to tell Jacob when to marry Omotola because Paul was a sadist—a selfish man who would punish people just for fun, without any pity for anybody.

Moji had loved Paul immediately after she knew she would be marrying him. A week before their marriage, she'd woken up each night gasping, yearning for the day she'd marry and be under the roof of the lovable boy almost all the girls she knew drooled over. One of her friends was so green-eyed with jealousy that she had refused to attend her wedding with Paul.

The second day after their marriage, she knew Paul had never liked her and never would. The marriage was a sham. And Paul wouldn't have married her in this world if Gbadamosi hadn't been trapped, if he hadn't owed her father a lot of money. Her father had written off the debt when Gbadamosi had agreed to her father's demands: cancellation of his debt in exchange for Paul's marriage to Moji. She learned all this at the time from her mother, whom she had not talked to since, confused and unhappy with her role in the scheme. Paul was far away not even a week after their marriage. He took a shine to Adewumi, "the beauty." Moji was devastated.

Moji wasn't beautiful as a young girl. In fact, none of her father's daughters were, but their father loved them so much, along with their mother, that he had resolved to marry them out to the most eligible handsome bachelors, not the old-timer goats around town. He didn't need their bride price. He only wanted his daughters' happiness and lovely grandchildren. There was one other thing. Moji's parents had believed that the offspring of their marriages would be lovely, but sadly, her six children—four boys and two girls—took after her. Not a single one had Paul's good looks. No man had come forward to propose marriage to any of her two daughters.

Moji's father was a short man without outward merit of beauty, but with a strong determination of heart to be successful. And he was. As a result, throughout Moji's life, she and other siblings in his household had been treated like princes and princesses. He was a man with a large herd around the area, a moneylender, and an occasional farmer, but for that part, he hired laborers.

Moji never thought she could lack anything until she married Paul. She realized that Papa couldn't fix everything. Sex had been the one thing her father couldn't buy for her. Since she had been left in a Dumpster after a few days of marriage, as Paul went after Adewumi, she organized herself to get what Papa couldn't fix or get from Paul. After all, Paul had started it.

The only man she could get, who was willing, since no other man passed a second glance at her, was Jacob. She'd met Jacob for the first time with Paul, on their wedding day. Jacob wasn't good-looking either. They were two people who found themselves in the dark. She was a beggar without any choice. He would do.

Part Two

ॐ

Chapter Ten

All Saints Primary School, 1945. Five years later.

Even though the home was chaotic and pupils in All Saints Primary School were mean, Omotola was still the best in her class since Primary One. She was becoming a woman, and that bothered her. It could take away what she loved, valued most in her life—Western education. She could be forced into a loveless marriage.

The school bell rang for lunch. In one of the elementary classrooms, Omotola sat up straight, frightened. Absentmindedly she closed her math notebook and looked through the classroom window. She could see the other pupils walking toward the cafeteria. The lunch would last forty minutes. During those forty minutes, she'd prefer to sit in the classroom by herself, out of the range of insulted from Dupe Akindele and her gang, who had wanted pieces of her since her first day in school.

Since she'd met Dupe and her friends on the school field years before, they had bullied her for coming from a poor home with a shabby appearance, and strongly suggested that she leave school because they were jealous of her intelligence and good grades. But she was blessed to have Sister Teresa, her first teacher in the school that strongly believed in her, and that is what made her stay. Apart from Sister Teresa, all other teachers that had taught Omotola liked her, all agreeing that she was a brilliant girl with a great future in education.

Each grade level had three classrooms. The three classrooms of the sixth grade were directly in front, facing the vast playground that separated it from the principal's office and the teachers' lounge. And the other grades, three classrooms each, were lined up behind it. The cafeteria was at the far end, on the left, a bit further from where the restrooms for the students were.

At most breaks in Elementary One and Two, Omotola would run out of the classroom to sit under the oak tree near the exit of the school. And she was always in tears. She feared the kids in her class, especially Dupe's gang, that targeted her and pasted insults on her at every opportunity, even when she'd had a bad morning at home and her legs hurt like hell.

Sister Teresa would always find Omotola during recess and lunch, making her a priority because she knew what torture Omotola faced every day, both at home and at school. At the onset of Elementary One, Sister Teresa had made her believe that she had talent, that she had great potential. She'd continued to sit with Omotola under the oak tree until she knew the child had grown stronger, replacing tears with children's books that she and others had provided for her.

In Elementary One and Two, when Omotola wanted to shy away from activities, Sister Teresa would have a smile on her face and would say: "To underestimate oneself is bad. It diminishes potential, but trial, persistence, and endurance are the keys to success."

Omotola didn't understand most of the words, but Sister Teresa had taken out a dictionary and read the meanings to her. It took her time to explain further in simple words: "Winners never quit, Omotola. They do stumble, and when it happens, they pick themselves up and try again until they achieve their aims."

So many encouraging phrases offered at her lowest point helped her persist. As she finished Elementary Two, she'd realized the sister was right—she wasn't less of a human being than the rest of the students in her school, just because they were children of the rich and famous. She had the highest scores on all of her exams. She knew she had an edge, and finally gained the nerve to talk back to them. She would laugh at anyone who insulted her and say: "You're stupid, even though you are from a rich family. Your report card said so…"

She made them cry, as they had made her cry in the past, until one day, during the early part of Primary Three, she had given Dupe's best friend, Ibukun, a blow on the head. Ibukun had provoked her, standing in front of her in the morning devotion assembly, in front of all the students, calling out, "Stinking Shabby, go back to your hamlet." Omotola let her have it.

Ibukun had slumped to the ground. The teachers frantically tried to revive her. Miss Anne, the headmistress who loved and encouraged Omotola, just like Sister Teresa, was highly disappointed in her. Her half-brother, Kola, had taught her to pray to God in difficult situations, so she had prayed to God then for divine intervention—

for Ibukun not to die and not to be sent out of school.

Sister Anne had strongly warned that the school wouldn't tolerate such barbaric behavior. Next time it happened, Omotola would be expelled. Since then, she'd decided to skip lunch in the cafeteria in order to avoid the rally of insults that only served to infuriate her.

She couldn't eat in the classroom, as it was prohibited. But as soon as she arrived home, she would eat her lunch in a rush. She loved school. She was extremely good at it. But the two-week Easter break was coming, and she was afraid it might soon be her last day of school, because all the indications of her becoming a woman were there. She'd started menstruation months earlier. Even though a child inside, her body said otherwise. Omotola had wondered—why does starting puberty equate to marriage? She might be married away to Jacob, a man who had been paying her bride price since her birth.

She hated her luck for having a father like Paul, who saw nothing good about school and only wanted her in an arranged marriage. Most of all, she hated having been born into a polygamous home that was also full of dysfunction.

She knew she had to share her fear with Kola, so they could both look for a solution. She needed him, as always.

"Omotola, what are you doing in the classroom when you're supposed to be in the cafeteria eating?"

Omotola was too carried away with her inner thoughts to notice her teacher had approached her. "I'm sorry, Miss Harriet," Omotola said, adding a lie, "I was copying everything on the blackboard. I'll go for lunch now." She stood up.

"Omotola, lunch is very important; the copying of

the exercise can wait," Miss Harriet said softly. "Anyway, Miss Anne wants to see you in the office. Go and see her, and come to the cafeteria for lunch immediately after."

"Yes, Miss Harriet…"

* * *

"Good afternoon, Miss Teresa and Miss Anne," Omotola said as she faced Miss Anne, the headmistress, squarely. "My teacher said you want to see me?"

"Yes, please sit down."

Omotola was fully attentive as she sat next to Sister Teresa on one of the three visitor seats.

"Your entrance exam to secondary school came back." Sister Anne hesitated. "But I'm glad it's as Sister Teresa predicted. You have one of the highest scores in the whole country, and the church has given you a full scholarship to any secondary school of your choice if you decide to skip Primary Six. The choice is up to you."

Omotola was stunned, just like the time Sister Teresa and Sister Anne had called her in, wanting her to try out for the exam. They had assured her it was *no pressure.* It was just to rate the school's academic performances. Omotola had agreed.

"It's unbelievable," Omotola finally said.

"No, it is not," Sister Teresa said without any doubt in her voice. "For a long time, I have known that you can do it. And I'm going to assure you that if you decide that you want to go to secondary school next year, you'll be as good as those finishing Primary Six, who passed this year to go to secondary school. As Sister Anne said, it's up to you. But I got you something for passing. You didn't let me down."

She gave Omotola a book from her handbag: *The Merchant of Venice.*

"I don't think that's appropriate. It will be too complicated," Sister Anne said with disapproval on her face. "Shakespeare is for—"

"No, it's not," Sister Teresa butted in gently. "She has already finished a good deal of this kind of literature—including *Julius Caesar!* Omotola, tell Sister Anne how far you've gone in literature."

Sister Teresa beamed.

"Yes, Sister Anne, I have read a great deal of literature, including *Julius Caesar.*"

While Omotola's schoolmates fooled around—her friends at home in marriages, Kola in the Lion Club—she had occupied herself with books. They were her companions.

"And, you understand them?"

"Yes, with the help of Sister Teresa."

Omotola had dipped her hands into strenuous literature like *Julius Caesar* because Kola wouldn't shut up about the book. He had been highly depressed about how difficult it was to understand. And out of pity, Omotola had gone to Sister Teresa for help, since the book was all Greek to her, just as it was to Kola. The nun made it interesting, explaining from A to Z what the book was about. Since then, Omotola had been in love with Shakespeare and had read a few more titles.

"Amazing, that's amazing!" Sister Anne nodded several times, unconsciously, as she stared at Omotola. "Anyway, as I said, it's your choice if you still want to stay and finish Elementary Six. I'm proud of you, Omotola. You are one of the greatest kids I have had the chance to meet in life."

Omotola felt perky.

"Can I tell you my answer later? It is a bit confusing right now."

"Sure, Omotola. Any of your decisions are fine by me. You can go."

"Thanks," said Omotola as she stood up and bowed to the two nuns.

She left the headmistress's office and went outside, onto the field, where she saw Dupe and her gang looking her way.

An "*Oh, no!*" invaded Omotola's head. She would have to dodge them, she decided.

Dupe and her friends had been playing around when Dupe saw Omotola going to Sister Anne's office.

"Look over there! I think Miss Stinky-Shabby-Crazy Hurricane Brain is in trouble," Dupe had said joyfully.

"Well, we'll wait and find out. For once, I want her to be in trouble. I hate her and her stupid brain. She makes all of us look dumb," Ibukun said as she watched Omotola disappear into the headmistress's office.

Before her quick escape, the seven-strong gang caught up with her, ready, as before, for full, bull-like aggression.

She had done all she could to make Dupe like her. She had agreed in Primary Three to Sister Teresa's suggestion to help Dupe with math since they came from the same town. She had arrived at Dupe's apartment unit accompanied by a guard from the front gate, who scared the hell out of her. Omotola had seen Akin on the balcony at close range— so rude, so snobby, too big for his boots to open his mouth to reply to her greetings. And as if that wasn't enough, Dupe had turned on her heel and shooed off Omotola like a dog. She would always hate all that came from the Akindele family.

"Omotola, no, that doesn't sound right," Dupe said, correcting herself. "Stinky-Shabby-Crazy, that's better."

The others laughed, stationing themselves in a circle around Omotola.

"Where are you coming from, and what is that?" Dupe said, pointing to the book in Omotola's hand.

"Where I'm coming from is none of your business or what I have in my hand. Now, let me pass."

"It's my business, parasite. Your kind is not welcome here. You have to leave like the rest. You can't finish Primary Six. You can't graduate with us. Get my point?"

The two other girls who had come from surrounding hamlets, who had started elementary school with Omotola, who had the same background as Omotola, had left the school. They couldn't cope with the insults. But Omotola couldn't leave. She had to stand firm and stay if she didn't want to be shipped off to the home of a crazy husband, who had been waiting for her for a long time. As long as she was in school, she would be protected. Besides, she loved learning, and learning agreed with her.

"Suit yourself. Give way!"

Omotola was ready to push one out of the circle, to liberate herself at all costs. She walked toward Dupe, the ringleader, ready to hit her.

"If you touch me," Dupe warned, "I'll fall on the ground, and others will scream that you hit me intentionally, and you know that has happened before. Only this time, you'll be out of school."

Dupe gave Omotola the evil eye.

"So, tell me why you went to the headmistress's office, and then beg for pardon."

The rest of the girls got ready for action while other students on the field watched the show. Omotola knew none of them would help. As a matter of fact, they would be ready to testify against her. Dupe Akindele controlled everybody. Nervously, Omotola was praying, looking around for a teacher to show up. In a flash, Ibukun snatched the new book from Omotola's hands, tossing it to Dupe. Dupe dodged it and backed off. The book landed on the ground with a force that tore off many pages.

"Ew, don't you ever touch a thing she's held in her hand," Dupe shouted. "She has a smelly secretion in her hands."

"Oh, God, you are right. I'm contaminated!" Ibukun shouted, looking horrified. "C'mon, let's go to the tap so I can wash my hands."

She turned, breaking into a run. The others followed.

Dejectedly, Omotola picked up her book and the pages that had fallen out, and walked towards the oak tree, her only friend in the school. She sat under the tree and wept for a long time.

❧

Chapter Eleven

Since Kola had finished elementary school and Ibata-Itan didn't have a high school, every day, Kola walked with Omotola to her school. And he continued his journey to his secondary school, Itan Central High School in Ajoni-itan. In the afternoon, he would walk to Omotola's school, and they both went back home together.

A few yards from the entrance of All Saints, Kola watched Omotola rushing toward him. All of a sudden, a green snake raised its head. She froze in her tracks.

"Omotola, don't move," Kola called out as he saw the snake lifting up its head, hissing. "I'm not going to let it harm you, not this time."

Kola dropped his school bag on the floor, picked up a stone, and threw it in front of the snake. The snake leaped into the bushes.

Kola ran to Omotola's side. "Are you all right?"

"I think so," she said, feeling weak. "Why do horrible things always pick on me? If you were not around, it would have hurt me, like before."

Omotola had been bitten by a snake on the leg on their way home from school a few years back. Kola had torn his uniform and wrapped it around the leg, carrying Omotola on his back for miles before finding someone that helped. Omotola had a high fever even after the town herbalist had chanted incantations to neutralize the poison and said that the worst was over.

"I don't think it intended to hurt you," Kola replied, trying to allay Omotola's fear. "It was as scared as you, but one wrong move from you, and it might have bitten you. So, how was school today?"

"The same. Dupe and her group picked on me again, but I know I only have to endure them for a little while longer because … I've decided to go to secondary school next year."

"What are you talking about?"

"My high school entrance exam came out," Omotola said casually. "I nailed it and have a scholarship to any secondary school of my choice. Sister Anne told me. The missionary granted the scholarship," Omotola said, looking relaxed. "Kola, I can go to any secondary school of my choice in the country!"

Kola hugged her. "Omotola, I know you can do it. You are never a quitter like the others. I'm happy. Please choose my secondary school. I don't want you to go high school in another town. That means you'd need to be in boarding school."

"Kola," Omotola said, "I'd be stupid not to choose your school. I'm sure I would hate boarding school. Besides, going far might kill my mom. And I know I'll need a lot of help with a lot of things, and I can count on you. I'm going to attend Itan Central High School. I'll tell them my decision after the holiday."

"Omotola, you will never regret this."

"Kola, I'm worried. Do you think Papa will still force me to marry Papa Jacob?"

"He won't dare do that," Kola said seriously.

"Are you sure about that?" Omotola said soberly. "Yinka's in-laws have asked her father for a wedding date. You think that won't gear Papa toward marrying me out soon?"

Yinka was Omotola's best friend. She had tried to talk Yinka into going to school, like her, to avoid the crazy wedding, but Yinka had refused. She always had wedding plans on the tip of her tongue, which irritated Omotola and stopped her from visiting her childhood friend, who happened to have a crush on Kola. She had tried to convince Yinka that going to school would make her wishes of marrying Kola come true, but to no avail. She seemed brainwashed.

"Your case is different from that of Yinka," Kola said firmly. "Papa would be crazy to do that. The missionaries would send him to jail, where he belongs. No, Omotola, he won't—trust me. I promise, during this holiday, I won't be far away from you. And any movement of such from him, it's likely I would kill him if the missionaries don't arrive in time. You have my word; he will never drive you to a sick marriage because of his selfishness and greediness."

"Thanks, Kola."

"You are welcome. Let's go home."

Kola and Omotola walked to the place where Kola had dropped his school bag. He bent to pick it up.

"So, you don't have any training in Lion Club this holiday?"

"None that I can think of," he said, standing up.

"Most of the members will be on holiday. Some will be on vacation overseas, so I heard."

"It's a shame that girls are not allowed in the club," she said, confessing, "I'd have loved to join. I hate when you have to go to practice and I have to be all on my own. Anyway, I'm glad you have no program for this Easter holiday," Omotola said, looking contented.

The Lion Club was founded by Akin, and it welcomed its own kind—rich boys with excellent academics and athletics performances—but it had little tolerance for boys from feeble families, except for a few chosen ones. Kola was fortunate to be one of them, and he hung out in the club by a fragile spider's thread.

Kola's favors came from Akin, the founder. They had both attended All Saints Primary, and were presently in Itan Central's High School in Ajoni-Itan. Akin was aware of Kola's talents since they were both in the same inter-house of Watermore, and both competed in the hundred meters and relays in the Western region. They had won many cups for the school.

Akin dictated the tune of the club. Nobody was accepted without his stamp of approval. Only a few males from humble families were initiated. Even a few girls from rich homes, with excellent academic qualifications, were excluded. "Girls are distractions, too weak and stupid to withstand the rigorous exercises designed by the author of the Lion Club." This was always broadcast by the members to any kind of girl who sought to join them—"No."

The boys in the club were the chosen few from all four corners of the British protectorates. Akin wanted the club to be global. Lion Club recruitment qualifications were: male, in secondary school, excellent academic and athletic performance, sound background a bonus. All applications must be submitted to the Akdrend group of companies' headquarters in Ladden. These requirements were stated prominently in all of the widely circulated newspapers in Nigeria.

When Kola joined the club, it was life-changing. Apart from his being snatched from the jaws of bullies in the school that were afraid of the upper-class members of the club, Akin turned into a pal who helped Kola materially. Initially, Paul's unwillingness to send him to school had given him the tough skin of an elephant. He also had the strong foot of an elephant, as it wangled its way through the thick forest—Kola went without shoes his first year in primary school, until the headmistress, Miss Anne, let him choose footwear from the lost-and-found unclaimed goods of the rich kids. It was there that he did his "shopping" until Primary Six. Since then, Akin had been a cool provider of all his essentials. Probably out of pity or friendship, Akin would walk Kola into a whole room full of clothes and other things, called a closet, to choose whatever he wanted.

Kola and his sister left the school gate and set out along the path they took home daily.

"Omotola," he said earnestly, "I'm not leaving you alone, especially when that cripple might…" He stopped, motioning for Omotola to stop too. He whispered. "Over there," and he pointed. "Papa Jacob! What is he doing around here?"

Jacob stood, examining some leaves.

"You are right; it is him," she said, looking terrified. "I don't want to talk to him."

"Me, neither," he said with hatred. "He is a creep. We'll wait and see what he is up to."

Jacob left the path, entering the bush.

They both sighed, walking faster past that spot.

Kola hated the way Jacob had jumped in front of them out of nowhere. "I'm going to talk to a Rev father about this," he said.

❦

Chapter Twelve

The Akdrend building in Arasola Street, Akuta town—owned by Simon Akindele—was easy to recognize. It was a tower of five stories with low buildings around it. His towers had the same features, the same character in all the big cities in Nigeria. Just as in all the cities, Simon's office was on the third floor, while his workers' offices were beneath and above him.

Akdrend Tower in Akuta was the regional headquarters for raw materials export in Itan Land. Today, Simon sat with a pale face in his office. He had frequently had a pale face in the last two years, around the closure of the academic year, when his children's performances would be revealed. But this only April. Simon had received a letter from the principal of Itan Central High School, Reverend Thomas. He requested a meeting immediately after the Easter holiday about his boys, Akin and Olu.

Since Reverend Thomas replaced Simon's old pal, Reverend Philip, in Itan Central High School two years earlier, Simon had been worried. The new principal showed him how his boys were doing in school each time he called upon him. And each time, one of his son's behavior was alarming. Olu was on the verge of being expelled.

The first time Simon met the Reverend, he knew straight away, he wasn't an easy man—not like his predecessors, whom Simon had used as playdough, to mold into whatever he wanted. No, this was a mean, tough, strict man. And any attempt to mold him, Simon sensed, would explode in his face. During Thomas's two years in the school, he'd expelled a lot of students that used to have a free hand in everything. Simon knew this because he was the chairman of the parent-teacher association of the school. And Thomas had warned them all clearly that any students who refused to shape up would be out like the rest of the undesirable in his school. Simon was uncomfortable with his unfriendly and rigid attitude. In fact, he was the first British man to get under his thick skin. To Simon, all men had their price. But he wasn't so sure about this one.

At Itan Central High School's inception, when the protectorates' governor, Sir Bernard Bourdillon, mentioned at a dinner that Archdeacon Watermore wanted the Anglican Communion to build a high school in Itan Land, Simon had promised his undying support. In fact, he would have lobbied for the secondary school for Ibata, his people, if it wasn't absurd, because his people were still in settlements, aspiring for sovereignty. Priority was given to an established town, the metropolis of Itan Land: Ajoni-Itan. So, Simon had obtained All Saints Primary School for his people instead. Meanwhile, he had been providing the undying support he had promised to the letter. The Anglican Communion counted on him for almost everything.

The school had claimed excellence from the start. At the end of form six, the first set, ninety-nine percent of the students who had sat for external final exams passed with the highest scores in Nigeria. When Akin and Olu had taken the entrance exam to the school that Simon had helped build, which was A1 in Nigeria, they passed. Simon was insane with joy. He was also thrilled that his boys would be attending a secondary school where his bosom friend, Reverend Philip, was the principal. The reverend was more or less the two boys' godfather. Simon had jumped like a frog everywhere, telling everybody the news.

Over the years, Simon had gone the extra mile to make both sons comfortable. The comfort, he knew, had gone to one of his son's heads. Olu was still in Form One, even though he'd started with Akin, who was now in Form Three. With this poor performance, Olu might be expelled like the rest of the undesirables in the school, Reverend Thomas had warned.

It seemed that Reverend Philip's early concerns that Olu's behavior was getting out of hand at the beginning of Form One were coming true. He'd called upon Simon and said that Olu was found in a compromising position with a girl, Janet, in the chemistry lab—as he had put it, "interacting with nature in the chemistry lab." The reverend made it clear that this must not be taken lightly. He emphasized that if Olu's behavior was not nipped in the bud and dealt with quickly, Simon risked having his other children follow suit. He'd told the story of Eli and his boys in the Bible to buttress his point.

When the Reverend Philip suggested that Olu and Janet go to separate boarding schools for their genders, far away from home, Simon had laughed in his face. He said the reverend was exaggerating and blowing things out of proportion. Simon was adamant that his son would never leave that golden school to be confined to a boarding house that was more or less a jail. He insisted that Olu was just in the wrong crowd of nonentity boys of the school— the children of the expatriates and Ladden boys who had known what sex was all about since they came out of their mothers' wombs.

"Olu was never a bad seed until those boys befriended him," Simon had told Reverend Philip. He refused to blame his lifestyle as the cause, the linchpin of Olu's renegade behavior, as Philip had cleverly pointed out once.

"Children learn by imitation," Rev had said.

"If it's the cause, why wasn't Akin affected?" Simon demanded, looking irritated.

"One child is different from another."

Simon was not buying it. Instead, he had hated the reverend for saying that. He had always been a caring father. He gave them the world. He told Reverend Philip this. He had believed that all of Olu's nonsense was just a phase, that he would get over it. In a way, Olu reminded him of himself. Simon had slept with countless girls for fun during secondary school, and he had turned out fine. He had argued, refusing to accept the theories and solutions the reverend had proposed. For peace to reign, to make the scandal go away, he'd convinced the parents of Janet that *she* should change schools since he arranged that Olu would marry their daughter as soon as he was ready.

Simon was more concerned about Akin, his firstborn,

the heir to his empire, his eventual successor, who had a cool attitude toward the world around him. His companions had been books and horses since his mother left. In fact, Simon was afraid he'd lose Akin to the priesthood. He hung around Reverend Philip too much. It happened to many young kids hanging around the Catholic churches and Catholic priests a lot. Anyway, if Akin did break away, he had a substitute: Olu.

Simon finally got the hint at the end of Form One that Olu's behavior was a bigger deal than he'd thought. He realized that Reverend Philip's premonition could come to pass as Olu skipped school to go to parties. He moved to his grandparents' house to play havoc with girls. Simon knew he should've listened to advice instead of assuming Olu would turn out fine. Still, he could've just counted on luck now, shrugged, and ignored Olu if his behavior hadn't been more terrible than ever. And if, as Reverend Philip predicted, this started to have an impact on his other children, things would only get worse. That was starting to give Simon sleepless nights, as most of his children were carbon copies of Olu in behavior—they started to hide in their grandparents' houses, skipping school. Even though some were still in primary school, they started to "interact with nature." Simon had been aware of it, hearing from their drivers who reported back after a journey. Olu started it, and all the others followed in his footsteps, like good patriots.

Out of Simon's six children in All Saints Primary School, on his last visit for the distribution of the report cards, Dupe's report, in Primary Four, was the only one without blemish. Akin and Dupe were both children from his first marriage. And despite their mother being long gone, leaving the two behind, their teachers had always had good things to say about them—from punctuality in school to taking part in all the school's extra-curricular activities. Their teachers were proud of them, as Simon had been proud of them.

The teachers of Simon's other three children, from his second wife, Arinola (the mother of Olu) and the teachers of his other two, from his third wife, Dola, had a lot of bad things to recount—skipping school, insulting teachers when they finally did show up for classes. When their teachers pointed out their errors and punished them, the wayward kids never failed to throw into the faces of their teachers that their father would make their lives hell if he knew they had been punished. After a time, they just overlooked their errors.

Simon Akindele didn't come into a fortune by accident or by sitting on his hands, waiting for miracles to happen. He had become rich by dedication and hard work, and he seized opportunities at the right time.

Simon's father, Kanbi, was a wealthy cloth merchant with two wives and six children. While he rode horses to trade far and wide, he always aspired for his children to do better than him. So, when a primary school opened in a neighboring town not far from Ibata-Itan, Kanbi was the only father that enrolled all his six children in school.

One by one, unfortunately, after a certain time, his children dropped out of school, including Simon. While Kanbi's five other children had chosen different paths in life as he had urged, Simon, the last boy, the most educated out of the siblings, had left school at Form Four. He'd left Victor Boys High School in Ladden, frustrated after repeating Form Four twice. He had opted out of school before he could be advised to withdraw. He got a clerical job in a bookshop as his father had wanted, in order to gain experience. And later, he'd joined his father in trade, selling clothes far and wide in the Western region. He later went into exportation overseas. That was how he made his fortune.

While he was building his prospects, Simon married his first wife, his sweetheart Joyce, from Josi. Joyce was a woman of ravishing beauty: fair skin, slim body, oblong face, pointed nose, and long, black, glossy, silky hair. At the time, he was at the onset of becoming a wealthy, powerful man—not only as a clothes merchant but by opening many depots and grading cocoa and other cash crops for export in the Western region.

When Simon was tapped by colonial masters to represent the farmers in the Western region of Nigeria, *Agbapo*, the farmers' union, Simon not only grabbed the opportunity but quickly bought up acres of lands from the kings and landowners. He acquired many uncultivated, abandoned lands as plantations for cash crops in Itan and its neighboring lands, and employed many locals to work for him. Within a few years, Simon Akindele's name opened doors in Nigeria and beyond. Simon single-handedly put the Ibata-Itan people on the map.

Simon married his wife Joyce in a small church near her house in Josi, despite both sets of parents objecting to the wedding almost until the wedding day. Joyce had been betrothed to a native, while Simon was to marry a native too. Kanbi had chosen a wife for him and planned an unbeatable wedding when Joyce came along. The whole family was disappointed. In fact, only a few members of Simon's family attended the ceremony, which may have been the glitziest society wedding of the time.

Simon's family complained that they knew little about Joyce, but he was unconcerned because he loved Joyce to death. He promised to hold the sacrament of marriage—until death do us part—to the end of his life. He began, but persisted for only a month. His father and family got to him, convincing him that he needed to marry the native, the one first set aside for him, for whom all bride prices were paid, as in the custom.

"Polygamy is not a taboo," Kanbi had said. "Your first wife has to live with it."

Simon had agreed. He'd married Arinola as his second wife, more to please his father than anything else. He had refused the elaborate wedding Kanbi wanted and prepared for. He said it wouldn't be fair to Joyce. Months later, Simon came from his hometown and told Joyce he had accepted a second wife from his father and that she was pregnant. Joyce was pregnant with their first child, Akin, too. After much persuasion and sincere apologies, Joyce had accepted the second wife in good faith but made Simon promise he would have no more wives. She moved with Simon to Ibata-Itan, and his second wife ushered in his subsequent polygamy.

Simon Akindele's two-story building in Ibata-Itan, his first property, was built to cater to his need to become a polygamous man. The main house was joined at the back with a stretch of self-contained apartments and a servants' quarter, far at the back. Within a few years, Simon married another wife, Dola, and Joyce left. Her disappearance was told in different versions.

At the time of Joyce's disappearance, she and his second wife, Arinola, lived in the apartment units in the backyard, while Simon's latest wife lived with him in the main building. And that latest wife was about to be moved to one of the tasteful backyard units since a new wife was arriving to take her place. Akin was sleeping in the second bedroom of the apartment occupied by his mother, while Dupe slept in the same bed with her on the day she left. It was Sunday.

Usually, on Sundays, Joyce woke them early, bathed them, and made them have breakfast with their father in his living room. But when Dupe awoke, she found that her mother was gone.

Dupe shook her brother from his bed. "Akin, wake up. Where is Mama?" Dupe had asked.

"Go back to bed, Dupe. Mama will soon be back." Akin waved her away so he could go back to sleep.

Dupe had gone back to bed. And hours later, she came back to Akin's bed to wake him up again.

"Akin, I still can't find Mama, and I'm hungry," Dupe had lamented.

The brightness of the sun filtering through the window blinds made Akin realize something was wrong because by then, their mother would have bathed them and would have taken them to have breakfast with their father before he went to his depots or settled down to read the newspapers. It was a ritual of bonding between Simon, his first wife, and the children. For reasons that were unclear to Akin, Simon never encouraged his second or third wife and children to eat with him.

Akin sat up. He said, "Okay, Dupe, I will go and ask Papa if he has seen Mama. You wait here."

Akin had left to look for Joyce while Dupe lay on his bed. He got to his father's living room. Instead of him finding his father dressed, waiting at the dining table for them to arrive, he had a bottle of gin in his hand and looked disturbed. He had put the gin bottle on the floor and buried his head in his hands.

"Are you okay, Papa?"

"Yes, Son, I'm okay," he mumbled.

Akin watched him remove his hands from his face, his eyes red and strained.

"Where is Mama? She is not in her room."

Simon stared at the floor for a long time without an answer. As Akin stood, wondering about his father's state and mother's whereabouts, his father cleared his throat and said, "Your mother left me; she ran away, left you and your sister behind..."

Joyce was never seen again. According to Simon, she was a callous woman, without a conscience, to have abandoned himself and her two children. Simon went on a rampage, acquiring more women like he was acquiring properties of choice.

Despite being almost illiterate, building wealth was as natural as breathing air to Simon. Market strategy had been his strongest point—going to Europe to front cash crops exportation. At home, though, he was less focused. He was incapable of loving one for long. He just got bored easily in relationships. After the first child, he tossed them to the back of his house, picking a brand-new bride as if they were new cars, the culture giving him a free hand in marrying as many as possible. Women were his greatest flaws.

However, while Simon built an empire for himself, he never forgot his regrets. He regretted never completing higher education. True, at times, it was difficult for him to negotiate the price of cocoa for the benefit of the hard-working farmers, without an interpreter—without Boyede, his assistant who had a master's degree in economics from Oxford University in London. But the dawn to that darkness was in sight. His son, Akin, was destined to be a lawyer, to take over the empire.

But to acquaintances, those who knew Simon in and out, his greatest regret in life, the one he could never conceal or find a solution to, was the disappearance of Joyce. It was a vacuum, they all said, that no woman could ever fill.

$$\mathcal{R}$$

Chapter Thirteen

The first week of the Easter holiday went by so fast that Omotola and Kola hadn't seen many people and were left mostly on their own. Their neighborhood was like a desert. The second week wasn't any better, and they started playing a game called *arin* in the front yard.

Taking a closer look at Paul's house and its surroundings, it was as if everybody in the neighborhood had shifted to another arena, but the truth was, everybody had gone to the farm. The two women who could have been at home—Rolake (Omotola's mom) and Adewumi (Kola's mom), since Paul took their lands—were doing labor work from one farm to another.

Playing the game of arin had become Kola's and Omotola's usual habit since the holiday started, once they were fed up with reading and it was too early for exploring. The game consisted of twenty arin seeds placed in front of each competitor, with a demarcation line in the middle. And there was a never-to-be-crossed stop line at the end of each section of arin. Twenty arin seeds were used as strikers, to displace the seeds in front of them. Whoever got the most arin seeds displaced on the opponent's side emerged the winner. Omotola was on a serious winning streak.

"God! Omotola, you cheated again," Kola shrieked.

"That's a lie," Omotola cried, agitated. "I won again, even if you hate losing to your little sister."

Omotola had been truthful. She had won three rounds before the one Kola complained about.

"You've stepped beyond the line. I'm not lying. We cancel this round and start again," Kola said.

"No, we're not canceling anything. I won. You know what your problem is—you are distracted."

"No, I'm not. I'll show you I'm not distracted," Kola said, with determination all over his face.

"So," Omotola said lightly, "no cancellation then?"

"Have it your way, Omotola." Kola said, placing the seeds back in their place. A voice buzzed, and then two people popped into view. Kola and Omotola stood face to face with Bayo and another boy in a security uniform.

"What the hell are you doing with your sister?" Bayo asked, frowning.

When you are born in a wacky home, schooled in hell, you are bound to have an attitude. You are bound to be aggressive and defensive, with punk words that flow out smoothly, or with a telling look. Omotola was, and she gave Bayo a *"you're not welcome"* stare.

Bayo's background was similar to that of Kola, or worse. He had been taken out of his hometown, Amokin-Itan, because of the unending violence and havoc caused by his father, at a tender age, when he started school. He had been chaperoned by a catechist and his wife until he had a full scholarship and could stay at the boarding school. He had been accepted into the Lion Club, like

Kola, but they had a common fear and a common enemy by the name of Wole. He would have made their lives miserable, if not from time to time cautioned by Akin, who had once before threatened him with expulsion.

"It's good to see you, Bayo," Kola said, to break the ice between the two.

"Anyway, Akin sent me with his butler to summon you for a meeting about Lion Club recruitment," Bayo said, letting go of the rift between him and Omotola.

"I didn't know we were having a meeting today. I thought it was next week, when we are all back in school?"

"Well, Akin wants it today, before the holiday ends, so let's go," Bayo said, ready to leave.

"I don't know," Kola said, looking worried. "I'm the only one at home with my little sister, and I can't leave her alone."

"What do you mean?" said Bayo, slyly. "Your sister is not little. She is a girl with a lousy attitude."

This isn't school. I don't have to walk away as Kola insisted because of the threat of expulsion. Bayo is trespassing. Omotola was ready to give it to him loud and clear. "You're such an idiot, with a big head full of crap," she said, smiling.

"Stop, both of you!" Kola snapped. "I wish to go, but..."

"Did I tell you Akin is sitting on his seat, *waiting* for you?" Bayo said, with an emphasis on "waiting."

Kola fidgeted as he turned to Omotola.

"Please, Omotola, I have to go. We can finish our game when I come back."

"Can't I come with you instead of being alone in the house?" Omotola said, pleading. "Please, Kola. I'm scared."

"Can I take her along?"

"Are you out of your mind? Wole is there too. And you should know by now what he'll do to you," explained Bayo in anger.

"He is right, Omotola," Kola said, unsettled. "I can't take you along, but I promise to be back really quick."

"Who is Wole? Another idiot? Why are you scared of him?" Omotola said, concerned at Kola's forlorn expression.

"Because he is scary. He'll eat a lousy, mouthy girl like you alive," Bayo said, full of hatred.

"Shut up, giant head. I'm talking to my brother." Omotola sneered.

"I'll tell you about him later," Kola said, then added nicely, "Please, Omotola, I have to go."

"Go, then, with your stupid friend to the stupid club meeting, but be back quick," Omotola ordered.

"In a jiffy, I'll be back," Kola promised. "Count on it. As soon as the meeting is over, we'll resume our game."

Sadly, Omotola watched them stroll away.

She tried to play the game by herself, but it wasn't fun, so she decided to sit on the bench positioned under the odan tree.

* * *

"What in the name of God got into you, Omotola, that makes you behave like a careless child?" Rolake yelled, looking upset. She had a large basket on her head, full of edibles. "Where is Kola? He promised to look after you."

Rolake couldn't believe her eyes as Omotola's body curled into a ball near the bench. Apparently, Omotola had rolled off the bench twice as she lay sleeping, waiting for Kola. Eventually, she had slept on the sand, since she was scared to enter the house.

"I'm glad you are back, Mama," Omotola said as she brushed sand and leaves from her body. "Kola went with his friends to Akin Akindele's house." Omotola looked around. She could see that the sun had almost set. "He should have been back by now. You know how I hate sleeping in the empty house by myself."

"I'm sorry, Sunshine," Rolake said.

And another voice joined in. "I'm sorry, Omotola," Kola said.

"No, you're not!" Omotola said, with a look of continued dislike. "I'm sure if that idiot Akin called, you'd go. By the way, you're turning into his slave too."

"I'm not," Kola said, correcting her softly. "He is my friend, and he is nice to me."

"If he is your friend, why hasn't he left his royal seat for once, to come to *your* house instead of sending a butler, an errand boy, that Bayo—who I wish to meet again—and who I'll insult 'til he drops dead in shame!"

"I'm sorry. We'll continue our game tomorrow. And if you want, tomorrow we could practice more of the exercises of Lion Club too."

Since Kola had become absorbed in his Lion Club activities when he was less busy, Omotola insisted on knowing the drills of the rich boys' club for her recreation. She committed to the tips of the club exercise. So, when Kola was feeling expansive and wanted to please Omotola—as he did now, feeling guilty about abandoning her—he taught Omotola the drills of the club. He was ready to please Omotola with what he knew would make her happy.

"I'd be stupid to trust you again—that tomorrow will be without a hitch."

"I mean it," Kola said, seriously.

"So, if Akin sends for you to play ball with him, you won't go?" asked Omotola, impatiently waiting for answers.

"I'll…" Kola stammered.

"You're as stupid as them all. I hate you. Mama, I'm going inside."

Omotola ran inside the house, mad at Kola.

She hated Akin for having sent for Kola, turning him into his page boy.

✤

Chapter Fourteen

Paul sat at his favorite palm wine bar on earth, the bar near the town market called Oja Oba, (King's Market) and a few blocks from the king's palace, chatting away in total merriment. The bar was a hut. In the middle of the hut was a long bench surrounded by a dozen chairs made from bamboo. All seats were taken. Some customers stood, sipping their wine inside, while some were outside, trying to avoid the congestion indoors. Aduke, the proprietress, sat in a corner with gourds of palm wine, ready to attend to the needs of her customers. The palm wine was great. Paul loved it.

"Aduke, your palm wine is delicious tonight," one of Paul's drinking buddies said.

"*Awe,* you read my mind," Paul said, raising his calabash to sip. And then he saw Jacob. He stopped, with shaking hands, placing the calabash on the table.

All he wanted was to run, but how? Jacob was entering through the only available exit. He plastered a fake smile across his face, waiting for him.

Jacob walked in, standing near the exit, his eyes scanning for Paul. Their gazes met.

"Paul, Moji told me you'd be here," Jacob said.

That was just the tip of the iceberg of what Moji had told Jacob. She'd told him a lot. She'd wanted to start the ball of war rolling between Paul and Jacob. She'd wanted to destroy Paul and his family. At all times, Moji had her ears to the ground. She was over the moon months earlier, when she heard a conversation between Omotola and Rolake that proved the girl was no longer a child but a woman. She'd started her menstruation. That same evening, she had told Jacob it was time to start getting ready to marry Omotola. If he waited too long, other men could come forward with a larger bride price on Omotola, or Omotola could have her own fancy man come forward to pay her bride-wealth.

Moji knew these were lies. Paul wouldn't dare sell Omotola to another man because of the missionaries. And the last thing on Omotola's mind was a man. All she cared about was school. Gently, Moji had said to Jacob, "Paul is a pig that does piggy things." With that phrase, Jacob had sent the elders in his family in the morning, as the culture stipulated, to ask Paul for a wedding date and the list of the rest of the bride price to pay.

Paul had demanded more time. Afterward, several times, Jacob had gone to Paul on the same issue. Paul had always dodged him with one excuse or another, full of mumbo jumbo. Jacob had enough. He needed a date for the wedding, along with the bride price Paul would want, so he could work toward making them available.

Moji knew Paul was a greedy man who continued to accept incentives on Omotola, despite the fact that she could never be Jacob's wife. Paul could never marry Omotola out, since the missionaries were at his throat. He would never want to go to jail. Moji advised Jacob to snatch her off the street as soon as possible. She'd advised Jacob to start a war if Paul became unreasonable, wanting Omotola back. She had loved that part, as Jacob agreed. It was better than the "competition." It was an instant live bomb explosion. Paul and his family could never win a war against Jacob and his family because they were many, and the majority were soldiers for the town. She knew Paul and his family wouldn't survive the war, as they would rush into it blindfolded, and they would all perish. It would mean that her solemn wish granted—kill many birds with one stone. Paul would be dead, along with his family. She'd vowed a long time ago to destroy Paul, and all that was related to him for the evils he'd done to her.

Stupid woman, Paul murmured to himself. "Jacob, you are back early from the farm today," he said vaguely. He turned to face Aduke, who was in a jovial mood because there was a new client in view, and said, "Serve my friend a drink, and add the bill to the original one."

Jacob was unlike Paul when it came to being a farmer, though they shared the same chaotic lifestyle. Just like Paul, he was a farmer who was barely capable of taking care of five wives and children in his den. But, unlike Paul, he was a dedicated farmer; he left for the farm with his wives and children in the early hours on Monday morning. They would all stay in huts he'd built on his farmland. His family usually came back to town at midday on Friday, while he would arrive back in town at dusk.

"I can't do that, Baba Paul," Aduke said, complaining. "You're overdue for the areas' payment, except if…"

"Never mind about the palm wine," Jacob said. "Anyway, I'd like to talk to you in private."

Jacob stepped out of the room and Paul followed, staggering and mumbling swear words at Aduke.

"Paul, I'm here about my bride, Omotola," Jacob said, with steady eyes on Paul, who was swaying from head to toe. "I want the finalization of the wedding ceremony arrangement. And I'll be happy if you choose a day, so I can prepare for the remaining bride price items."

"Jacob, I know you're impatient to have your bride," Paul said in a friendly way. "Can we have this discussion another day?"

Paul prayed inwardly that Jacob would go with no hassle. He had been drinking, but not to the extent of being drunk. He was faking it so that Jacob could leave, come another day, or never again in life, which would make Paul happy.

"You don't know how impatient," Jacob said, smiling as he rubbed his bumpy face. "As I see my bride blossom into a woman with incredible beauty and features on her that makes me…" Jacob stopped. It wasn't appropriate to drool over your bride in front of her father.

Jacob had fantasized countless times about Omotola, especially their first night together. In private, Jacob sometimes tailed Omotola, unknown to her. The other day, Kola and Omotola had seen Jacob on their way home from school. Jacob was checking on Omotola again. And if possible, and she was alone, he wanted to woo her, talk to her. He wanted Omotola more than anything. Nothing could ever stop him from marrying Omotola, he decided. And seeing her that day, again, brought another strong urge to take his bride before losing her to a higher-paying suitor. Paul was not a reliable person, Moji had said, severely.

Even though Omotola was from a hell hole, it never showed in her body. She would have been an excellent replica of Paul, had she been a man. She was tall and slender, with figure-of-eight curves that stopped men to stare. She was an exotic beauty, with voluminous jet-black hair, a face that harbored exquisitely long eyelashes, stunning eyes, and delicate lips that covered a lovely set of extremely white teeth. To make matters worse for men now discovering her beauty when she sat on Paul's porch, she had firm oranges on her chest, and flawless skin that glowed between ebony and a brown chocolate color. It was unimportant to those who were after her to know of her genius value and her strong ambition to be somebody—an academician, one day.

Paul could have got twice as much for her had Jacob not come forward at her birth, or now, but jail hung over his head if there were negotiations for more. Omotola's life and death lay in the Oyinbo's hands.

"I understand your word, my friend, but Omotola is still young to be married."

"That's untrue. Many marry younger than her, and I think it's time I make her my bride. Please, Paul, name your price, and I'll meet it. Your daughter pleases me a lot."

"Jacob, you have to have a little more patience," Paul mumbled. "It's a little complicated at the moment."

Jacob had enough. He was angry.

"Where is the complication? When you took everything I provided, it wasn't complicated then," Jacob sneered. "To make things clear, Paul, I'm giving you three months to undo the complication. Either you give me my bride, or I snatch her off the street. And if you become stupid, I'll wage war on you, Paul. I'll make your life miserable, like that of your stupid drunkard father."

"Whose father are you calling a stupid drunkard?"

Paul glowered with rage. *Biff!* He gave Jacob a dirty slap. Jacob retaliated. People rushed to separate them.

"It's your father, Paul."

"You know what, frog face—I'll pay you back everything you've spent on Omotola. Get this—my daughter will never marry you, period."

"How are you going to do that, drunkard debtor, Paul? Whether you like it or not, your daughter is going to be mine in three months. The complications will be between you and the missionaries, liar!" Jacob said, snatching his body away from the man holding him off Paul, and left.

Omotola sat on a mat in a corner in the bedroom that she and Rolake shared, reading Merchant of Venice with an *oguso* candle as Rolake was getting ready to go out.

"Are you sure you are okay on your own, since Kola's not at home?" Rolake asked in an agitated way.

"Mama, I'll be okay," she said with a smile. "Go! I'll see you later."

"Omotola, you can come with me instead of being on your own," Rolake said, pleading. "You need fresh air."

The last thing Omotola wanted was to see her mother's friend with her recent third baby. She hated being an only child. She wasn't ready for a scenario that would bring pain.

"No, Mama, I'm serious! Go!"

"The reason I'm asking is that the crazy Moji's daughters are roving around. I don't want you to be their victim. You could go and see Yinka."

Moji's daughters were tall and lanky, a replica of Amazon women warriors. Omotola, even though tall, only reached their shoulders. Three years earlier, Omotola had taken a serious beating from Moji's youngest daughter, who had accused her of bad-mouthing her eldest sister. Rolake had been scared. The beating had taken place because Kola was away. Kola had a hatred for the two since he knew they were out to get Omotola, because of her going to school. The girls were strong, but never strong enough to match the wrestling skills of Kola in *ijakadi*. And when he came back and saw Omotola's face and body, it had been war. He had started with beating the eldest, hard, while the youngest flew away. However, Kola was waiting and descended on her with a *koboko* as she reared her head. Paul wasn't bothered when their mother reported this, crying. Since then, the two had behaved, but since Kola was not at home, gone to another meeting at the Akindele's house, there might be another chance.

"Mama, I don't want to see Yinka. All she ever talks about is her upcoming wedding," said Omotola, feeling bugged. "She even has a name for her firstborn. Isn't that stupid, Mama? Marrying a man with two wives and still proud of it? She is really crazy."

"I know it's a little out of place," Rolake said with sadness.

"Mama, it's not out of place. It should never be! I'm happy I've chosen to go to school. Probably, I would have been with that insane man with a face like an uncemented wall!"

Rolake laughed at the comparison, although it was a bitter one. The danger of her daughter's shipment to Jacob's house still loomed large. That wasn't disclosed in order not to frighten her. For quite a while, Rolake's joy of the day and night had been like the dew of the morning and evening, which never stayed … never long enough.

She slept with one eye open, full of worries, full of fear since Omotola had produced the first menstrual blood months earlier. To be honest, Rolake had prayed for her daughter's slower growth in all the areas that could possibly draw attention to adulthood. She had prayed that all features remain in hiding until Omotola could finish secondary school.

But, alas, it seemed that God was mocking her, turning a deaf ear to her prayers. Omotola's body bloomed, especially her chest, which had developed into small firm oranges instead of limes. As a result, she knew that it was just a matter of time before Jacob saw her, grabbed her off the street, and forced himself on her—and marred her for life.

"If Yinka's attitude gives you a problem, you can go to Iya Abiye to while away the time. She will be ready by now to start the evening tales."

Iya Abiye was a storyteller whose house Omotola never missed going to as a child. In fact, she was among the midwives who delivered most babies in the town. Omotola was one of the children she had brought into the world. All those she had brought to the world saw her as a second mother. Children visited her house whenever they wanted, and they were always welcome. Besides, Iya Abiye was an eloquent orator and storyteller. Omotola had loved listening to her as a child, but she had passed the age of sitting down, anxiously waiting for an oral story that was sometimes a repetition of what she had heard before.

"Mama, I'm no longer a child who listens to tales when I can read them myself, on my own. Mama … I'll be fine. Go!"

"I'll get you another *oguso* candle to be able to see well, then."

She said, "Thanks," barely looking away from the novel in her hand.

Chapter Sixteen

The following evening, Kola was in casual dress and on his way out again. Omotola ran up to him.

"Where are you going?"

"I'm going to a short Lion Club meeting at Akin's house. This Saturday is Lion Club recruiting."

"What about the book report you told me you were going to write tonight, due in a short time?"

"It's one scary book I'm not going to need in life; I'm not doing the book report."

"Anyway, this Saturday, can I tag along and…?" She trailed off.

"Tag along to do what, Omotola?" asked Kola as he laid one hand on his chin, studying her.

"Well, to try out."

"Seriously, you want to try out in for a club exclusively for boys?"

"Why not? You trained me, and I think it's high time to show if you are a good teacher."

Omotola's decision to want to be in the rich boys' club wasn't because of its prestige or wanting to run with their crowd, or even to prove a point—far from it. She still hated most of them, who trash-talked girls like her and had attitudes as if they owned the world. She just tired of being alone most of the time, since the majority of her friends were married, and the rest lived in different worlds from hers. Kola often promised to stick around the house but sometimes snuck out for hours with the club members, even outside of club activities. If she wanted to spend quality time with Kola, the only person who understood her, she would have to be in the Lion Club. If able to join, she would never be left alone in a ghost-haunted house by herself. Another two months' "long vacation" was approaching, and she didn't want to spend it like the last one. The scenarios during the Easter holiday—when Bayo and Akin's butler came to collect Kola, and when Kola went out to play ball with Akin day after day—had finalized her decision to join the club at any cost.

"No, Omotola! See you later."

He turned to leave.

"I mean it. I'll follow you on Saturday."

Kola turned to face her again. He snapped. "No, no, and no, Omotola." Kola shook his head vigorously, almost off the hook. "You're not following me to the recruiting on Saturday. Understood? The club is only for boys. They never accept rich girls, not to mention girls like…" Kola stopped, looking timid.

"Girls like what, Kola?" Omotola snapped. "We're poor. So what? You of all people should have known by now they're not better than either of us."

"They are stuffy rich kids. I'm hanging out in the club as if by spider webs. And taking you for recruitment will definitely make the threads snap," Kola complained.

"You don't know that, Kola."

"I know that most of the kids in the club hate me. Akin keeps me there."

Plan B, premeditated plan, you're on! Omotola muttered in her head.

"Kola, if you promise to take me along on Saturday, I will do your homework in literature—your book report on *Julius Caesar*—after school tomorrow."

"You'll do my assignment on *Julius Caesar*, really?" Kola cut in, looking surprised.

"I read it when you kept on ranting about it," Omotola said softly. "Actually, it's not all that bad. In fact, it's a piece of cake. You want me to quote some of the lines I like in the book?"

Kola looked at her in astonishment. Omotola liked what she saw and went to work.

"This is from Mark Anthony at Caesar's funeral: "Friends, Romans, countrymen, lend me your ears. I have come to bury Caesar, not to praise him. The evil that men do—"

"All right, all right, I know you've read it," Kola snapped again. "How did you understand the book and I didn't?"

Omotola shrugged and wouldn't reveal the source of her knowledge, in case Kola wanted to tap the area, the source. She needed him to need her.

Kola lost himself in contemplation and Omotola waited for his decision. It didn't come as quickly as she expected.

"Kola, I'll do your assignment on the book, and I guarantee you a good mark," Omotola assured him.

"You're sure you will do that for me?"

"I promise."

To assure Kola of her promise, Omotola then put the second finger of her left hand before her lips and pointed to the sky—the sign to affirm her words, and that God was a witness.

"You are on. But let me do all the talking."

"My mouth will be sealed until you want me to talk."

Again, her finger touched her lips, then pointed skyward.

✿

Chapter Seventeen

The bedroom door slammed shut violently. The pen in Omotola's left hand dropped to the floor. She looked up from Kola's book report to see Yinka pressed against the door, looking terrified.

"What's wrong with those gorillas?" she asked, panic-stricken. "Mama Moji's daughters—they were both in my face asking what I wanted, immediately after I stepped in front of your house—as if I'm new around here. When I refused to answer them, they got angry, wanted to fight. That's why I ran inside. They are insane."

Omotola gave her a quiet look and said to herself, *They are nuts, and you know why? Because you are about to marry, and they are not!* Omotola didn't dare say that out loud because she risked losing all composure completely if she had to enumerate on a subject that might make her puke.

Lately, Paul had been unkind to Moji's two daughters, hurling sinister insults at them. He'd called them ugly, wanted them to find a husband and get out of his house. Out of annoyance, the two sisters went on the rampage. Paul had gone to beg, proposing the two of them to Jacob, to replace Omotola. Jacob had refused the proposition, saying that he wouldn't marry a beast to replace a beauty, but he promised to get his bride, lawfully or unlawfully.

"I'm sorry about them," Omotola said and went back to the book report.

Looking at the sheet of paper on her lap, Yinka asked how everything was going and then jumped to the reason she was there. "Anyway, I just wanted to tell you that my in-laws came. And a date was fixed," she said, blushing.

"Oh, congratulations," Omotola said, pretending sincerity as she looked up to give the "good wishes" speech.

"Thanks," Yinka replied.

"When is it going to be?" Omotola asked without any eagerness.

"It will be in August. The first weekend in August. I just wish you could marry Aba Jacob at the same time, and we could both settle in our husbands' houses and see each other always. I hate you going to school, Omotola. You know it will…"

There it is! thought Omotola, in a rage at Jacob's name, the bile starting to rise in her throat.

"Yinka," Omotola said shortly. "I have to finish this assignment for Kola. I'll come over as soon as I'm done, so we can talk."

"You promise?"

Omotola nodded.

Yinka continued, "I've finally come up with a name I would prefer for my firstborn."

Another name again! Omotola thought as she looked at her friend dubiously, but said, "Good! I'll see you later."

"You didn't even ask what name it is."

"Sorry, what name?" Omotola asked, unconcerned.

"*Omotola* will be perfect. I like your name a lot."

"That's groovy! I'll see you in a few minutes."

Reluctantly, Yinka left, murmuring, "I hope those gorillas are not out there."

⚜

Chapter Eighteen

Omotola dressed in her most valuable clothes—a pink T-shirt and brown khaki shorts. They were part of the wardrobe Sister Teresa had given her earlier that year, those she reserved for physical education. She accompanied the outfit with *"jalawoota,"* a pair of almost worn-out flip-flops, rubber slippers that threatened to melt, or tear off underneath the pads of her feet because of the heat of the day.

Omotola followed Kola, who was dressed in the cute uniform of the Lion Club—white T-shirt, black shorts, and black sneakers. She hated the promise of the day's weather, especially the heat. The temperature at eight o'clock was about ninety-five degrees Fahrenheit. The sky was a clear blue without an inch of gray. No chance there might be a downpour so that the heat might be swept away.

They walked through a dense forest and finally arrived at an overgrown path. The path showed a long-term lack of use that left it traceable only by those who frequented the forest. Kola seemed to know his way around. He pushed tree branches away with his hands, revealing the small line of the path visible on the ground.

Omotola followed—unconditionally, determinedly.

Omotola looked at Kola's sagging shoulders as he walked fast. Without saying a word, she understood that taking her to the club caused him some regret. If she dared complain that her legs were burning and that he should slow down, he might snap and send her back home, so she kept quiet. They roamed the forest for more than an hour, and finally arrived at a tarred road. Lined up on each pavement of the tarred road were fleets of the most luxurious cars Omotola had ever seen in her life. In the cars, drivers were waiting.

They crossed the road and walked onto a vast acreage of carved-out terrain. It was on the outskirts of the town. Simon Akindele had bought it and handed it over to his son, Christopher Akinrinola "Akin" Akindele, for his indulgence. It was just the right place to use as headquarters for a nationwide, grand club for boys like him. Its surroundings included natural rock outcroppings, a waterfall, and an untrimmed jungle. The carved-out terrain was full of man-made facilities—gymnastic poles erected along with tire rings. Part of the land was graded with soft sand, part-covered with low grasses, and part with newly planted trees, each edge marked out by stones.

Everything Akin had wanted done on the land had been done. The area stretched out to the Esa waterfall in all its beauty, graced by rocks and encircled by picturesque mountains, which in this singular locale made it seem a paradise on earth. Omotola gasped and blurted out, "Oh my God, this place is beautiful, despite it's in the middle of nowhere."

Immediately, Kola walked away from her, as if he embarrassed at her outburst. If he stayed within her radar, she might embarrass him more. He left and stood at the far end of the Esa waterfall, far away from her, where he couldn't hear her breathe.

Omotola felt alone and abandoned.

She walked slowly towards an assembled troupe of opulent-appearing boys, most of whose eyes were transfixed on a small pamphlet, as if studying for exams. Omotola was eager to know what the pamphlet was all about. The few who bothered to turn her way wore a look that could instantly cut her dead, like a dagger.

She shivered from head to toe as she remembered that she had seen those looks before. History was repeating itself. It was like her first day in elementary school. She was instantly hated by some students and looked down on by some parents at that tender age, even at a time when the world was not supposed to wear its dirty prejudice like clothes. She was a laughingstock to some of the girls. At that moment, right there, she had hated herself. She'd wanted to run back home and never return to school. Kola had squatted in front of her and made her understand that dreams can be broken, can be shattered by so many, but the passion and desire to succeed determined the final result. His talk, and many other teachers' talks afterwards, had made her determined to stay in school. She was glad she had, and had sailed through primary school with flying colors instead of running and hiding in the closet, losing the gift God had bestowed on her, as Sister Teresa said all the time.

Sister Teresa's encouragement had helped her pass through elementary school and had made her a celebrity—the only girl going to secondary school from such a family as hers, in her town and its surroundings.

Her guiding angel, Sister Teresa, had beamed, with tears in her eyes, as she announced her decision to go to secondary school without finishing Primary Six. And she had said, "You're one of a kind, Omotola. You have to believe that. Believe in yourself. Don't let people bring you down."

She'd tried everything in primary school, sometimes her heart's desires, sometimes her heart's foibles that arose from being pessimistic, in fear of disgrace that could have literally led to death. Sister Teresa had taught her how to combat this anxiety disorder.

"Take a deep breath, Omotola, as long as you want, and give your best shot."

She did as she was told and gave her best shot. She was always successful. Sister Teresa was always right—she made her a winner throughout primary school. Yes, a winner never quits.

Now, Omotola needed the club. She must be in the club, even though it was off-limits and beyond her. She couldn't let Sister Teresa down. She might be watching. She nodded several times like a frog and smiled in spite of the uncertainty of her fate as another phrase of Sister Teresa rapped in her brain. "You're a winner, Omotola. Never in life underestimate yourself."

She knew she had to be strong, ready to do the extraordinary, and take many deep breaths in order to join the exclusive Lion Club. She took a long gulp of air, released it gently, and smiled. "Trial inevitable."

Omotola knew she was supposed to maintain peace, ignore their lot with cold-eyed and boyish attitudes, and walk away from them. But she wanted to mingle. She decided to take a step toward being friendly.

She approached their group without fear. She could smell their breath, just as they could smell hers. And like deer spotting a hunter, they all stopped what they were doing, standing with strained faces that carried alertness.

Omotola murmured, "Hello," and none answered. They all stared at her like a piece of rag. Their hostility was not hidden.

"That's rude," Omotola said aloud.

She decided not to be bothered or scared by their exhibition of enmity and contempt. *You are just brats with fates as shaky as mine. Be as unfriendly as you want. I'm used to it,* she murmured inwardly and moved away. She decided to walk around the site to lurch into serious thinking on strategies to win and belong.

From afar, Omotola assessed the boys and herself. The boys dressed in immaculate T-shirts, khaki shorts, and brown sneakers as it should be for supplicants. And not as it should be, was she in a lousy pink T-shirt and brown shorts, with slippers that belonged in the garbage. The gap was lengthy.

But right away, she shredded the negative thoughts. She recited her new mottos since Primary Two. That was when she realized she wasn't less of a being than them. "It's not your fault, Omotola, that your household is poor. It's not your fault you were born into destitution and fathered by a crazy man. But it's your fault if you don't go for what you want in life. Ignore the visible hatred. Stay, Omotola. Never run away from hurdles in life. Winners never quit."

She tucked the bottom of her T-shirt into her shorts—the torn, ragged end of her dress shirt, worn out from daily use in physical education classes, and she removed her flip-flops. She walked onto the soft graded portion of the acreage, nearer to the waterfall. She climbed the mountain to dive from, more or less around fifty feet high, and at its summit, the water looked friendly, smiling back at her with a gentle gush. She heard its sequence of waves and its smells, all pure like the world should be….

Omotola cast a glance at the people below the stone—they all looked like ants. Instead of being scared, she laughed at how small they were going to be when she belonged. She closed her eyes and imagined inwardly how to dive into the cool water with style. For a few minutes, she stood at the top—stood in her world that brought the beauty of belonging to a club like the Lion Club. A new beginning, a new onset, a rail away from loneliness. And, paramount to this, was not cutting a journey short, not feeling sorry and going home, as Kola's attitude had expressed, as written on the faces of the other boys.

"Omotola, you've got to do your thing," she muttered aloud.

Eventually, she descended and wandered around a bit. Finally, she came back to her original spot before migrating to greet the rude people.

She waited like the others. The gossiping of the boys was all about her. She could tell, since almost all of them looked at her. Some of them laughed, some whispered, and some had a disdainful look.

Instead of taking to heart their disapproval, paying them back in their own coins, raining down abuse on them as she knew how from the home in which she was born, she applied a brake to her lips. Just as a duck shakes off water from its back, so was their conversation to Omotola.

She sat on the grass like a guru master in meditation. She closed her eyes, and then a tiny fear crawled into her head again as she remembered she hadn't met the real members, especially kooky Wole, and their leader, Akin, whom all, including Kola, worshipped like a lord. Akin was a pompous, autocratic snob, mostly without any sense of humor and more, a brother to another pompous bully called Dupe. Omotola had had no choice but to share classes since Primary One with his worthless sister, who had made her life a living hell and insulted her on a daily basis.

Omotola had been to the Akindele's residence once. And she'd seen Akin on his father's mansion's balcony at close range—he'd ignored her greetings, giving her a look that made her feel like nobody. She hated him, and yet, she felt something for him—and that's something she would take to the grave, would never share with anybody. It was stupid. She was stupid. She felt unease. She preferred to quit. She didn't want to face the snobbery and kookiness.

Omotola looked around, wondering how to get home, which she knew would be a huge task. She didn't even know exactly where she was. Her mind turned to negative thoughts: *This is not one of the primary school things that you can handle, hailed and encouraged by the teachers. This is an isolated event, and you are solo in it. You are an intruder, on private territory where you will never be welcome. You're poor. You're a girl. You'll be thrown out of the grounds by the members. Omotola, how many more wrongs will convince you? Go back home before you regret it.*

She trembled, her heart racing like hell. She was short of breath. She was having a panic attack, just like a few she had had in elementary school. She felt disoriented.

She closed her eyes, taking in deep breaths like Sister Teresa had taught her, until the flush of fear drained from her head, and she could breathe comfortably again. She thought of the reasons she had to be in the club, and that allayed the negativities. She decided to stay until she was thrown out. In a short while, she could hear someone approaching, but she refused to open her eyes to discrimination, to hatred. Whoever was coming should go to blazes.

"Omotola, it's a bad idea for you to stay. You've to go home," Kola said.

She opened her eyes to face Kola, who squatted in front of her.

"I'll stay, Kola. I don't want to go home."

"The members won't like you or like that idea. You just have to go home now, Omotola."

"Please, Kola, let me stay. In the long run, the members may like me if they see I've got potential. I promise I'll never embarrass you."

"No, Omotola. You have to leave now." Kola placed his left hand on Omotola's shoulder. She shuffled it away.

"No, Kola, I'm staying; I'm not going home. A promise is a promise. You promised to sneak me into this site if I did your homework in literature, and I did. Now it is your turn to fulfill your part of the bargain. I'm not moving." Omotola looked wearily around. "I don't even know where I am. Or how to get home from the forest that looks like a jungle."

"Omotola, I thank you for my homework. Quickly, I'll help you trace your way back home before the members arrive."

"No, Kola, I'm staying."

Omotola looked back to Kola, who seemed about to cry. She shrugged again.

"Omotola, listen to me." Kola resorted to a last-minute appeal. "Thousands of boys put in their application for membership from all over Nigeria. And only a hundred and ten were selected. The boys standing on this terrain have it all. You don't."

Omotola was angry, and her eyes shot arrows at Kola. One thing that made her stubborn and boiled up was telling her she couldn't do something without trying.

"No, Kola, I'm staying." Omotola looked furious. "A deal is a deal. I'm as good as those boys over there." Omotola pointed to them. "I'm staying, and that's it."

Kola was angry. He stood up ranting, walking away at the speed of a millipede, finally going back to his former position, vesting his anger in kicking the sand into the waterfall.

"A deal is a deal," Omotola muttered.

She continued to sit like a yoga master with closed eyes until she heard footsteps marching toward her like soldiers. She opened her eyes, and the members of the Lion Club went to the soft graded area that Omotola had visited—eighteen boys in number, all in white T-shirts with the conspicuous logo of a Lion, black shorts, and black sneakers, like Kola.

The supplicants stood at attention. Omotola stood up and joined them.

Akin sat on one of the stones not far from the boys while his fellow comrades arranged themselves. A short, stocky boy walked out from the crew that had just arrived. He had a whistle on a chain around his neck, indicating his function. Omotola could tell right away from Kola's description that his name was Wole, and he was the trainer.

He looked fierce, like a starved dog. In fact, the members of the Lion Club called him a bulldog behind his back. He had the look and the attitude of a bulldog in one of the elementary books—aggressive, with saliva flying from his mouth when he was angry. Kola had described him to Omotola a few days after Bayo came to collect him for a meeting at Akin's house. Kola also called him the number-one bully in the club. His specialty included inflicting pain on members from homes like Kola, and greater pain on newcomers, encouraging them to quit training and go home.

Another boy set out a booklet like a register and a pen, perhaps to record the names of new inductees.

The remaining members divided into two groups— seven boys on Akin's right side and eight on his left side. Kola bowed his head, walking to join Akin on his right-hand side.

Wole and the other boy with the booklet stood in front of the supplicants. Instantly, Wole looked Omotola over with disapproval. Finally, with a smug look, he posed a question to her.

"Since when does the Lion Club for boys attract the feeble sex?" He laughed, and without waiting for an answer, he continued. "This is a Lion Club for boys, not Lioness Club for girls. Before counting up to three, I want you, you ragged girl, out of my sight."

Omotola glared with hatred as he made her his primary prey. She pasted a look on her face which said, "I'm not leaving."

Wole saw the sign and shouted, "Where did you come from?"

Omotola would have spoken, but she had sworn to

Kola to remain silent, leaving the conversation for him to handle. She remained silent to see what direction the ball would roll.

"Are you dumb? Get lost now."

Wole's ranting didn't scare Omotola. In fact, he sounded like her father, Paul. Besides, she had seen worse in school, and in her house. Neither did the staring eyes of the boys around her, like hundred-watt lightbulbs, affect her aims. But she was slightly disappointed about Kola's muteness; she knew she was on her own.

"Listen to me, baby girl, your gender is incapable of the exercises we do here. Go back home."

Omotola stared at Wole resolutely. She couldn't help but wonder about the mentalities of boys and men that made them think women were vulnerable and weak. She attended school with them and whipped their butt when it came to grades. In gymnastics, she was more accomplished than this bunch.

She continued the staring game, adding folded hands around her chest to confirm that she would not move until removed. She remembered that there was only one person with such veto power, as Kola had said, and that was Akin. And he hadn't said a word yet.

Omotola shifted her eyes to look at Akin. To her surprise, he sat staring at her with a poker face. She felt weak as his eyes burned into hers. He refused to avert his gaze. Omotola's body felt rigid, and for a few seconds, the clipper of her courage unclipped itself. She seemed bewitched and scared at the same time. She knew that with one word from him, she would be removed from the premises and instantly dragged away like a slaughtered animal. Like a coward, she pulled her eyes away from Akin to concentrate on the ground.

Wole shouted, "Boys, form a single file." He pointed and added. "Toddler, over there. Go home now!"

Wole's voice brought Omotola's brain back from transit to resume work. She raised her face to meet his, ready to prove she belonged.

"Good response, boys," Wole remarked.

The boys formed a file in a jiffy. Omotola arranged herself in the line, standing before the last boy.

"Toddler, get out of the file!" Wole snapped.

Omotola didn't understand what "toddler" meant, but she was sure it was another insult. She promised herself she would look it up in the dictionary as soon as practice was over.

Omotola cold-shouldered Wole's word again. And, temporarily, he gave up. He moved over to the boy with the register, nearer the waterfall.

"As I call the next in line, you state your name and be ready for the first test. In fifteen minutes, you are to climb to the top of that rock and dive from its peak into the water without disturbing it," Wole instructed, pointing to the rock Omotola had climbed earlier. "Got it, everyone?"

Most of the boys groaned aloud, and one in particular said, "But in the pamphlet, the climb and dive time is written as twenty minutes. Why change it to fifteen minutes now?"

"That's a new bar set, folks, but you can quit and go home like a sissy…"

Wole's face flashed disapproval at them all. The boys recoiled in silence.

Omotola finally realized that there was a pamphlet she was supposed to have read. Many surprises were to come her way, she assumed.

"The drills commence!" Wole shouted. "First in line, state your name, town you are from, and come over for your first test."

The boy stated his name as Sam Bartend and Ladden as his town of origin. The boy with the booklet wrote them down. Wole stared at a watch on a chain. Omotola's mouth dropped open like a basket. She had learned about the boy's great-grandfather in history. His grandfather was considered one of the founders of Nigerian nationalism, a profound activist against colonialism.

But Sam's performance put an end to Omotola's awe. The Laddencian sausage couldn't even get halfway up the rock in sixteen minutes, and he panted as if he was going to die. Wole looked up from the watch and shouted, "Stop; next!"

The boy stood at the foot of the waterfall, humiliated. Omotola felt sorry for him.

She quivered as she heard the surnames of most of the boys—children of the well-to-do from all over Nigeria, the surnames you only read about in history books or newspapers. But she was consoled because, even as their names filled the air, the macho power attributed to some of them proved false. About twenty boys were disqualified. They were to pack and go home.

Now it was her turn. She moved forward. Wole shouted, "You can't dive, Missy. Girls are taboo here. The last boy, move forward, please."

Omotola struggled hard not to insult the sexist jackass. She wished she had not sworn to Kola that she would remain quiet. She wished he would speak up for her.

She decided to move forward for the first test, pretending she hadn't heard Wole's command. At the foot of the rock, Wole intercepted her and placed one hand on her shoulder. Omotola shoved his hand away. Wole grabbed her by the collar of her T-shirt. The collar pulled out of its socket, dangling like a rag down her back.

Omotola was mortified. Wole shrugged but instantly let go of her shirt.

The atmosphere was confusing. Some boys were laughing. Some were stunned. With frustration written on Wole's face, he turned toward the rest of the Lion Club members and said, "Who brought this taboo into our midst?"

"That w-w-would be me … she's my s-s-sister," Kola stammered and raised his right hand, falling out from the rest and standing next to Omotola.

Deafening laughter erupted.

"What did he say?" one member asked.

Kola was cursed with the defect of a stammer, especially when struck with fear or anger. When he was little and the defect surfaced, Adewumi would tell him to take a deep breath, organize his words in his mind, and tell her everything at his own pace.

"Kola, take your time; I'm not going anywhere," Adewumi would say. And he would follow her advice and manage to express himself. Gradually, he was growing out of it and getting better—but not today. Each word came out with a great effort. His lips trembled, his eyes blinked, and he had to jiggle one hand and slam one foot down several times before he could finalize his speech. He was like a live fish struggling on land, or a snake flailing out in the open.

Omotola stood rigid, feeling for him. She prayed inwardly for God's divine intervention.

"If she is your sister," Wole said, laughing, "how come she is a beauty in rags, and you are a beast in polished clothes, huh?"

Kola dropped his head in shame. Wole continued with jests and insults. From the corner of her eye, Omotola saw Kola gripping both his hands, using the method to stand still. Pain and humiliation were written on his face. She hated what she saw—a dejected boy with a broken spirit. She looked away swiftly. She couldn't watch.

She felt sorry for the havoc she had caused. She ruined everything. She wanted to shout and rain insults on Wole but decided against it swiftly, as she had decided she couldn't just turn back and walk away. The deed had been done. Unfortunately, she had to wait until the bitter end. She remained mute, so as not to worsen the situation, wishing that something, anything, would stop Wole.

"Are you stupid enough to bring a toddler? Not just any toddler, but a girl?" Wole asked.

Kola was dead quiet.

"Remain dumb like your sister," Wole said. "But I've news for you, Kola. Pack up and go home. You never belonged."

Omotola's eyes scrutinized the terrain. Most of the boys were chuckling. Akin, as usual, still sat on the stone, and as before, concentrated on studying Omotola with a poker face. Defeated again, she turned her face away from him as one member shouted, "You heard the man, Kola. Get your stuff and leave with your toddler sister!"

"You're not in command, Femi. Shut up," the register boy said.

"I'm in charge, so the two of you get lost," Wole said with a grin. "No offense, little girl—girls are not allowed in Lion Club because they are stupid, weak, and they are taboo. Go, and take your stone-faced brother with you."

There was a pause. But Omotola had had enough. She was at a boiling point. How dare he humiliate her half-brother publicly?

"We are not stupid and weak," she spat, hissing like a cobra snake.

Kola touched her on the shoulder to stop her from talking, but Omotola wriggled free. She clenched her fists and got ready to punch Wole if he hurled more insults or ventured to touch her. She tried to hold her tongue, thinking, *Kola is worth a million more than you assembly of rich crusts that bred on your parents' glory. He is a mentor, and role model, one of the best students in high school, with a full scholarship. He's the most talented athlete that the Western region of Nigeria ever produced, also a compassionate, self-made man. And I'm not weak, either. I could withstand all your devilish exercises. Kola has equipped me with all that's necessary. I dive like a dolphin, climb a tree like a monkey. I could memorize your stupid pamphlet in ten minutes. All these things I learned entirely from my mentor, Kola.*

"Yes, you girls are weak and lazy," Wole shouted, interrupting her thoughts. "Get lost before I ask the boys to drag you out, along with your ugly brother."

"My brother is not ugly! You're a bulldog," she said, then stretched out her left hand to pull off the dangling collar of her blouse, and threw it on the ground. "I'm going to prove it to you right here, right now—that what boys can do, girls can even do it better. I'm not going anywhere."

She gave Wole a cutting stare. The crowd chuckled. Wole's face went from glory to doom. He turned in the direction of Akin, searching for help, for Akin to give the order to quit. Omotola knew Kola was right—Wole was just a gofer. Akin was the one that called the shots.

Her heart pounded as she looked at Akin, waiting for his decision. Omotola held her breath. As Akin shrugged without a word, that was the green flag for Omotola to go ahead.

In a fury, Omotola climbed to the summit of the diving rock. She heard a member shout, "Twelve minutes, impossible!" There, as taught, she stood still, gulped in air, closed her eyes, and launched forward without waiting for orders.

There was a commotion of boys drifting to the edges of the waterfall, staring in disbelief. Even Akin left his royal stool to watch.

Omotola shot down into the profound depths of the water like an arrow. For a few seconds, no bubble was visible on the surface until she zoomed back up, with hardly any disturbance to the glassy water. Stylishly, she swam to the bank of the waterfall, exited, dripping, and she smiled as she walked up to the others who waited.

Mouths agape, sharp drawing in of breath and murmuring, like battalions in the thousands. No! Wait! Like honeybees buzzing as Omotola passed the boys looking for Wole. She suas used to these reactions in the gymnastics hall. She knew the reason—her T-shirt was clinging to her body and showed her breasts. Boys were stupid, even though they claimed to be the strongest. Their thoughts showed on their faces like oil slicks on top of the water. They were mesmerized by the slight visibility of breasts—one would think they had never seen them before, despite their proximity to their mother's chests from birth, or the physiques of so many women in their lives. This was weakness, plain and simple.

Omotola didn't care. Even if she cared, what could she do about it? She was wearing what God had given her. In addition, she had passed their test without a hitch. She could die a happy girl. At least, she had proved females are as good as males.

Her eyes searched for Wole. She found him staring at the water like a moron.

"In your face, bulldog!" she said. She found Kola and maneuvered her way next to him.

Kola beamed as he said, "That was good, sis."

"You made me the best—"

"Haaa…"

Everybody suddenly turned their attention on Wole, who was yelling as if he'd gone mad. He continued to yell like his butt was on fire. After a while, he stopped, and without another word, flung the whistle into the bush and rushed away, into the trees.

Omotola noticed the members sticking together. Bayo looked from Kola to her with disapproval.

"I'm disappointed in Akin's nonchalant attitude," Bayo said.

"What do you mean?" Kola asked.

"Are we going to have a girl in the club?"

"Are you feeling threatened?" Omotola sneered.

Those nearby chuckled. Bayo wasn't worth her time. She had wanted to tell him off since the day he came over to their house, but for Kola's sake, she let it go and turned to check on Akin. After all, only he mattered. The errand boys could crawl into a hole and die.

She noticed that Akin seemed to be smiling at his stirred-up friend, Wole, who had stomped off into the bushes like a baby. Then he brought his eyes back up to meet hers… A wink? He winked? No! Yes! He seemed to have winked? Omotola wasn't sure, since Akin quickly resumed his poker-face and addressed a boy beside him.

Meanwhile, an unfamiliar boy with a fit, athletic body ran to pick up the whistle. He automatically took Wole's position as the trainer, ordering the boys back to their positions. The members flanked their leader, Akin, who took his formal seat before the supplicants in line.

After hours of and testing and proving the skill of the prospective members with the drill, all exercise came to an end. Omotola had nailed the other tasks one by one. Even though she had done her best, she was apprehensive and shaky. Her faith still lay in the hands of Akin.

As so many had failed before reaching the top, or even while still close to the bottom, all of the Lion Club hopefuls were able to move swiftly through their tests. One by one, their grit and determination would prove successful within the allocated time, or they would fail quickly and have to move aside for the next.

The remaining supplicants were asked to form a line. Omotola was proud to be among the forty who had done the best. Four members of the club, including the register boy, squatted near Akin and conversed in silence. After deliberations that seemed like ages, but only took thirty minutes in reality, Akin stood up and called the names of the accepted new members to step forward. Omotola gasped as she heard her name.

Those whose names were not called were asked to

move aside. Omotola was among the new, shorter line. These were subsequently cut down to stricter standards, and Omotola was among the ten who were finally taken to join the club.

After her name was called, she was stunned, standing in a trance, barely hearing what was going on around her. Some boys murmured compliments in awe of her accomplishments. Some flexed muscles. Some barely understood why Akin allowed a girl into the club, especially a girl with a background such as hers. She let their reactions wash over her, unconcerned.

Akin walked up to her. "You're a pro and natural. Congratulations, and welcome into the club," he said and winked.

He did wink! She saw it clearly this time and came out of her trance. "Thank you."

Akin left her side. She took a long breath, releasing it slowly. This was the experience of a lifetime. How did she rise from rag to throne? Perhaps it was divine intervention. It's an end of an era, she said to herself, convinced that the fat lady had sung.

Omotola was thrilled. Her eyes roved around, and she could see and hear boys starting to talk again. To her surprise, Wole wobbled over to her from his hiding place in the bushes. He said, "Don't get fooled. You'll never be welcome in the club."

He walked away.

"Members, join the new members for an address from the Lion Club's president," the boy with the register announced. Akin stood next to him.

As the members were taking their positions, murmuring was intense.

"Great Lions!" Akin saluted, shutting them all up.

"Great," the original members of the Lion Club replied.

Three times Akin saluted with "Great Lions," and three times, the original members replied, "Great," which was their official greeting. Akin cleared his throat.

"Listen up, everybody. The general meeting will come up soon, and the new Lion Club uniforms will be distributed at the meeting. We'll all have our photo taken for the year. The date, I'll communicate as soon the uniforms are ready. In the meantime, I want everybody to fall out. Great Lions, I salute you all."

Akin rounded up his speech. He turned to leave, and six old members of the club ran up to him—three on his left and three on the right. They formed an entourage to escort him away. Omotola stared at their backs in astonishment. She still couldn't believe it had all happened.

The left-over rich kids, including Wole, were rooted to the spot, producing sneers and slurs that could convert enough energy to erupt a volcano. Kola walked up to Omotola, lifted her off the ground, and spun her around as though light as a feather. Gently, he placed her back on her feet.

"Against all odds, you made it free and clear into the Lion Club. Sis, I'm so sorry to have doubted you, and…" Kola hesitated. "Sis, I'm proud of you. You're a shining star."

"Are you sure I'm not dreaming? Because my head is still woozy from everything!"

"You are not dreaming, little sis. Akin confirmed your membership. Do you know what that means? You are in the richest boys' league of Nigeria. God, you'll be the envy of all the girls around soon."

"I feel like a giant."

"You are. You're a giant, you've always been outstanding, and you'll continue to be. You'll show the girls of our background that all things are possible with determination."

"You're a hell of a poet. Thanks a lot, Bro; I couldn't have done it without you. You're a great coach." She laughed.

Kola's eyes shed tears, which he made no effort to wipe off. He just let the tears run. He opened his mouth for a second without a word coming out. Omotola knew it was tears of joy. She knew Kola was overwhelmed again, that good and bad emotions could hit him hard, render him speechless. She knew what her achievements meant. They were from a poor family. They would never have been accepted into the club if not for the fact that Akin, unconcerned of gender, cared more for potential.

"Today is one of the happiest days of my life," Kola said. "Let's go home, Sis."

"Just a sec, let me look for my slippers."

They both looked and found one buried in the sand; the second had disappeared.

"It doesn't matter, Omotola. Let's go home."

Barefooted, she obeyed. Kola wrapped his right hand around her shoulder, leaving the bunch of angry, rich brats staring. They walked home, babbling about the events of the day, musing about what the future would hold for her in the Lion Club—one woman in the midst of boys.

Finally, they fell silent, their minds traveling down

memory lane—the darkest moments of their lives in the crazy house they were born into and the path they each had chosen to follow. Their shared history had proven what they both had learned: you could always become what you aspired to be, with self-determination and help.

Chapter Nineteen

Abstract: [Extract "The conception of the aim of education was that it should make useful citizens, and when we say useful citizens we mean literally citizens who would be of use to us. They were to be taught trades that they might be more usefully employed, not that they might have a fuller enjoyment of life." H. S. Scot, 'The Development of the Education of the African in relation to Western Conta, Usill,ed… The Year Book of Education 1938 (London, 1938) pp. 737–738.

So, the purpose of education during British rule in Africa was to teach their sovereigns to be useful to them, not the other way around. Primary school dropouts worked as their household help. With Primary Six average certificates, the British were clever enough to provide the locals modern school and "all shallow schools" to enable the indigenous people to fill low-paid jobs. Dropouts before secondary school could become clerical officers in a British corporation or go to teacher-training school to obtain a certificate to teach primary pupils.

To go as far as finishing secondary, but with a failed result, the British provided "kangaroo" colleges, institutions like College of Technology, for vocational training. And to finish secondary school with an average grade, entry into a school of nursing was one of the options. To finish high school with an excellent grade was another matter. That enabled pupils to obtain a scholarship to study abroad, to further their education. The British in Africa were not keen on establishing domestic colleges, institutions with credibility, because the end products could challenge their authority.

"Education is a light to darkness, a path to freedom, a power to be autonomous." The British knew all this, and as a result, the scanty higher institutions provided in West Africa were intentionally worthless. Only a few students— poor or rich—made it abroad, and only a handful throughout Nigeria had enough qualified education to tell the British to pack up and go home.

Itan Central High School, the first secondary school in Itan Land, was to serve the entire sector. Its front gate opened onto a vast field used as the devotional assembly for its pupils in the morning. And, nearby the assembly field was a parking lot, with a few oak trees here and there. A few yards from the assembly field was a "crescendo," a building used as classrooms. Classes for the first-year students were on the ground floor, while classes for seniors were on each level of the five flights of the building.

The back buildings included a principal's office, plus a teachers' lounge, gym, science labs, chapel, library, and a multi-purpose dining hall. Further down were dormitories and a residential bungalow for teachers living on site.

On school days, Kola couldn't wait to be with his club members. It had become the edifice of Kola's life. And, with Omotola being a member of the club since last

Saturday, Kola was in a happy mood more than ever. He entered the gate of the school just as Bayo came into view, looking mad.

"Are you such a bonehead to have brought your baby sister for recruitment on Saturday? And to have allowed her to rage at Wole like that? Well, I have a newsflash for you. You're going to be terminated, and so is your sister."

"No, we're not. She made it into the club."

"No, she didn't make it into the club. The boys said Akin promised to reverse his decision after Wole talked to him and said that girls are liabilities. You know Wole has influence over him. He's Akin's brother-in-law to be. Wole is engaged to Dupe. You probably know that already."

"Yes, I know Wole is engaged to Dupe," he replied. "But Akin—"

"There is no "but," Kola!" Bayo cut him short. "You and your sister's explosion is done. All Lion Club members I've seen this morning are singing the same song. I'm terrified. And I don't want to be part of it."

"What are you saying?"

"Kola, I'd rather die than be expelled from that club. So, we're no longer friends. See you around. I don't want to be associated with you anymore. I don't want to be swept away by the flood you created for yourself. See you around."

Kola stood, confused, watching his fair-weather friend walking away.

If expelled, Kola knew life would end for him, just as Bayo had said. He would have to say goodbye to the only leverage he had over some other kids of his kind. It would mean that he would have to come back and face the bullying from upper-crust pupils who had left him alone since he'd been accepted by a club to which they themselves could not dream of belonging. They had stopped harassing him, afraid of the people he was in fellowship with. Akin ruled everywhere.

Kola knew that if he were cast out, every pleasure he had gained from the club as a member would vanish, along with his life. It would leave him worthless, meaningless, and back to square-one, at the depths of the sea. He might never have the courage and strength to swim to its surface.

He would blame the book that gave him nightmares, even at a mere glance at the first page—the book that terrorized him because of its old-fashioned English blank verse, which his teacher called "iambic pentameter." Stupidly accepting Omotola's help was about to cost him a lot. His shortcut had got him into a jam.

Kola never had to doubt academics with Omotola, as she had a rare IQ. He wasn't surprised that the words from the book flowed from her in recitation. She quoted from the book, and that make him look like a dork. He couldn't even remember a word from the first page he had read so far.

Kola hated everything that wasn't science. In fact, he preferred working on ambiguous calculations meant for university students rather than a glimpse at art subjects. Art subjects were his weakest link, but literature and English were compulsory subjects. He had no choice—he had to face Shakespeare. And that year, literature's axe to grind was *Julius Caesar.*

He knew he shouldn't have stupidly assumed that Omotola would run back home as soon as she realized she'd be the only girl. Kola wanted to cry, and instead of going inside the school, he turned back to the exit of the gate to avoid talking to someone else and hear how foolish he was. He was about to be dumped by the one person he counted on to have his back anytime.

Maybe it was time to accept his inadequacy and thank his lucky stars. Probably, this would be a blessing. Omotola would be in his school, and he could hang around with her after school—stay and be with her, as she wanted. And do what? Kola regretted and mourned. He closed his eyes in sorrow as he found a spot to hide in some shrubs on the side of the school gate, where he couldn't be easily spotted.

As the morning devotion bell rang, he emerged and walked slowly, deciding to line up behind a junior class. He queued behind a boy, watching the group he normally couldn't wait to meet on the morning devotion assembly field, happily chattering their heads off. Yes, he'd been expelled.

Dejectedly, he looked away and stood there until the bell rang for students to go to class. He waited and climbed to the third flight after the seniors had gone. In the corridor to his class, at the end of the passage, he saw pupils who had never bothered to look at him or even regard him as a human being, looking his way, smiling. He was more puzzled than ever. They had likely heard about his doom. He was about to fall from grace to disgrace, and they either wanted to show sympathy or mock him.

Though he was in a hurry, some girls flagged him down and planted themselves in his path.

"Kola, you got a minute?" Kike said.

Kike had ignored him from primary school to secondary. So had her friends, four in number, who now stared down at him with obedient eyes. *What do they want?* he wondered.

"Not now, Kike. I've got to go."

"How about after school?" Kike said. "We wanted to—"

"Okay, I've got to go. After school, then," Kola said hurriedly.

"Thanks for listening to us. You're a great guy. We would like to know you better. We will see you later."

"What?" Kola asked, frowning in bewilderment. Their sudden change of heart and gentleness unnerved him more than the fear of being expelled from the club. Then he saw Femi walking toward him. Femi was a member of the Lion Club and a dear friend of Wole, who gossiped worse than girls. Quickly, he added, "See you later! Bye!"

Kola was fearful as Femi came closer, as he seemed to be on the warpath and might blow a fuse. But, to Kola's relief, he passed by without a word. Kola sighed and paced off toward his locker.

Nothing was making sense. His club's blue-blood wanted him dead, and the rest of the crowd wanted to cuddle him? Either his classmates had gone nuts, or he was simply dreaming again.

He once had a dream when he was in Primary Two, in which he was a giant on the planet called Earth and in command of the boys of his age. He was extremely happy in the dream, as the rich kids in his class were mini people and afraid of him. He had to walk around them with caution so as not to crush them to death. Not only did he wake up panting for air, but it was the worst day of his life. He was pushed down the stairs that day, bullied by a notorious group of rich students who were jealous that he got the best results in their class. They called him "Stupid Brainy," just for being smart. It was a day he would love to erase from his memory forever.

Since then, he had never believed in dreams. Since then, he had developed a thick skin against bullying. And since then, as one of the minorities in a rich-kid majority school, he had developed a shutdown device—to shut out unnecessary noise that might make him think less of himself.

At the far end of the corridor, he went to unlock his locker. He wanted to get his books and run to the classroom before meeting another set of kids who had previously shunned him and suddenly had a change of heart. It was maddening. He ignored two boys who seemed to have love in their eyes as they stood watching him at his locker. He was about to close his locker when he spotted Felix and six of his boys approaching.

He gasped.

He looked back inside his locker, as if memorizing its nooks and corners, trying to become invisible.

Felix—he could break him with a thumb. Kola had learned *ijakadi*, self-defense, because of boys like him running wild. As the leader of a mob, Felix walked around with his brutes after primary school, and they ambushed their targets in broad daylight. Sometimes in the evening, if it pleased him. Felix and his gang were uncultured rich boys who made life a living hell for guys like Kola. Felix was a buffoon, rooted in Form Two, despite the fact that he was supposed to be in his final year of high school. Even though he had repeated the program several times, the entire academics of Form Two were still vague to him. In short, Felix was a senior boy in Form Two, whom Kola had met there and left there. His gang rushed boys, and there was nothing anybody like him could do about it. They even scared the shit out of the poor teachers. Felix might be out of the school that year if his life yielded no progress. Reverend Thomas was prepared to get rid of rotten apples. Everyone knew that.

Felix was perpetually at Kola's throat until he made it into the Lion Club and had rich boys as friends, especially Akin Akindele, whom nobody ever wanted to mess with.

Felix had tried to join the club twice, but he had failed. Now that the privileges and security of club membership were about to be flushed down the drain, putting him back in Felix's sights, Kola was shaken.

He was staring at his locker, thinking of a way to escape the oncoming gang, when he heard a "Good morning" from Felix. It sounded so strange, so far away. Kola checked around to ascertain he was being spoken to, and then he realized—Felix was speaking to him. He also realized that he was the only one in the corridor who was shoulder to shoulder with Felix, and his boys had formed a semi-circle that almost enclosed him. Three were on Felix's left wing and another three on his right wing. They were just a copycat of a Lion Club's standing arrangement.

Kola stared curiously at them. They were probably buying time; they might attack any minute. For sure, what came from his mouth could determine his fate.

He chose to ignore him. He then concentrated on putting the books he needed in the class on one arm to hide his trembling frame, and solemnly, he prayed that

Felix and his buddies would leave him in peace. He was running mad with fear.

"Good morning, Kola. I know you're mad at me because I was an ass back then, but it's all over now," Felix said. "Can we be friends?"

Weird again, but better than being kicked in the ribs. Kola clung to a glimmer of hope but did not fail to wonder what was wrong with his erstwhile enemies. Why soften toward him? What was going on? Kola had no answers. Why did everyone all of a sudden want a piece of him? What brought this weird affection? It was unreal and unnatural. He must be dreaming again.

He blinked twice and opened his eyes wider. Felix and his comrades still stared at him firmly. Oh, boy! It was not a dream; it was real. Kola studied Felix a bit and decided there was no harm in being friends with an enemy. It would mean only having to double up on prudence, and to be on alert most of the time. After a second of hesitation, Kola spoke.

"Good morning Felix. What do you want?"

"We're now friends, right?" Felix stuck out his right hand for a handshake to seal their friendship, which Kola ignored, but nodded at him instead. He'd like to know what Felix was getting into before a seal of friendship that might end up in a fiasco. Satisfied enough with the nodding, Felix went on, "I learned that your sister genuinely insulted that irresponsible good-for-nothing bully Wole at the Lion Club initiation last weekend." He paused and smiled, adding, "They said she had destabilized his bulldog hegemony, and now she is a member of Lion Club."

So, this was what all the softness of the spoiled rich

kids was about, why they had melted like condense oil in the sun. Kola tried hard to suppress laughter. Surprise, surprise—Felix called Wole a bully. *The pot is calling the kettle black,* he thought. The world must have turned inside out since the weekend: Felix had apologized and recognized a bully. Kola would have loved to laugh, but instead, he said, "I'm not sure about insults, but my sister made it into the Lion Club, and there are complications…" Kola trailed off. He was picking his words carefully.

"I learned you trained your sister. You've got to help me with the training for next year. Please, I'll pay you for it."

Bully Felix begs for help! Wonders would never cease.

"I don't need your money," Kola said. "But, I'll see what I can do. Okay? Right now, I've got to get ready for classes."

Kola closed his locker with a slam and vamoosed before Felix could delay him any further.

He had to go down to the chemistry lab. That was his first subject. It was housed in one of the buildings behind the classrooms. He couldn't see any of his classmates. It seemed they had all gone already. Kola galloped through the corridor and cold-shouldered the other pupils who wanted to talk to him. He saw a friendly face, Tade, emerging with a gymnastic bag from another arm of Form Three. He was among Kola's few pals in the club. His father owned a construction company that had built almost all the existing infrastructure of the country. As Tade turned toward the stairs, Kola ran after him. He tapped Tade on the back.

"Wow, you're a very difficult man to find," said Tade in surprise as he turned. "I looked for you in the morning to know more about your sister, and…" He stopped and then added. "And why didn't you join us in morning devotion?"

They descended the stairs together.

"You didn't know?"

Both temporarily stopped walking. Kola's face wore pain as Tade frowned. "Know what?"

"That I'm about to be expelled from the club because of my sister."

"Whoever told you that lied, because I personally dig your sister and all her moves. She was incredible." He grinned. "Akin confirmed her membership. For real. She is a member."

"That's what I thought until Bayo said otherwise this morning. That's why I stayed away. I saw Femi a while ago. He was as moody as a stirred-up storm."

"That woozy, lousy, leech Bayo speaks for himself. Akin won't cave. You should know him by now. He is a man of his word. Besides, I'm sure he was as glad as me that a girl as lovely as your sister made Wole cry like a baby. In the case of Femi, pay no attention; he is nobody of importance when it comes to Akin. C'mon, let's go."

As they finally came down the stairs, their destination in sight, Tade said reassuringly, "You will be the last man out of the club, Kola. Akin likes you a lot."

"I was such a dodo to have accepted Bayo's words without a blink. Thanks, man. See you later."

He felt more at ease than he had all morning as he ran to the chemistry lab. He was sure he was two minutes late.

* * *

Morning devotion of pupils and teachers on the field of All Saints Primary School was on as usual. The pupils queued behind their class captain while the teachers stood a few meters away from them. One of the teachers rang the bell to bring silence. As all were quiet, Sister Anne offered the morning prayers. And after the last "Amen," she asked the students to open their eyes.

"I've a great announcement to make," she said, smiling. "We picked one of our pupils to sit for the high school entrance exam because of her excellence since class one to five. I'm proud to announce that she passed with flying colors. And yesterday was the happiest day of my life as she told me she'd skip Primary Six. I'm happy to announce that Omotola Olorunfemi will be going to Itan Central High School, Ajoni-Itan, as of this September, with full scholarship. Omotola, come here."

The Friday before the recruitment, Omotola had walked into Sister Anne's office, and Sister Teresa was there as well. She had told both of them she'd love to skip Primary Six and go to secondary school. Both women had left their seats and hugged her firmly, one after another.

Omotola felt like she was walking on air toward Sister Anne. She stood next to her. Affectionately, the woman placed a hand around her shoulder. Delighted, she continued. "Omotola has promised to come to school every day, to help other pupils that have difficulties with their studies, 'til the end of June. Isn't that wonderful?"

* * *

From morning until later in the afternoon, almost every pupil outside the Lion Club wanted to talk to Kola. He was afraid half of his brain might be paralyzed from talking. He hadn't been used to such conversing since birth. A lot of pupils outside the Lion Club wanted the tittle-tattle confirmed, wanted info on Omotola's performances, and wanted his help to meet the next recruitment. At any given break, he had someone looming around him to ask about just anything. He was exhausted; he'd had enough conversation for a day.

He sat in the math class, copying the assignment written on the board by his last teacher of the day, and he gasped as he realized: he still had to face a lot of pupils he'd have gladly avoided for the rest of his years in secondary school. The ones who had made him late to almost all of his classes because he was trying to be nice, listening to their inquisitions. That had to end now, he decided. All he needed to do was to escape the school premises like a lightning flash. He hated being the most wanted, most famous boy in school right now. Overnight fame and glory were overwhelming and sometimes too difficult to bear. He hated fame.

The success of Omotola making it into the Lion Club spread like pure oxygen over the school. Likewise, the humiliation of Wole by Omotola spread like polluted air. Even the big fish that never ventured to say hello to Kola bowed and wanted help. Almost everybody wanted him to train them for Lion Club recruitment next year. And many wanted to meet Omotola. Crazy! Omotola was now called a "wonder woman." Some believed that her performance and boldness were extraordinary, and that any myth about her must be true. Kola would swear that if he claimed that Omotola were an alien with body components of iron, the majority would eat it up without any doubt.

He smiled—his little sister, once called a dirty girl from the gutter, would have pupils asking for her autograph come September, in Itan Central High School. And she might be a cornerstone to be reckoned with. Kola understood that her rejection, like a leper, by most pupils in primary school had molded, sharpened, and made her stronger than a nail. What cannot kill you definitely will make you stronger. Omotola had grown a thick skin like an elephant, and became bold like a lion.

Kola snatched his books off the table and dashed out of the classroom. Narrowly, he dodged the set of girls (Kike and friends) who, right away in the morning, wanted to talk to him about a thing—The Thing, he already knew. He must leave school at once, get Omotola from her school, and both walk home before classmates bombarded him like locusts invading an unfortunate farm.

Half running, half walking, avoiding eye contact through the long corridor, he finally reached his destination. He placed his books back in the locker and was about to lock it, but he abandoned the task as he saw Bola elegantly walking towards him. In slow motion, he assimilated her body movement.

Bola wasn't just any girl. She was Bola Rawa, a beauty. Classy and brilliant, Bola was born to parents who owed their riches to banking and business. Kola had loved her since day one, when he sat next to her in Primary Three. And all the time, he'd wanted her. She was his chosen girl—the girl of his dreams. He'd have asked her out, but his background and his tics hindered the move. She would probably shun him as she had in Primary Three, or laugh at him. And, what was worse, she'd tell everybody in school. And everybody would make him their laughingstock, an insult punching bag, again.

Moreover, every popular girl in the school loved Akin. And when they couldn't get him, they settled for his entourage. Bola had settled for Femi. Kola had felt a sharp pain through his chest at the last Lion Club bash as Femi's and Bola's mouths locked together. He couldn't stay there, watching them. He'd left, since the pain was unbearable.

Kola looked toward Bola again. Instantly, he wanted to launch his intent—take the chance of a lifetime—capture her world, as she had captured his. Suddenly, he felt nervous, and his throat was dry. He knew he'd have his old enemy back if he talked first, and that would be disastrous. He stood, waiting for Bola to reach him. As she did. Seductively, she touched her long Rasta hair, pulling a strand up a bit, as if showing off. Kola stared in admiration, dazed.

"'Hi, Kola," Bola said with a smile. "I learned your junior sister made it to Lion Club. What is she like?"

She is actually in front of me, talking to me! Slowly, Kola came around. He grinned. The insecurity alarm in his head went dead.

"Yes. She made it in all right. She is terrific."

"I learned Akin is thinking of removing the bar." She smiled, twisting a strand to flirt again. "And allow girls to join the club if they meet the requirements?"

Kola swallowed hard as he could see the beautiful gap in between her incisors, her teeth as white as cotton wool.

"Well, I'm not sure about that since the club hasn't met since the recruitment day," Kola confessed. "And a date for the next meeting is not yet fixed, so I'm not sure of Akin's intentions."

"You trained her, right?" Bola said, blushing. "I'm wondering if you can give me some tips on how to make the team, and of course, meet your darling sister, my hero."

More grease to my elbows; even better than I thought. Kola's brain calculated immediately how far he could go. *As a private tutor to a beautiful girl, I could touch, look, and feel. It's not a crime. It will be like a cake on a platter—it will be so delicious. During the course, I will make my intentions known.* Kola's body felt alive.

"I'd love to," Kola said. "You just tell me when you…"

He couldn't finish his sentence before Kunle, another member of the Lion Club, walked up to them. Moodily, he said, "Akin is in the parking lot. He would like to speak to you, Kola. Immediately."

As soon as Kunle said it, he turned and walked away. Hastily, Kola said, "I'll get in touch, Bola. See you soon."

"Thanks," Bola said.

Bola retreated with a backward glance and a smile. It told a lot. Kola was amused. He grinned to let her know he would be at her service as long as she wanted. Kola locked his locker quickly because when Akin Akindele wanted to speak to you, you dropped everything and ran to meet him.

Kola disappeared toward the stairs, praying inwardly that his meeting with Akin didn't mean he had changed his mind about Omotola staying in the club. As Kola trod from the stairs to the parking lot, he felt unsettled, like a bird on a rope. He saw Akin standing off in the midst of his entourage. Even though he knew he should take to heart only the words of Tade, discarding what Bayo said, it was too soon to relax. He had seen some of Wole's groupies in pain, but he couldn't say "hurrah" yet.

With Kola's classroom at one end of the corridor and Akin's at the other end, the space between the two classes was a blessing, both a shield and a sword of protection. Apart from morning devotion that he attended with Akin, and all of the other activities that were compulsory, Akin's leftover time had been private. One had to be invited to be in his presence, or so the boys around him portrayed to the world. Since Akin's bodyguards and entourage included Wole, and the chosen ones that circled him like an electric circuit round a gem, Kola never searched for Akin in school except when called for. He connected to Akin on another level: sport.

Akin thought of Kola as a god who didn't need his father's money to stand out among his peers. His beauty he had inherited from a fair-skinned mom, a Bulane descendant. Kola was once told that her beauty made other women cry out in frustration of being plain, no matter how beautiful they were. And her beauty was known by men from Ibata-Itan and other places far and wide. Unfortunately, he didn't know her.

Akin was an introvert. And that made most people assume he was pompous and a snob, but the fact had always been there—boys wanted to worship him as a god, treated each word from his mouth as an utterance from God, circulated to the world the fairy tale that sounded too far from who he was. In all senses, Akin was a cool, level-headed bloke when Kola got to know him on a personal level. They had played ball together at his father's mansion, and on every occasion, Kola had been welcome. He always went home with goodies, from shirts to shoes to backpacks. There was never a time Akin had lorded over him or thrown his background in his face. He would hold on to those personal assessments of his friend until he decided against Omotola, Kola told himself.

Akin leaned on the car that would take him home: a Cadillac. He was talking to about eight boys, including Femi and Wole, when Kola arrived.

"Good afternoon," Kola said nervously.

"Good afternoon, Kola," Akin replied. The others just stared at him, unfriendly.

"Guys," Akin said, annoyed. "I thought a comrade just said good afternoon."

"Sorry, we didn't hear you," Wole replied. They murmured, *"good afternoon"* like the buzz of bees.

"Okay, anyway," Akin said tightly, "I'd like a private word with Kola. See you all tomorrow."

"We could wait until you finish, and we could go to your house," Wole said.

"That won't be necessary. You all go home, and I'll see you tomorrow," Akin insisted.

Kola watched as the boys shot deadly looks at him. It seemed they made a promise to kill him the next time they met. Reluctantly, they went to their various cars. Their drivers drove off fast and furiously. As Kola's eyes roamed around, he also noticed that some boys who were supposed to get inside the car with their drivers stood watching with amazement as if watching Poseidon—god of the sea, god of the earth, god of horses, the greatest god of Greek times—had landed on the Itan Central High School parking lot. Akin probably had not been seen lingering so long in the parking lot before.

"I'm sorry you had to watch that," Akin said, his

voice carrying an apology.

Kola's attention came back to Akin, who seemed indifferent to the spectators around them.

"I'm okay. It's nothing," Kola said.

"No, it's something bad, not acceptable," Akin said, concerned. "We are comrades, and we should be without enmity. I'll have a word with that bunch soon."

"Thanks," Kola said. "Kunle said you would like to see me?"

"Yes. I want to ask about our football game next Saturday. Are we still on…?" Akin's voice shook and eventually trailed off.

Kola knew this was about more than their game. Probably, Akin was unable to voice a dead-cert decision yet. Crowded with worries, he replied, "We are on, as you wanted it."

"Good. So, how is Omotola doing?" Akin said, looking straight at Kola.

Kola fidgeted, uncomfortable. He wasn't sure how to answer, so he finally said, "She is fine."

"How does she feel about being the sole female out of the bunch?"

Kola heaved a sigh of relief as audible as the worst snore. "She is as tough as a nail," he said. "She'll cope."

"Happy to hear that." Akin asked curiously, "Is she still in Primary Five, like my junior sister? If so, would she have the time for training with the battalion? If not, I could arrange a special…?" Akin said, all in a rush, eventually fading out.

"Actually, that won't be necessary. Come this September, she is admitted into our school with a full scholarship," Kola said smoothly.

"That's a great relief." Akin's face broke into a smile. "I don't have to be worried that she won't show up for practice. She is a great girl. She earned her membership, hands down."

Kola watched as Akin's face widened and softened into a smile.

"Greetings to her, and don't forget our football match this weekend. I'm prepared to beat your butts," Akin said, changing the subject.

"I'm glad to hear that. Looking forward to the game. And let the best man win."

"Would you like to ride home with me?"

Kola would've loved to keep on chatting with the guy he respected with all his heart, hop into a luxurious car, and let the other pupils see he was riding with a god. But he had to say no.

"No, I've got to meet Omotola at her school."

"I guess I'll see you on Saturday then," Akin said.

"Can't wait," Kola said. "Bye."

Akin got inside the car while Kola went to meet Omotola.

$\mathcal{S}$

Chapter Twenty

Simon sighed and pressed a bell to call his messenger from the adjacent office. Immediately, a tall, well-dressed man in a *buba* and *sooro,* with a lively face walked through the half-opened door to his upscale office. He bowed.

"Go and get Boyede for me," Simon said firmly.

The messenger left. Within seconds, a man in his early thirties wearing a gray suit entered Simon's office. As he entered, he put both hands together in front of his genitals, bowed, and said, "You would like to see me, sir?"

Simon looked wearily at him.

"Yes, cancel all my appointments for this afternoon, and reschedule them for another time. I have to be in my children's school to collect their report cards."

"I'll do as you wish, sir. That means I'm not going with you then, sir?"

"'No, that won't be necessary. But be here and rearrange all my visitors' appointments."

"I'll do that, sir. Is there anything else you'd like me to do?"

"Thanks for asking. Take my bag to my driver. Tell him to get the auburn convertible sedan ready in front of the building. We are going to Ajoni-Itan."

Simon had met with Reverend Thomas after the holiday. The meeting didn't go well. Olu wasn't progressing academically, his continuous assessments were poor, and his behavior was nothing to write home about. For over an hour, the principal had talked about him. Simon had just sat, unhappily listening, as the Reverend revealed Olu's latest evil deeds in the school. At the end of his speech, he sounded the last warning: that Olu must buckle down or he'd be tossed out of the school. That night, Simon had called Olu to echo the principal's warning in his ears.

Again, a few weeks later, Reverend Thomas wrote another pointed letter insisting that Simon see him that day in school, after which he would have visited each of the two boys' classroom teachers.

Simon's driver opened the door for him. He stepped elegantly out of the car. He was wearing a luxurious, light-blue linen walking suit and handmade crocodile-skin, black leather shoes from Italy.

Obediently, Simon walked toward the teachers' lounge. Its door was ajar, from which he could hear the teachers' banter, but they fell silent as soon as he was in sight. They all stared, startled, at Simon as if they were looking at a ghost. Who could blame them? Simon's face was as widely circulated in all the newspapers as the famous faces on banknotes.

Simon cleared his throat. "I'm sorry to have frightened everybody. The door was open." Simon's voice was unsteady. "Anyway, I'm here to see Akin and Olu Akindele's teachers. Is any of you Akin's teacher?"

Eventually, everybody recovered from the shock. The

men bowed, females curtsied, and a nun fumbled with her glasses as she introduced herself as Akin's class teacher. In haste, she picked a folder from a cabinet and ushered Simon to an inner private room for the visitors. She sat down to explain the splendid aptitude of Akin toward school. Simon sat in silence, without an interruption, and at the end, the nun handed over Akin's report card. Simon glanced through it. Everything was perfect, as he'd had in mind, so he struggled not to shed tears of joy in front of the woman staring at him.

Gently, he placed the paper on the table and heaved a breath of relief. He'd needed good news first, and he got it. He was so impressed with his elder son's performance that he wished to stay with his teacher forever, but the bell rang. He had no choice but to face Olu's teacher, his panic rising.

Olu's teacher was summoned, and he started talking without a blink, without stopping. Simon felt stuffy within two minutes of the soliloquy. The man wouldn't shut up. He kept on and on, like a woman. Simon just sat listening and hated every minute spent with the woman in a man's body. That was the image of this teacher in Simon's brain.

His two sons' performances were two parallel lines that could never meet. Olu was so bad that Simon felt like crying, calling it quits, and running away. He did not want to have to look the new principal in the eye—the man who took no rubbish from anybody. He'd had enough for the day. Finally, he deduced from the teacher's last words that Olu hadn't passed out of Form One, even though he was supposed to have passed to Form Four, like his half-brother Akin. The boy would still be in Form One.

Simon's head throbbed gently. As if what he'd already heard wasn't enough to run a father insane, the teacher finished: "Sir, Olu could never go higher in education with his attitude. Since I have been his teacher and watched him, there is no hope that he'll progress out of Form One. He is a kid with the worst attitude I have ever seen. He has lost interest in school."

Conclusively, the teacher handed over Olu's report card for Simon to see. Simon took it and folded it without giving it a second glance, then stood up.

"Thanks," he mumbled. "I need to see the principal."

"Would you like me to take you over there, sir?"

But Simon was out the door without answering the teacher's question.

* * *

Reverend Thomas was signing some papers when Simon got to his office. Briefly, he rose for a handshake, sat down again, and urged Simon to do the same. He handed one of the sheets on the table to Simon, who read it in silence. He was too late. Olu had been expelled.

Simon closed his eyes for a second. He didn't know what to say. The reverend watched as Simon stood up and said, "Thanks a lot, sir."

He didn't wait for a parting handshake. Simon left the principal's office and staggered toward the parking lot as if drunk. Yes, he was drunk with grief; yet he wondered if it were not too late to turn Olu around.

Simon wished to yell "stupid" at the top of his voice to himself. He knew that wouldn't help the situation and would only make him look stupid in front of passersby. His children were not duty-bound to go to school, but they did have to learn a trade they could fall back on in life, just like he did, he resolved within himself. Before it was too late, before it was too hard to carve like a dry fish, he must have a meeting with his children and their mothers to express his final warnings.

"This very evening, I will lay down the ground rules of making a choice," he muttered to himself, walking toward his car. "And those choices will be made plain in front of their mothers, who did nothing to stop their children's futures from being flushed down the toilet, right underneath their noses."

Simon recalled how some of his classmates who had fallen out of school became bums because of a lack of proper orientation to the future. They had quickly found their lives out of balance, especially those who had refused to learn a trade and do something constructive in their youths. He had some of them, now grown, depending on him for daily bread.

Safe in his car, Simon's mind went briefly back to his occasional bewilderment since Olu had turned out to be the black sheep of the family. Why was there a gap between his children from non-native mothers and native mothers? He had briefly concluded, as he always did, that he was an idiot to have married the natives, who were barely concerned about their children but were highly concerned with ostentatious society. His second and third wives would crawl to hell to attend a prominent function.

He cursed under his breath the day he decided to listen to his father, to marry natives who bore irresponsible children. Had he stood his ground, he would have stayed with the wife he married for love. Also, he wouldn't have married the third wife that he had faintly loved in his youth. And if he wanted to sow more oats, he would take non-native, as he did now. Lightning might strike again. Simon had switched to non-native civil servants—two of his secretaries were his wives, and his latest wife had been an attorney in a law firm in Ladden before he married her—to test his theory. He would patiently wait for their infants to start school, and if his experiment proved positive, then he would shift his interest permanently. He relaxed as if the experiment would absolutely work.

"Sunday, do you know the road to Teniola's house, our representative in Ajoni-Itan?" Simon said abruptly.

He had meant to see Teniola, his foreman in Ajoni-Itan, and ask about the cotton plantation in his area. Cotton was about to be approved as a cash crop for export, and Simon decided that instead of burying himself in sorrow, he decided to at least kill two birds with the same stone.

The driver started the car. "Yes, sir, he lives not far from this area."

"Good, let's see him now."

The driver turned the car to a small road as soon as they were out of the school compound. Within minutes, they were in front of a bungalow, in front of which three girls of varying ages were playing.

Immediately after Sunday parked the car, one of the girls dressed in ordinary pants ran up to the car without listening to the others shouting her name, telling her to stop and come back. Simon wound down the window as the little girl approached.

"Are you Teniola's daughter?" Simon demanded.

The little girl pressed her body against the car. She placed both hands on the frame of the window and smiled.

"You don't know I'm his daughter?"

Simon was bemused by her confidence and her fearless attitude with a stranger.

"No. So, what is your name?" Simon asked with a frown.

"My name is Titi, and my father is Teniola. He is not at home. He is at the farm. You can come back if you want."

"No, coming back is impossible, Titi. But tell your father Mr. Simon came to see him. And he should see me tomorrow morning in Akuta."

"Do you have sweets in your car?" she asked, peeping inside.

Simon shook his head and murmured under his breath about nobody teaching manners anymore. "No, adults don't eat sweets. Tell your dad I came."

She didn't reply and seemed angry.

"Move away from the car, Titi," Simon ordered.

The girl did as she was told, reluctantly. Simon tapped Sunday on the shoulder and said, "We go to Ibata-Itan now."

Chapter Twenty-One

S imon's domestic lifestyle wasn't any different from that of his father, Kanbi—well, with a few exceptions. Despite the fact that Kanbi was one of the richest of his time, and he could stuff women like sardines at the back of his house and have a sea of children, Kanbi had only two wives for a long while. Both wives and children lived in separate self-contained apartments at the back of his villa. And when his wives were advanced in age, he married a beautiful young girl to see to his old-age needs. He was moderate, and channeled his energy toward other things, like a horse ranch, as he was a horse lover. Simon was too, until he had an accident while riding and was then afraid of the animal.

Simon was glad that cars had replaced the damn beasts as a means of transportation. And he had been acquiring cars in different shapes and sizes and colors, just as he had been acquiring women and *ale* (concubines). The wives and his children were stacked in self-contained apartments at the back of his mansion, while his mistresses were far from his home, where he provided for them. So far, there were four wives in accessory dwelling apartments, excluding the live-in wife in the mansion, and also excluding Joyce, the runaway first wife, and the runaway bride, Sarah. There was uncertainty about how many concubines were in the diaspora. His three older brothers were well-to-do, but not as rich as Simon, who wined and dined with the dignitaries of Great Britain.

Simon's compound occupied about twenty acres of land, while his newest, dream mansion—his third in Ibata-Itan—sat on the land next to his current manor house. The new one was under construction, too vast to quantify both in size and space. He hoped for it to be completed as soon as possible, since his present dwelling wasn't big enough and wasn't pleasing him as it used to.

The front of the residence had a fine, large lawn manicured by three gardeners, and in the rainy season, even more. The chief gardener saw to that every time. A parking lot was built on one side, and on the other side were residences for the more elite servants. There were gigantic playgrounds, including a soccer pitch and a tennis court. And not too far away, but at a certain distance from the playground, were the quarters for the other servants. Whatever Simon saw abroad, he copied.

The hall of the mansion was immaculate cream color with high-ceiling columns designed and heavy chandeliers from the King George IV era. Each chandelier weighed a ton and shinning it best. A cream marble staircase descended to a dark brown shaggy rug in the hall. The left and right of the hall displayed sculptures and heart-attack-if-broken antiquities, including large vases, gourds, and beautifully mahogany cupboards at corners. The sculptures and vintage, expensive objects made the hall resembled a museum worth a fortune. Three footmen stood, alert, as though guarding the treasures. Magnificent dual grandeur staircases climbed upstairs, opposite directions. Each led to an apartment block with a gasp-for-breath–sized living room that stretched out like an ocean, exhibited an exclusive blaze-brown granite floor, polished Isfahan rugs, along with finely styled Victorian couches imported from Kingly furniture shop in London, which was highly recommended by Reverend Philip. The luxury of each parlor was brought to life vividly with the authentic sculptures of Oduduwa, Yemoja, Ori-Olokun, and ancient gods and goddesses, as well as paintings from overseas that cost a fortune. Next to each living room were five bedrooms, decadent and equipped with bathrooms and toilets. Their designs were lifted out of the best British interior decoration. One of the apartment blocks was for Simon and his latest wife, Peju, the former attorney.

The other half was for important guests that, as rumor had it, included Sir Bernard Henry Bourdillon, the former governor and commander-in-chief of Nigeria and his wife, plus other prominent dignitaries from Great Britain who lodged there from time to time. The rumors had encouraged a lot of wanderers, who entered the compound aimlessly, even though it was secluded. This was the reason the mansion was fortified with walls, surrounded by barbed wire, and guarded by uniformed security men. There was also a rumor that Akin occupied one section of the ground floor, directly below Simon, so that he could be called upon as the heir to Simon's empire at any given time, to meet and dine with important guests, without having to include other members of the family. In the other half, on the ground floor, there was a lounge, a ballroom, a drawing room, a dining hall for the entertainment of close guests, a kitchen, and storage.

These rumors were true.

Akin lived in a similar space to his dad's. His space started with a vast living room dotted with articles such as sculptures and paintings tagged "one million pounds." The living room was surrounded by three bedrooms, three bathrooms, and three toilets, for Akin and his visitors. The other two rooms were used as dressing rooms. It said loud and clear: Simon was a lion ruling his household like a king, and Akin was a cub with a brilliant future, waiting for the mantle of power.

Akin's apartment also reflected his own taste, as he wanted it—framed posters of Allan Lane, best actor in *Red Ryder,* were hung on the wall. Simon had brought the first comic book series home when Akin was little, from one of his trips abroad, since he was aware that Akin adored horses and he was also aware that the boy sometimes sneaked away to Kanbi's ranch. Akin had read the comics from cover to cover many times over. When Allan Lane was nominated best actor for his depiction of the hero, Akin had asked Simon to lay his hands on his posters at all costs.

Encyclopedias, and books as heavy as encyclopedias, lined the shelves. A turntable record player. Scores of record albums, Akin's ornaments, and shiny trophies won for academics and athletics, which were as radiant as the sun, were all on display. There were selected pictures of Simon in black and white, shaking hands with dignitaries in London. And, the best goody of all, Simon pictured with Sir Bernard Bourdillon, and with Sir Arthur Richard, the present governor of Nigeria. Akin had met and dined with them both.

Dupe was in her apartment living room having

breakfast—bean cake in one hand and the other gripping a spoon of pap. Akin slipped in to talk to her. Dupe's personal maid bowed to Akin and left, closing the entrance door behind her.

"Akin, you had breakfast already?" Dupe glanced up, asking.

"No, I'm not hungry. I'm here to tell you that one of your classmates is now a member of the Lion Club."

Akin's voice was wobbly, Dupe noticed, and as a result, she placed the cake and the spoon back in their respective homes—bean cake on top of a pile of the same, and the spoon into the pap bowl. She gave full attention to Akin, who was looking nervous—a first time for her big brother, who was usually confident.

"I thought you must be in secondary school before you can be eligible to be a member?" she demanded.

"Yes, but she was exceptional, and plus, she'll be in secondary this September."

"You allow a "she" in the Lion Club?" she screamed at Akin's deadpan face. The identity of the "she" slashed across her brain: "Stinky-Shabby-Crazy!" Dupe screamed, looking edgy. "Oh, God, don't tell me you allowed Omotola to join the club?"

"Yes. She has all the merit, and I don't see why not."

Dupe stared, and Akin looked away.

"But you only admit boys from exceedingly rich homes. Why a girl, especially that one from an abject home?"

Akin dragged his eyes back to look at Dupe.

"That's not totally true," he said. "There are other boys from unknown…" Akin drifted off.

"Oh, God!" Dupe exclaimed. "When will she stop

being a parasite? Omotola is a dirty, dowdy, skinny girl with a hurricane brain that absorbs all she's taught in a gulp. What's more, she's a parasite. She lives on others to grow. She was the pet of all the teachers in the school, and they all provided for her needs at everyone else's expense. I hate her. So does every other pupil. Akin, it will be a huge mistake if you allow her; she will eventually bring her kind and pollute the club in the future. Chase her out fast."

"I can't. She earned her membership fair and square. Besides…" Akin hesitated.

Dupe's eyes were intensely focused on Akin's face as he failed to complete his statement. A possibility dawned on her. "God! Not you too. Brother, don't tell me she crawled under your skin, and you think you like her?"

"Well, I like her for her courage—a bit. Maybe a lot … I don't know. I've just never felt this way about any girl before, and…" Akin scratched his head, eyes on the ceiling.

"You can have all the feelings you want. Papa will never let it materialize. Chase her away whilst she's still a maggot and save yourself a lot of trouble," Dupe insisted.

"I can't do that," Akin said with conviction. "I'm going to talk to Papa about her right now, so he can do what's necessary."

Dupe's face altered to black, glaring without a word. And since there was silence, Akin said, "Talk to you later." He left for the main building.

For days, Akin's mind had been in pain as it focused on the girl he'd seen at Esa waterfall—the girl whose wet T-shirt clung to her body as she came out of the water and aroused murmurings among the boys … the girl whose beauty left him stunned, made him speechless. Akin had admired Omotola straightaway, as soon as he laid eyes on her. She gave him feelings he'd never had before, emotions that still surged within him, even though the recruitment was long over.

Thinking of her made him shiver, want desperately to touch, to cuddle her. "Too crazy," he'd told himself at the Esa waterfall as his body temperature rose at the sight of her. He'd had to shove away those feelings with great effort, so as not to look like an idiot in front of his friends. He'd made up his mind since she had dived into the water that she belonged to the club. Now, as he left Dupe's presence, he made up his mind that they belonged together. Omotola had the three Bs: beauty, brains, and boldness—three things he'd always wanted in the woman of his dreams. He ran through them in his mind.

-Beauty: tall, with a curved, slender body that seemed frail and weak … but that was deceitful, to Akin's wonder, because her body surged into action beyond imagination as she performed each drill of the club more brilliantly than ever expected, even better than most boys.

- Brains: everything confirmed it. Even his little sister hated her for her intelligence. Omotola would skip Primary Six, as she had passed her exams to secondary school with flying colors. She would have a full scholarship to his secondary school, starting in September! He still found it hard to wrap his head around the possibility of a Primary Five pupil passing the entrance exam to the most excellent school that only selected the best students nationwide. It was too unbelievable, beyond imagination.

Boldness: a salute to her exceptionalism in her

gender, as no female had ever ventured for a trial for Lion Club before.

She brashly broke the hegemony of "boys-only" rule in the club. As the founder of the club, he'd be lifting the ban on girls in Lion Club, and the legacy would be everlasting—that was final. "Yes, she'll be the one," Akin murmured as he left Dupe's apartment to see his father.

Since the recruitment, Akin had never been the same. He kept on remembering the girl in a pink T-shirt, with brown shorts and worn-out slippers. At first, he was scared, and eventually convinced himself that he liked Omotola. No! He was in love with her. The more Akin thought about her, the more he wanted to be with her, and the more he wished to touch her, hold her close to his heart, and tell her he'd give her the world.

She was special, he had concluded, and he wanted her at any cost. But he needed to act fast—before another boy grabbed the opportunity, wanting her as their future bride, or before she liked another boy in the club. He'd heard that many of his Lions dug her already, and he understood what it meant. If he waited to act, Omotola might fall in love with somebody else. He couldn't afford that. He must involve his father straightaway. It had to be official, he decided.

Akin was young but acquainted with the drills of the town he lived in. Arranged marriages were as routine as breathing air. A father organized a wife for a son. A father married his daughters to the best suitors. A man took wives as often as he wanted. It was all part of the great Itan Land custom that made men superior to women and let them live lordly lives in their households. Children who chose partners to marry were very rare, and many times brought the wrath of a father who generally believed he knew better than his offspring.

A few years earlier, Akin was told about the match made between him and Solape. He wasn't bothered, because he was determined to go into the priesthood and immediately move from Nigeria to study in Great Britain. Six months before he formally met Omotola, he was introduced to Solape. His father told him their wedding would be before he left Nigeria to study. Then, Akin was concerned he would be forced into a marriage he had never agreed to. Even though he knew Solape and her family inside out and knew that the matchmaking reflected the love that the two families had for each other, Akin had told his father to count him out. But Simon wasn't giving up. He was of the belief that "time heals wounds, as time brings two people together to love each other." But Akin had insisted, "Love is not a feeling you grow into, like growing into a dress or a pair of shoes—especially when you have nothing in common with the person in question!" Despite all his objections, the marriage would happen.

Solape "dolled" over him, he could tell, but for him, the spark didn't happen. On the official introduction day, he was forced to spend with her, he'd questioned her a lot, easily realizing that she had no ambition, and indeed, was another artificial, delusional brat. She'd rather settle down, have babies, and become madame of the house rather than pursue any goals. Akin hated the idea of living with a nudnik as much as he hated the idea of marrying a girl from his circle—one who was as dark as charcoal, but who pretended to the world that she was as white as snow.

It wasn't his problem that Tunde Ogunlade had been

his father's best friend in the world since childhood. Akin hated to be the sacrificial lamb for their friendship to grow, to continue. He could have been a priest. He thought he wouldn't mind embracing life like his mentor, Reverend Philip; that is, until Omotola showed up, and that changed everything.

Akin, whom the girls called "Mister World," had seen many girls and could have bedded as many girls as he wanted, like his half-brother Olu. But he didn't want that. Akin knew he'd been waiting for Omotola. He was happy he'd found her. It was love, period. He wanted a woman he loved, chose himself, rather than having one chosen for him. He cared nothing for the custom. He wanted to marry the girl he was madly in love with at present, and would be for eternity. He prayed she felt the same about him. She just had to. He was on his way to see his father.

Akin walked back from Dupe's unit to the corridor leading to the main building. Two footmen on the corridor bowed their heads as he traipsed an exclusive Kerman carpet in a long, wide corridor displaying sculptures and antiquities left and right as well. Instead of heading toward his apartment, Akin went to the staircase leading to Simon's apartment.

"Master Akin, your butler was looking for you. He said your breakfast is ready," one of the three footmen in the hall said quickly.

Akin stopped and turned to the man. "Thanks for the message. Please tell him I'll eat later. I've got to see my father now."

"Sir, would you like me to escort you up to announce your arrival?"

"No, thanks," Akin replied with a smile. "That won't

be necessary. I'll do this alone."

Simon's house rules were that no member of his household or visitors were allowed to see him without an appointment that he permitted. Everyone had to be accompanied by a footman or an escort and announced to Simon. Simon would decide if he wanted to attend to that person, but Akin was the only exception—the only one who could walk in to see Simon without accompaniment or an agreed rendezvous. With all due respect, Akin came first in everything in Simon Akindele's house, even before Olu. Simon's special affection toward Akin wasn't hidden; it was obvious to the rest in the house and the world, and that caused much jealousy. Simon didn't care. "A son after my own heart," Simon always bragged to friends and business associates. He loved the boy more than life itself. They all knew this.

Akin climbed the stairs and briskly traversed the living room to Simon's bedroom. He greeted his father's latest wife, Peju, and a maid who was placing Simon's outfits for the day on his bed, and dashed to the bathroom, where he knew his father would be at that moment with Ojo.

He knew Simon would be undergoing the morning ritual of receiving barbering, shaving, a manicure, and a pedicure by his trusted servant, Ojo. The barber was much more than a servant, but a close pal and Simon's grapevine communicator. He could gossip about everything to Simon, including who had farted among the crowd in his household when he was away. Simon had brought him all the way from Ladden to cater to all the barbering and other household needs. Akin would find his father with Ojo.

⸙

Chapter Twenty-Two

Simon sat on a lovely Victorian chair, paying little attention to Ojo, who rested on a cushion on the cream-colored marble tiles with dark brown veins running through them, performing a pedicure. As the servant cut Simon's toenails, babbling about the new maid who was still excited to be employed, and as a result, dropped things. Simon scanned the news—the *Nigeria Daily Times* first, followed by *The Daily Mirror*.

He folded the two papers on his lap and glanced at the barber. With a bored look on his face, he demanded, "Ojo, did you see Olu recently?"

Gently, Ojo put the nail clippers on the floor. He looked at Simon and said, "Not recently. He seems to have fled from the area and its environment, though he was seen in Ladden recently. If you want, I can ask one of the drivers to go to Ladden and check where he was seen last." Ojo's face was full of concern.

"That won't be necessary. I'm sure when he runs out of resources, like the prodigal son…"

Akin walked in.

"You, I call a son. Come over here, Son," Simon said, looking revived.

Ojo retrieved the nail clippers, rose, and backed away a little. Akin moved and stood in front of Simon.

"Good morning, Papa and Mr. Ojo," he said, looking impatient. "Can I talk to you in private, Papa?"

With a nod from Simon to Ojo and a simple wave of his hand, all the other attendants dispersed from the area, giving privacy to father and son to talk behind closed doors.

Simon's affection for Akin had a lot to do with his mother and with the way in which he was conceived. Akin was among the few Simon could aver that he fathered without any doubt with his semen. With the others, he was mostly wasted. He couldn't recall his first time with Arinola, as he never liked the woman. As for his other wives' children, he knew about their births from other people, especially the servants who come running, congratulating him on another little baby—but it could have been congratulations for another little bastard.

But Simon had sweated like a pig as he waited in the antenatal ward's corridor when Joyce was giving birth to Akin. She was in labor for hours. He was almost out of his mind with worry and begged her not to go through pregnancy again immediately as he finally laid eyes on his adorable son. At that instant, he had experienced an overwhelming love that persisted until the present. And then came Dupe. He was too scared to be at Joyce's side at the hospital, but he prayed profoundly and even tried to bribe God. Akin was a child conceived in love, with a woman he loved.

He always remembered their first time together, on their honeymoon, when he took away her innocence. She was the woman he'd loved with all his heart, to whom he gave his heart and also gave the world. The woman who Simon also vowed to kill with his bare hands for ridiculing him, for leaving him like forgotten goods at a rummage sale, for making him cheap. There was a bounty on her head. If he found her, she would be eliminated, silently, without a fuss. She was damaged goods to him. He would rather stick his rod in a python's mouth than sleep with her. He didn't want her, and he couldn't bear the pain of someone else having her, either. She needed to be silenced.

Akin was Simon's pride and joy—a son who never failed to uplift his name both in academics and sport, news of which was splashed all over the papers. Simon almost died from over-excitement the day he was called upon by the headmaster to learn that Akin was the top pupil in Primary One. But he went out of his mind with worry when Akin became Reverend Philip's disciple. Sometimes he was afraid that Akin might never settle down as Simon wanted him to, afraid he might take off and pass on his heirship. He was bleeding inside but managed to keep up appearances. He never told anybody. And it was a relief when the reverend left Nigeria and Simon got back his son—his beloved son who wouldn't end up in the priesthood. His pride and joy wouldn't shun the path he wanted him to follow. He was delusional with happiness.

Since Akin became more and more introverted and reserved after his mother left, Simon tried to give him everything to make him happy—to make up for his mother's disappearance. Simon couldn't wait to bring Akin to a suitable apartment as his heir toward the end of his Form One. Well, there could have been sibling rivalry, but Olu was in his own world, settling for a furnished, tasteful apartment at the back of the mansion, where he'd see less of Simon and do his own thing.

Simon didn't give it a second thought when Akin wanted acres of land for a club—the club that had become a success, with unquantifiable publicity in all the newspapers and parents coming to solicit his help in getting their kids into the club. The club news overshadowed nightmarish captions like "Baron's wife shagged by a postmaster, what is the thrill?" to cartoon sketches that showed him as an angry husband. Even though his name wasn't mentioned in all the rubbish in the newspapers, his close pals knew it was him.

Simon looked at his son and realized he looked as weary as he used to be when his mother first left. Although, that had changed since he started the club. When in his presence for one thing or another, he saw smiles, but these weren't present as he watched him now. Simon was concerned.

"Son, what can I do for you?"

After a pregnant silence of a few seconds, Akin looked at his father and said, "Papa, I met a girl the other day. I kind of like her." And he looked away.

Simon stared at his shy son and realized he was in love. And not a puppy love either, but a real one, with a one-way ticket to the point of no return. Simon had had that once with Akin's mother. He knew the effect.

Joyce had been a cloth-selling apprentice in Simon's father's shop in Josi. She had stopped schooling after Primary Six and had developed an hourglass figure, with a curved, symmetrical face that could stop traffic, making most men's mouths drop wide open. She was a lot more than a beautiful woman. She had something in her, in her body language, that made a man like Simon refuse his chosen bride or any among a string of girls, mostly from well-to-do families, without a second thought.

Arinola, Simon's father's chosen bride, was from an acclaimed rich family whose patriarch was a childhood friend of Kanbi. Kanbi was so proud to have selected a woman from his backyard, and greatly disappointed when Simon announced his first marriage, to his apprentice. And he went through with it. Joyce was the only person who could make Simon roll off of any woman—any day, anytime—by merely calling his name. He might never have leaped and married the third wife if he hadn't hated his second one so much, the longer she lived in his house. If he hadn't wanted more kids, he wouldn't have taken the third wife, Simon had explained. He had been afraid he might lose Joyce to pregnancies one day if he overworked her with having more babies. His friends knew better than to believe that. Why not stop after the third wife? Why Sarah? Why others?

Simon's addiction was women, period. Even the great love he had for Joyce couldn't stop him from toying with other women. He once admitted to a friend that he loved to sample different appetizers, even though the main course at home was so satisfying. The rumors had it that his lewdness in chasing after other women had driven Joyce to open her "thing" for a man not worthy of being a gardener in her husband's house, and to run away with him eventually.

"Serves him right," said most of his friends, who had been dying and praying to have one time with Joyce.

"Simon has *Okin,* the peacock in his yard, and chases after *awon Igun*, the vulture and the scavenger unworthy to carry Joyce's slipper," they all said. Jealous, they were all happy when Joyce did what she did to ridicule Simon. He was the architect of his own downfall, and most of them laughed their heads off behind his back as he grieved for days over Joyce's disappearance.

His parents were the worst. They pointed out to him that he was stupid to have married a non-native—that her history was like a shadow because she was a beauty. And that wasn't true, or perhaps wasn't the only reason. Simon marrying Joyce had little to do with beauty; it had everything to do with love. It was the one crazy moment of his life he'd never forget. No woman could ever replace Joyce, and Simon knew it.

Akin coughed, and it drew Simon's full attention to his son, who was staring at the floor instead of looking at him directly.

"Girl, you said?" Simon's voice trembled. "But I've chosen a fiancée for you already, as a father should for his son. You remember Solape, my friend's daughter? She is pretty, and she loves you."

Without beating about the bush, Akin said, "I don't want her as my wife. I told you already."

Simon said desperately, "Akin, listen to me. Solape is my dear friend's daughter. She is a lovely girl from a great family. She'll make an excellent wife. Son, I want the best for you. I want you to marry a reputable woman who I can vouch for, not a woman like your mother. You remember what she did to us? She abandoned us and ran away. Solape will make you an excellent wife. I'm positive about it."

"Papa, I like the other girl much better," Akin insisted, looking straight at his father.

"Son, remember your mother!" Simon said.

"Remember the pain she caused both of us when she disappeared without a trace? As your father, I know the girl who is best for you—who won't break your heart, run away, and abandon you and your children."

"Papa, I hated what Mama did, but that shouldn't be a stumbling block to marry the girl I love."

Simon had told Akin that his mother had run away, but later, he'd learned the ugly truth from his father's servants: that his mother had run away with another man—abandoning them, to be cared for by their father. Much, much later, he found in his father's closet all the nastiest things written about her in the newspapers.

At that tender age of six, Akin had summoned up courage as his father told him to long for her absence in secret and feel the pain in silence, which was sometimes unbearable and inexplicable. There was nobody in the family he could ask or consult who wouldn't spit on Joyce. Reverend Philip had been his father figure since Simon had thrown himself into his business and women. The reverend remained Akin's guiding light until he went back to Britain, but Dupe had no one. She was badly affected. Far from recovering, she frequently asked, "Where is Mama? Akin, when will she come back?"

"Papa, I do understand the pain her disappearance has cost us, and I know you mean well, but I prefer to choose my bride myself."

Akin finished and focused his eyes on his legs.

Out of all of Simon's friends, when Joyce ran away, Tunde Ogunlade alone stood with him as a true friend. Out of everybody Simon had mingled with before Joyce ran away to the moment when he gained the ultimate power, Tunde had been his trusted friend and confidant.

And those easy-to-come-by friends, he owned their existence; he could order their balls for his dogs as a meal. Watching Tunde's loyalty and seeing one of his daughters grown up with beauty and sophistication had been another bonus that brought Simon to accept the engagement and allow his beloved son to be matched with Tunde's daughter.

Simon was pensive as he studied his son intensively. No doubt at all, Akin was deeply in love, and he knew it would take the world to change his mind. He never thought a day would come when a girl would raise his son's temperature and make him shy off of the match. He knew he had to do something fast. *Geez! Boy meets world.*

As he looked at Akin, a thought occupied his head— as a businessman who wants success, Simon needed to be able to adapt, amend, add, and subtract when necessary. It was now time to do that. If Akin didn't want Solape as his starter wife, he could marry a woman of his choice from any upper-class family or any Highlife Club member—and later, he'd convinced him to marry her, just like his father did when he stubbornly clung to Joyce. He might even embrace polygamy early, like him. Simon finally concluded that it might work out. "This idea must work. Otherwise, I'll look like an ingrate to Tunde Ogunlade," he muttered to himself.

"All right, if you insist," Simon said reluctantly. "Give me the name of the girl and family name later, and I'll do what needs to be done."

"*Later* might be too late," Akin said promptly. "Papa, I've got her name right here. Her name is Omotola."

"Son, we won't go far with a first name; you have to add her surname," Simon said, smiling.

"Right, Papa," Akin said nervously, "Her name is Omotola, and her father's name is Paul Olorunfemi. She's from this town."

Simon bolted upright in his chair, as if he was pinched by a pin or something sharper in his back.

Akin had done his homework on Omotola's background before facing Simon. He even knew that his father's "absent bride," Sarah, was Omotola's aunt. Leye had soaked him in details.

Akin smiled, continuing, "She is an extraordinarily brilliant, beautiful girl."

Simon glared as Akin went on.

"She used to be in Dupe's class, but she's on her way to Itan Central High School this September. Can you believe that, Papa?"

"Oh boy, here we go again." It came out before Simon could stop himself. His face changed from pain to horror.

"Is there a problem, Papa?" Akin asked, looking perplexed.

"Where in the world did you meet a girl from that family?" Simon's voice carried more revulsion than his face. "Son, the Olorunfemi family is the craziest family in this town. You can't marry from that den of thugs. None of my children would be allowed to marry from such a home."

"Papa, you're wrong. Omotola is not crazy nor a thug. Besides, I'm a friend of her brother, and he has always been good to me. When I met her last recruitment, she was nice, and I love her, Papa. She is a great girl. As I said, she has a full scholarship to my school at Primary Five. Papa, I love this girl with all my heart, and I promise not to disappoint you like Olu did."

Olu had cheated on Janet on several occasions with some of her friends. And he'd told Janet that their matchmaking was a lie, never consensual. He would never marry her, period. And on several occasions, Simon had to do damage control with money, assuring Janet's parents that Olu would marry their daughter.

"She is a native, Son; native is not good."

"Papa, my mother was non-native. See what she did?" Akin had an *I rest my case* look on his face while Simon looked alarmed thinking about the Olorunfemi family. He knew a lot about the family, and what he knew was depressing to him. Simon's impression was that most of the adults from the house were ruffians and swine because their parents were the same. The few he had been to school with from the family were brainy, with attitudes, and also losers.

He stared past his son, looking at the huge Victorian bathtub in the corner of the bathroom. He was going batty, wondering how his heir could fall in love with a girl from such a house. What was the thrill? He remembered that he would have made the greatest mistake of marrying one of them, Sarah, for the stupid reason of helping with the cocoa price negotiation instead of using an intermediary. She was a brilliant, proud girl, and her father promised she would marry him. She had gone to the school of nursing at his expense and disappeared. He'd brushed shoulders with the family over her, not because he loved her that much, but because she had put on a sheet of paper that she wouldn't marry "a stark illiterate bully."

Simon had wanted Sarah's greedy father to pay. He hated the Olorunfemi family from the bottom of his heart as he had hated Paul, Omotola's father, for so long. Paul Olorunfemi was Simon's classmate in primary school for three years. He was the cleverest student in his early primary school, despite his truancy. He hated him then and even more now, as he turned out to be a pathetic alcoholic among the majority of his classmates who missed the high road. To be specific, it was *Ogogoro,* the local gin, and *Emu,* the white wine that had rendered Paul's brain useless. Simon knew about these. And his heir wanted to choose from that family? It would be degrading, insult his status, and bring problems.

Simon wondered why Akin had not hand-picked as many as he wanted from the children of the Highlife Circle, his inner circle or thick aristocratic circle—girls around his age from, who could satisfy both purposes of beauty and brains, if those were the cause of the commotion. Akin claimed to have little attraction to Solape because of her lack of flair for school, as he'd complained.

Highlife Circle were super-rich, the top echelon from esteemed families of the Western region. To be a member, you had to be from the money or respect crowd. Simon's inner circle and the aristocrat families, their children refrained from mingling with any Tom, Dick, or Harry around Nigeria. They went to the best schools, learned the proper fashions and behavior, and had never-ending debutante balls, called "in-coming" for youths to meet. At least, Akin could have chosen from his circle, and that would guarantee a reputation, born and groomed to the echelon of perfection. Why choose a child from a hell-hole who would lack knowledge of the dance, the laugh, the jokes, and comportment? A girl from an aristocratic family—that background, along with beauty, he knew Akin would need later as he attended functions with kings and queens. *It would be catastrophic if he chose a girl from an ill home. He would be a laughingstock.* Simon felt queasy.

Simon wasn't concerned that Solape had no intellect. Other things made up for that … he noticed her beauty and elegance flowing like a river each time he saw her. He had always been well pleased with her. He was on top of the world that her educational appetites were tiny. Akin could marry educated ones later, should he want to. Simon's latest wife was an attorney—Peju, who was grooming his bed at present. The higher certificate she needed was to satisfy him sexually and domestically, to the letter, or else someone else, with better qualifications, would take her place in a jiffy.

Since Solape wasn't brilliant, Tunde said he would be happy to marry her off immediately, when Akin was ready. Simple education was not a barrier. She wouldn't need the certificate for anything anyway. The one thing expected of her would be to take care of Akin's needs and to be glamorous at all the functions she would be attending with Akin as the CEO of Akdrend Worldwide. Simon had been happy for a long time that Solape would be ready to marry Akin as soon as possible, preferably towards the end of his form six. He would be over the moon to give the wedding bash of the century in a couple of years and in seventh heaven if Akin could knock her up before he bowed out of Nigeria.

"But, oh, no. Akin had to change his mind," he muttered to himself.

Why didn't you give Joyce up as your father wanted,

Simon? As much as his thoughts dug deep, excavating, he hated the question. And he knew love is schizoid, bizarre enough for a king to leave a throne, but he was worried that Omotola would be like Sarah. He would have to influence Akin to marry her later. She would compete for Akin's love like Peju, the one living with him in the mansion. He could marry ten educated wives in a day, and not a single wife could ask why.

"Son, you have a choice. Marry Solape first, or any other from my inner circle, then later marry Omotola. You know why Omotola has to come later?"

Akin looked at his father as if he was insane. He frowned as he shook his head.

"It's because a brilliant girl from a loony house would be too proud and tend to want to prove she is equal to any man."

Akin folded his hands around his chest and gave his father a stare that was hot, ready to blow a fuse.

"So, what's wrong with that, Papa? If you don't want to help me with Omotola, I'll do it myself. I love her, and nothing can change that, as nothing can change that I hate the idea of more than one wife in a lifetime. I'm not..." Akin stopped.

Simon was sad, leaning back on his seat as he watched Akin change from the shy type who had walked in, at first, to a man poised for action. Akin's stare, directed at him, unnerved Simon.

"All right, Son, you made your point. I've got to warn you this is a twisted situation that will need much patience, but I will see what I can do."

"What do you mean by 'twisted situation'?" Akin demanded. "It's good, right, Papa?"

"Yes, son, twisted is good. I'll see what I can do … find out…" Simon stopped short of adding *"if not stepping on another man's territory. Omotola could be engaged."* He knew it would confuse his son.

"Thanks, Papa."

"Son, I'll proceed as the town customs demand," Simon said casually. "Anyway, I'll try and do what needs to be done before we travel. You can go, Son."

Arms released from his chest, Akin's face softened to a smile.

"Thanks, Papa. I know nothing is impossible for you."

Simon smiled back. Akin walked away.

Simon knew Akin was patronizing him by saying, "I know nothing is impossible for you," yet it was true. His son had got that part right. Akin wanted a crazy wife from the crack house of Paul Olorunfemi! That's what he would get.

Simon sank into his thoughts. Paul Olorunfemi, the olori-ebi, the heir, the lord of his clan? He laughed as "the lord" sounded in his brain, picturing the man. Paul hated him for rubbing shoulders with his family. The hatred between them was reciprocal. Still, he would prevail at all costs in giving Akin what his heart desired. He could read Paul and the needy bum as he could read the back of his hand. Paul was a pathetic excuse for a man, capable of selling his whole clan for a shilling. In fact, Paul wouldn't be a "blocking stone" in the long run if he raised her bride price beyond other suitors' capabilities, but Simon's worries lay with Omotola.

Chapter Twenty-Three

Stanley, the assistant director of marketing at the Akdrend group of companies, London branch, sat in one of its fabulous exclusive lobbies at the main headquarters in Ladden, Nigeria. He was waiting to see Akin, the heir to the empire. His right leg crossed over his left leg, both of which didn't stop trembling as he anticipated meeting his future CEO on dual assignments—he had to deliver a sample of jersey uniforms for the Lion Club founded by Akin. As he understood it, the boy must approve the sample of the jerseys before the consignment could be shipped over to Nigeria, and at the same time, ask the lad what he would like as a treat on his visit to London. Simon wanted the boy's first time in Britain to be comfortable.

That summer, Akin would be in England for a month so that he could be brought up to speed with what was happening in the company. Simon wanted him involved from an early age, in case something happened to him. He'd have to take over immediately. He'd said years earlier—should he live to see his son graduating from college, he would transfer the full mantle of power to him on that same day.

The exclusive, high-priced Victorian sofas and chairs shipped from Britain, from the most notorious shop for the barons and moguls, arranged impeccably, didn't entice him—not today, anyway. On normal occasions, Stanley would have been wondering how the lot got rooted in the dying-to-be extremely tasteful room. He'd have been proud of himself to have the privilege of being in the exclusive lobby, not in the general lobby. And he would have happily told the others in Britain they'd missed out, but Stanley was not happy at all. In fact, each creaking sound around him made him crazy. He watched the door and mopped his face constantly, since the sweat kept dripping, even though the air-conditioning in the room should have frozen the glands, frozen his blood.

The last thing Stanley wished for was trauma or drama from the boy, dealing with a spoiled brat. And these dual assignments could have been postponed, since the boy would be in Britain in a few weeks for the summer. That might have delayed the about-to-be death-warrant if he was not liked by the boy. He was a desperate man with one wish: that the boy should be nice. Otherwise, he would have to start to look for another job. And what company paid a salary like the Akdrend Company in England? None. Simon Akindele was one of the highest-ranking business tycoons in Nigeria, and the number-one-rated investor in Great Britain. He took care of his employees to a fault. His logo Daws simple: "You take care of your employees, and your employees will take your business to the next level." Stanley had been in the company for years and never dreamed of leaving in his lifetime.

Twice, he had been to Nigeria. His first visit, he was

to deliver an urgent message on behalf of his department to Simon's immediate secretary. He had to fight through his teeth to come to Nigeria. The delivery was quick, and he had met Boyede, Simon's personal assistant in Nigeria. He had taken him around Ladden before lodging him in one of Simon's penthouses.

In confidence, Boyede had told him that each morning when he woke up, just like most of his friends in the Akdrend Company, he thanked his lucky stars. It was a dream come true to work for a company that only selected the best. He had added that it was great to work for the company, have a high-flying salary and mounting benefits that included clothes allowances every year, which most Nigerian proprietors wouldn't pay. But the greatest thing was to be in contact with the most powerful and richest men of their present age. Boyede said his suits were handmade in London. Simon made shopping for them compulsory every time both of them visited London. Simon wanted everything impeccable, not only in his men, but in his surroundings as well. It could not be overstated that his workers never wanted to leave.

His second time there, he was in a group of four delegates from his department in Britain to Nigeria. Simon's generous policies opened to a random selection of delegates from both ends. He was among the crowd, and that was easy. The two previous times, he'd never felt this tense. It was worth it, but not like now. He knew this meeting with Akin was going to be energy-intensive, since the mission shifted on to him compulsorily by the director of his department. He had ranted at him immediately after the details were handed over. His director had smiled and said, "Go do it, tiger."

Stanley had murmured, "Coward," as he left the man's presence.

The director, or any superior in the company, was supposed to go to Nigeria to handle this sensitive issue, to meet the boy, but not Stanley. They just shifted the burden onto him, and who wouldn't? He would've done the same: let someone else take the blame and be fired.

The door opened slightly. A secretary poked his head in, and Stanley looked at him suspiciously.

"Sorry to disturb you. Just want to check on you in case you changed your mind and want some refreshments," the secretary said.

"Thanks for the kind gesture. I'll wait until after the meeting. By the way, do you have a clue when he'll arrive?"

"No, but I'm sure anytime soon, since he'll be with his father, who has an important meeting with some delegates this afternoon."

Stanley wanted to know which delegates. He smiled to entice, but his face looked as if he was about to burst into tears.

"Which delegates would that be, from Britain?"

"I can't tell you, since I don't have a clue." The man shook his head and added, "I'm not the direct secretary to Mr. Simon. I'll see you later, Mr. Stanley."

Liar, he knows which delegates. Stanley tensed and resorted to last-minute prayers. He prayed for the young lad to be compassionate and without an attitude. He remembered one other thing to pray about: that Akin was less of a misogynist than his father. He prayed that his job description of providing "the treat" wouldn't involve getting him girls. That could be a problem, as Stanley was a happily married man. And with the little he'd heard about the big boss, Simon, from his personal secretary in London—who was sacked for disseminating secret personal information about Simon's company to his competitors—was that he made inroads anytime he was in London, when it came to women.

The secretary was friends with Stanley. He still caught up with him from time to time in an East London pub. He had said that Simon and so-called friends—especially his dearest mate Tunde Ogunlade—acted with the same trashy attitude of sleeping with women and discarding them the next day with a wave of the hand, when in London. They were identical in womanizing, misogyny, importing girls from all over the world, meeting in Simon's villa in London, and making merry. Even his British associates started to emulate him. Stanley used to disregard all these rumors, calling them blasphemy, until he was in the presence of Simon and the delegates and had heard his words on "why polygamy is as rampant as corruption in Nigeria, and why few women are making an impact in the country."

Stanley's jaw muscles relaxed, and he released a smile as he remembered the bogus story or myth Simon narrated to answer the question at Ibata-Itan, his hometown. Silence blanketed the entire room, just like darkness would cover a cold, dripping night, as Simon commenced a strange, degrading story about women.

"Women were cursed by a deity called *Ife*, and that's why they lacked love and lost prerogatives. My friends, the reason was because *Egbin,* a female deity of beauty, cheated on Ife, the deity of love, with another deity, *Ota,* who was a deity of enmity. Ife had cursed women that they would be numerous and never have him in their marriages. Men would pick and choose from their plenty, and treat them as they wanted." Simon sighed and added, "That's why women are plentiful, and men choose as many as they want, and put them in the kitchen where they belong."

He paused and continued. "The holy book, the Bible, even confirmed the curse. Eve, the first female representative on earth, tricked Adam to eat the forbidden apple, and there came curses on her from God. Genesis Chapter 4, verse 16: God said, 'With pain you will give birth to children. Your desire will be for your husband, and he will rule over you.' Simon stopped for a response.

Over the years, Simon had convinced himself that must be the reason why women were stupid—the reason that wanton Joyce opened her cunt to a postmaster and eventually disappeared with him. The last glimpse of respect he'd had for women flew away with Joyce. Women were objects to use and discard.

While everybody was silent, pondering over the strange story, trying hard to link the curse in the myth with the one in the Bible, Simon burst out laughing. When he finally cooled down his display, he said, "It has to be the reason. How do you justify women's behavior? Even the few that show love, misbehave. They are numerous, like a swarm of locusts, and the worst part of it—the more you marry them, the more they produce their kind. For balance and check of power, women must be suppressed and disciplined," he said strongly. "It's a man's ordained right to have many wives, many concubines, to marry native and non-native, to deflower at will many women. But it's a sin—a taboo—an abomination punishable by rejection and stoning to death for a woman to have husbands or secret lovers, to marry non-natives and not a virgin before marriage. Because men pay bride price before acquiring them, just like properties. If they violate any of these rules, they must face the consequences. As a young adult, a girl, if lucky, shall be plucked from her parents' vineyard like a fruit, then placed in her husband's vineyard, ready to be processed. A man shall process the girl's place in his vineyards to his taste, to his wishes. She has to be submissive to the wants and wishes of her husband, or else she will be disciplined. These are profound laws that are definite."

There, Stanley rated Simon's hatred for women eight out of ten. And the stale taste of the story and Simon's nonsense rendered his colleagues speechless, wondering as they compared notes later on who the woman was who had spooked the big boss so badly that it made him see no good in their kind. That made them realize that men like Simon had a long way to go in accepting women as equal. Simon was some men in Nigeria, armed with short court concepts to dominate women. The most aired concept was "discipline." All rights and powers were handed over to men, despite the fact that they were a handful compared to women—sad.

That same day, the entire delegation agreed and named Simon "King Solomon of Africa." Eventually, the press got hold of the name and established it in the newspapers. How they knew about the alias was still strange. Even though it had been long ago that Simon had told the revolting story he called a myth, it was jumpy and heart-aching each time. His mind never failed to rewind it. He wasn't surprised it came back to him, even though he was freaking out.

Stanley would gallantly describe Simon as statuesque, a plutocrat comedian, a shrewd businessman, and one of the worst misogynists he had ever known. Within the long length and the wide breadth of the five-story building, Stanley wasn't surprised that there were only a few women working for the company, just like everywhere else in Nigeria. It was sad. He knew that the beliefs of rich men like Simon relegated women to the background and squeezed out their voices.

There was a click, and a uniformed man opened the entrance door wider. It brought Stanley back into his surroundings. Quickly, he abandoned the crazy myth of Simon and the words about him as he watched a handsome young man, not a boy, in a lovely white silk dashiki suit strolling over to him, beaming. The entrance door closed behind him.

Stanley stood up wearing a convincing smile of welcome, projecting a good impression that would continue to earn him his daily bread with his future boss.

"I'm so sorry to have kept you waiting," Akin apologized. "My dad had a stopover at a meeting in Ija. I'm Akin Akindele."

He looked genuinely sorry, and for the first time since he had been in the room, Stanley felt good. Akin presented his right hand, and gently, Stanley clasped it in a warm handshake.

"Good morning, sir." Stanley said softly, "it's a pleasure to finally meet you."

"Likewise, Mr. Stanley. Please call me Akin." He replied with another smile and settled on the nearest couch that faced Stanley's former seat. Stanley sat back in his former seat, and he knew he could breathe. The first impression of the young man would last in his brain.

"Your father said I should show you the sample of the new jersey, with a better picture of a lion. He mentioned you complained that the lion picture on the old one wasn't bold enough."

Even though the greeting went well, Stanley was nervous as he brought out a T-shirt featuring a vivid image of a lion and handed it over to Akin. Akin took the jersey with both hands to examine it.

"Never mind, my old man. It wasn't a complaint, really. I just wanted the picture of the lion to be much bolder, like this. I like it. It is exactly what I want. Thank you."

Stanley loved the boy already.

"I'm glad to hear that. Since you like it, I'll need a number of how many you want."

"Actually, that could probably wait 'til I come over to Britain. But I'd love to have jerseys for girls, with the same logo—just not very sure about the color and the size—probably T-shirts in pink, and brown shorts, to start with. I'll have to talk to the girl in charge."

"That's fine with me, but one more thing—your father wants me to ask what else you would like. I mean special likes."

Akin said, "Convince my father to let me stay in Nigeria for the summer to be with my fiancée." Stanley's face widened with surprise. Akin smiled. "Never mind, Mr. Stanley, I was joking. He'll never agree to that. All I would love to have, tentatively," Akin said, grinning, "is a sample of jersey for a girl, about five pink T-shirts and brown shorts. My father's secretary will send the size to you through a telegram soon. If I want more, I'll let you know when I'm in Britain."

"Certainly. All will be in position by the time you arrive," Stanley said, looking pleased. "And congratulations on your engagement. Would the girl be coming to Britain with you soon?" There was sadness on Akin's face, as if Stanley had hit a wrong button. He quickly said, "I'm sorry to pry. I'm just thinking ahead." Stanley's voice went quiet. He was going crazy with worry.

"That's fine, Mr. Stanley. Really, it's fine," Akin said softly. "There are just some complications, and when everything is cleared up…" Akin paused, changing the subject. "Anyway, when I'm in London, I'll personally ask for your help on a lot of things. What a girl needs. I'm crazy about her."

"I understand, and I'll be highly honored," Stanley said again, gingerly. "Are there any special treats you'd like me to get ready before your arrival in London?"

"Nay, nothing I can think of. And if there is anything else, I'll let you know as soon as I arrive in Britain," Akin said humbly. "If that's all, may I beg to take my leave?"

"Of course. That's all."

Akin stood up and extended his right hand for a handshake again, and Stanley stood up, grabbing it as if his life depended on it.

"Good. Again, it's a pleasure meeting you, Mr. Stanley. See you soon in London," Akin said.

"Pleasure, sir. I mean, Akin," Stanley said, confused.

Akin smiled, briskly walking toward the entrance door. Stanley fell in next to him. Stanley opened the door for him, and Akin muttered, "Thank you.

Akin remained unruffled as people nearby stopped, staring at him as he walked with Stanley. Stanley escorted

Akin out of the building to a waiting car. The car zoomed off without delay.

"You just got yourself a new job—a personal assistant to a lovely boy," Stanley said to himself as he walked back to the building. He couldn't wait to tell everyone when back in Britain and make others jealous, especially that non-well-wisher superior who would have wished it was him.

The discussion was beyond his comprehension. Akin's demeanor was mature for his age; he commanded respect with outstanding English and good articulation. He was confident, asked intelligent questions, and waited patiently for answers. Where was the youthful delinquency, the arrogance of a spoiled brat that he was expecting from Simon's children, especially his heir? Stanley marveled that he found none of this with Akin.

Stanley was already passionate about Akin. He believed a star had been born, and at the same time, he could tell that the young master was deeply in love, and not a scent of a misogynist in him. He could love. His prayer was for the boy to come to London. He would be glad to be his yes-man, as long as he wanted. It meant a lot to Stanley's own future, because the young man was everything to Simon.

* * *

Akin had to leave in a hurry, since the person he loved and would have loved Stanley to meet—to talk to and to ask what she would like from Great Britain—was barred by tradition. He had talked to Simon the day before about inviting Omotola to come to the meeting with him.

"Papa, since I'm meeting Mr. Stanley tomorrow, I

would like Omotola to come along. At least, she could be there to design the new outfit for the girls who will join the Lion Club later."

"Son, how I wish it were that simple," Simon said. "Even though a lot has been altered from the tradition concerning the choosing of a bride, coupling, and marriage rites, certain elements never change. No matter how badly you want Omotola, it has to wait for certain reasons. Omotola has a suitor—her father's friend. And I need his approval to relinquish Omotola from his grip, as the tradition states."

"Omotola is engaged to a man as old as her father?" Akin frowned.

"Yes, son, she was to marry him when she reached adult age."

"That's stupid and disgusting, Papa," Akin said. "How could she agree to that?"

"Not as stupid and disgusting as not to look before you leap, Son. You don't go around another man's property without asking for his permission."

"Papa, Omotola is not a property," Akin cut in. "Why did you say that, Papa?"

"Son, I meant figuratively. I mean…" Simon was confused as to how to explain the facts to his son without betraying the opinion he had of women, and when he failed to find a nice avenue, he said, "Son, how would you feel if someone encroached on the land you're using for sport without your permission, just because he could?"

"Bad. But Omotola is not a property, and why such an engagement, Papa? Why did she agree to such a weird arrangement?"

"Slip of the tongue, Son. She is not a property. I value

her as you value her. But what I'm trying to say is that she has been betrothed to marry a man, whether she likes it or not. Her suitor has been paying her bride-wealth for a long time. If we get involved with her without asking for the man's permission—well, it is taboo and severely punishable. Son, Omotola marrying a man as old as her father might seem stupid and disgusting to you, but it's in the culture. Your mother was supposed to have married an old rag like that before I…" Simon stopped, looking ill.

"I never knew that, and I'm sorry I made you talk about her."

"It's all right, Son," Simon said reluctantly. "All I'm trying to say is that it's in our culture. It isn't wrong that an older man marries a young girl. And in the culture, you don't hang around another man's bride unless you're stupid, because such an act can bring a clash, even a duel, to the point of bloodshed. Besides, it's necessary to consult the Olorunfemi family for her hand in marriage first."

"Papa, do you think her family might refuse and the old man would harm me if I insist on marrying her?"

"Son, I can't say much about the Olorunfemi family yet, but the old man would be out of his mind to make such an attempt. But Omotola, on the other hand, could be harmed. She can be stoned to death if people find out you love her and are taking her to Ladden—that's part of adultery."

"What? Omotola can be stoned to death? *Why?* How?"

"Never mind about that, Son. Forget what I just said. What I'm trying to say is, since another man has interest in Omotola, out of respect, you should reach out to the man first. And that's what I've done. I'm just waiting for his reply."

"You think he can refuse? Papa, I love Omotola more than you can imagine. And I can't bear to lose her."

"You will never lose her, I promise. You're going to marry her. But to be on the safe side, in the meantime, you've to keep away from her until I assure you the coast is clear. Which means, Son, you've got to go to Ladden alone with me until I hear from her suitor."

$\wp$

Chapter Twenty-Four

I t was the second week of the long vacation. Tutu, the fourth and newest wife of Paul, woke up for the third time, full of excitement, like the previous two times she had woken up during the same night. She was over the moon that finally, she was back on Paul's sex rota, and that night she was the wife Paul invited to grace his bed, period.

"Yippee, he finally comes around," she said softly, lying on her back on a mat in her bedroom, faintly illuminated with one single *oguso* candle. The candle was at the far end of the room.

Paul's bungalow was in deplorable condition, nothing to write home about. The eight crappy rooms faced a rugged passage leading to the backyard. The backyard space was vast, but luxuries were scant: a hut as a pantry, clay pots of water, a bamboo bathroom, and numerous cages for animals that were resting underneath the trees.

The first two rooms, opposite each other and next to the entrance of the main door of the bungalow, were occupied by Paul. To the left of his parlor—full of old wooden stools from tree trunks carved like seats—was an outdated calendar from his golden years. On the right, his bedroom: a shrine his four wives visited in turns at night, furnished with a worn-out, wrecked mattress full of dirt and stains from sexual atrocities committed by Paul. A wall hanger, with not too many clothes, housed Paul's earthly possessions, as well as a clay pot that had to be filled with fresh drinking water each day.

The wives' rooms were not any better. Next to Paul's bedroom was that of his latest, Tutu, and her daughter. Opposite, on the left, was the room Omotola shared with her mother, Rolake. Further down, on the right, was the second wife's room—that of Adewumi and her last daughter, yet to be married. Next, on the left, was the first wife's room, for Moji and her two daughters. Last, on the right, was an empty room waiting, probably, to be filled with another wife. And the last, on the left, was a room occupied by Kola and two other half-brothers.

A few days earlier, Paul was sending Tutu outrageous love-making signals, and she loved it. Finally, on Friday, the same week in the afternoon, he came and whispered to confirm she was invited to his bedroom the next night. "It is happening. The night is going to be a good one."

She continued to lie back on the mat with her knees up, staring at the roof. Even though she saw nothing as she stared, her imagination was running wild, in advance of the celebration of what was to come. For a long time, Tutu had been forgotten by Paul, even though she was his latest wife—the marriage of just two years thus far. During the pregnancy and weaning of her baby, when her libido was frantic and alive, Paul wouldn't touch her. She was just brushed aside, treated like an outcast. She was absolutely insane with wanting Paul—wanting sex.

Hence, Tutu sometimes cried herself to sleep.

Moji, the first wife, had explained to Tutu one evening, "Paul has no interest or desire to butter bread in an oven. Immediately, from the time a pregnancy is visible 'til the nursing period, you are on your own. He simply switches to available wives or dashes to his concubines. It's painful." Tutu had been four months pregnant then. And she was so horny, so desperate for Paul, that she acquiesced to have the unsavory talk with her rival.

Moji had added, "You just have to live with the pain. If you're desperate enough to do something stupid in this town, like a hamlet, Paul will find out, and you'll live in pain more than Adewumi. That's if you're not stoned to death first. Tutu, Paul will come around when he is ready."

And briefly, Moji had explained what transpired between Paul and Adewumi, that Kola going to school was the cause. That was why the soft-spoken beauty, Adewumi, was out of Paul's sex rota and maltreated—why she walked around the house with a doleful face.

She turned on her side to look at her daughter. The baby was sleeping like an angel next to her. Her gaze focused on her baby while her mind was far away again. "Open your damn eyes, day, and run into evening fast. Because something magic that ceases breaths, that dazes the eye, is about to happen. It's not my fault I'm hooked on coitus—Paul did that," she said softly. She couldn't go back to sleep. The turmoil in her head didn't allow that. She rambled on the mat.

As the day was breaking, she decided to sit up. She cushioned her chin with her right hand, pondering over a chronological order of events to excite Paul besides the obvious: his favorite food. Paul had never been a man not to notice a cart before the horse, and Tutu knew this. Tutu was taught details, strongly advised on one shot, on one night to make her man want her forever out of his wives. Her mother, Maggi, had taught her this to the letter: what to do, what to make, how to lure and make vulnerable a man like Paul—to want more and forget the other three forever.

Maggi's *5 Golden Rules in a Polygamous Home* were:

Top on the chart, Rule One:

Self-Presentation: Make hay while the sun shines. Make use of youthfulness to wile and to wrap your husband around your waist, and your waist alone. Tutu's mother, Maggi, who had paddled her into the world, had said this and reminded her eternally.

Maggi Rule Two:

Girdle and disguise the unattractive early: Giving birth should never be an excuse, or you'll have a successor earlier than you expected. Men are pigs.

Maggi Rule Three:

Chicanery and manipulation are not the monopolies of any man: Be smart with what's taught, to get what you want. Get in there, do what Mama taught you, and elbow off the competitors.

Three to be explained now, and the other two would be later. Tutu hoped she succeeded this time around. Maggi wouldn't condone the excuse that Paul was a strange man.

On the first night of the honeymoon, Paul was waiting diligently in his room for Tutu, treating her with tenderness and care, as if she was the only woman in his life. She spent six days with Paul in his room, in an idyll.

There were six nights of heaven. Tutu was not in pain when she lost her *ibale,* her virginity. Paul talked her through it. She became a huge fan of sex by the second night—she wanted the touch, wanted all the trimmings that came with it, ate up whatever he dished out at any time of the day. She couldn't wait for the evening to crawl in. Paul knew how to do his thing. Tutu closed her eyes and could see her six-day honeymoon. She was getting more turned on, running crazy, gasping for more … and *Bam!* Paul had withdrawn on the seventh day. Her eyes flicked open.

The days after the honeymoon flashed through her brain, showing how Paul had put her in pending status, put her on hold, drew back, and waved to her from afar. She felt used, looking horrified when, on the seventh day, she was shoveled to her room—more like "driven" to her present abode. Since then, she'd had to wait in line until Paul wanted her and put her on the sex rota like the rest. This queue was not fixed; Paul could not be counted on to honor it. Then, *Bam!* Next came the pregnancy. With that, Paul just moved further away.

Tutu was unhappy with the way Paul had treated her. She had tried everything prescribed by her mother. Nothing worked. Eventually, she'd gone home in tears. Maggi had a frown on her face that told her she wasn't smart, that she should have been able to follow her mother's example and woo her man. But things were not the same for Tutu. She said to herself, "Paul is nothing like my father."

Maggi was the fifth wife in her household, and the last. She was the woman after Tutu's father's heart, his *"aayo."* She made him pant like a dog running a race. She made him lose the desire for other women. He would laugh like a clown and obey like a genie in the bottle as her mother insisted on having her way, gate-crashing the sleeping arrangements. And that secret, her mother said, was like a ray of sunshine that drew the man to you in the first place. Outwit the others with cleverness. Child-bearing would never be an excuse.

Maggi was clever as a fox, a dynamo using her preaching skills. She made Tutu's father conscious of her beauty at any given time, even though she wasn't a beauty pageant candidate. She brought out the radiance, the softness, the smoothness like silk in her face and her body by simple body exfoliation, with black soap in droplets of lime that she used once a week. And as for the whiteness of teeth, a rub with charcoal from wood, which amplified the everyday use of pako chewing sticks, was what she used once a week to brush her teeth. And that brought the smile of a star. She was always impeccable in appearance at any given time. It created jealousy and name-calling from the other women, which had terrified Tutu as a little girl.

Maggi was unconcerned when she was called *husband-snatcher, bitch, witch, tramp,* whatever. She always had that smile on her face as she discarded the names with a wave of her hand and said, "They can't break me, because I won't let them. Daughters! Take a leaf out of my book, my life. Do everything it takes to wrap your husband round your little finger."

And with that, Tutu's two sisters went into the world, into the dens of their husbands. And the news of them had been favorable. It was now her turn to add to the legacy that must be in continuation, as her mother wanted.

That same day, Maggi had given a new set of lectures

to Tutu. Tutu had then concluded when she left her mother's presence that if she had an opportunity again, she would play her cards right with Paul. She would play all the known cards tonight, as taught. She would take charge like her mother. She would wrap Paul around her wrist like a wristwatch and release him into the wild, to interact with other women—wives and concubines combined together—on her own schedule, on her own terms, when wanted, just like her mother. She wanted to be egotistical, like her mother. As Maggi said, "Selfishness is never a sin. Conscience should be a thing of the past when installed in a polygamous home. Daughter, a polygamous home is a jungle. And the motto is, survival of the fittest."

Tutu released her chin from the cup of her right hand. She sighed and stood up, ready to start afresh, start anew. And the way to a man's heart was his stomach. The first lesson in the marriage institution was universal. Learning to cook was paramount for girls, as early as possible and a "must" as far as their teenage years went. If mothers wanted their daughters' success in marriage, for them not to be brutally beaten like a cow, they had better learn to cook.

But Maggi's philosophy went beyond that. Knowing how to cook was of no value without cognizance of a husband's favorite food and the technical know-how to make it irresistible—as in textures, as in delicacy, deliciousness, and presentation. Maggi coached her daughters that one crucial way to delight a man's heart was to give him what he craved on a gold platter. Paul craved bush meats in *egusi* soup, and that was coming up soon.

Paul had told Tutu he would go out early on that

Saturday morning after being fed by Moji, who was on Friday night's rota. Moji's night shift finished with Paul's breakfast in the morning. Paul would go out to see people and come back early, at dusk, after bantering with John. She would prepare the dinner for him, and the rest would follow. Tutu tingled from head to toe as she wished the night would come fast.

But first, she would have to take care of her baby. As if in an Olympic race, Tutu clothed and fed her baby girl and then went on to get the egusi stew ready. She tasted the stew, and as she rolled it on her palate, she knew she had nailed it. The first success was a sign that tonight was going to be a good night again. After eating the main course, her body would serve as an elaborate dessert. Hmm… A pleasurable time for both. The waves of excitement spread over her body. She got tingles again and muttered, "Welcome back into my bosom, Paul."

She felt joy. All the effort was worth it. As a means of appreciation, Paul was going to give all he had to her satisfaction tonight. That should be it, Tutu smiled, thinking she should add glamor to entice Paul. Before dusk arrived, she would add the last touch, the last piece of the menu—yams pounded in a mortar to make them fluffy. Since it would be hours until then, she decided to dash to a hairdresser for a new hairdo, even though she'd had her hair styled two days earlier, which was expected to last at least two weeks. But, presentation! Maggi would rage if she didn't look her best this time around. Tutu knew her mother would be more than willing to redo her hair, even if it had to be every day, as long as it got Paul bouncing like a yo-yo.

Everything had to be perfect. As her mother had said

countless times, and was the last lesson she had delivered a few days before Tutu's honeymoon: "Perfection brings beauty. Brilliance in a woman goes a long way to run men insane, as it glues their two…" Her mother had not specified what part in men it glued. That part, Tutu had deduced herself.

* * *

"Tutu," Maggi said, objected to Tutu's initial hairdo suggestion, "Let's give Paul a hairstyle that will make his throat dry… one that would run any man out of his mind, that will make Paul want you forever."

Maggi predicted that the hairstyle she had in mind would enhance the romance of the night. As Maggi was rowing her hair for plaiting, she asked, "Tutu, how is it going with Paul?"

Tutu's face was worn. She gave a tiny shrug and said, "Okay, but I wish Paul were simple, like my father. He…" Abruptly, Tutu stopped, looking nervous.

"Look at me, Tutu." Maggi temporarily stopped the plaiting, making Tutu straighten her head. "Stop saying that, honey. All men are like your father. What you've got to do is get hold of his weak point with all I taught you, and then he'll dance to your tune. Look at your sisters— they're as established as a rock in their husbands' domains. You could talk to them if you want. Tutu, it's now or never, to hold the reins in Paul's house, not when you've a successor. Make the hay when the sun shines."

And true to Maggi's prediction, Tutu emerged from the styling with the sharp face of a goddess. That came from the effect of the cornrow-braided bun hairstyle that Maggi had made for her. The particular, irresistible hairdo she insisted on, only *"venustraphobia"* could resist. It was the hairdo Maggi used to get compliments for, one that brought ardor from men and made many heads turn. Then Paul had come along and swept Tutu's parents off their feet. Her parents loved Paul. He was intelligent, and physically, he was totally enticing, which assured damn good grandchildren with intelligence, or so her parents thought.

Men turned to have a second look, Tutu noticed, as she walked back to Paul's house. She felt happy that her mother was right about the hairdo. She walked to the backyard of the house to warm up pap for her daughter, who lay sleeping on her back.

Nearby, Moji gasped aloud, staring with awe in her eyes. "Wow, Tutu, you look great. You have to give me the name of your hairdresser. Mine is a dope." Tutu managed a fake smile and muttered, "Thanks."

She was ready to go. She wanted to stop talking to the woman. This was part of her mother's teaching as well.

Maggi Rule Four:

Never indulge or trust the others: Apart from your husband and your children, in a polygamous home, the others should be irrelevant. Steer clear of them because they are your competitors.

"You forgot to give me the name of your hairdresser," Moji said quickly.

Tutu stopped and said, "My Mama plaited it for me."

"Would she be interested in plaiting my hair? I'll pay if I have to. Please talk to her because I've a wedding to go to in a couple of weeks, and I want your style on my head."

What? sounded in Tutu's head. She wondered if Moji was stupid or just playing dumb.

You must be kidding to want my hairdresser, to want my hairdo! Maybe you don't know that I can't allow that because this hairstyle is designed to run our husband crazy. Steal him from all of you, and make him mine forever. Yeah, copy my ass, old woman. That was what Tutu wanted to say to Moji, but instead, calmly, and with a smile, she said, "I'll see what I can do. If my mother agrees, I'll let you know. And if you excuse me, ma, I have to feed my daughter."

"Of course," Moji said, looking relieved. "Thanks for agreeing to talk to her on my behalf. I'll see you later. I'm going to a friend's house."

Tutu wiggled her nose at Moji's back, murmuring, "Why don't I do that as if it was yesterday? I'm sure my mother will be happy to give you a sedative, powerful stuff. It will hypnotize you, so she can shave your head to the skull and spit on your face as soon as it's done. And shout that nobody rivals my daughter and gets away with it! Even if you're the first wife, you've got to leave the stage for my Tutu."

She knew Maggi could do it. She wasn't mixing words up. It was what Maggi could do.

She heated the pap over a wood-burning stove in a pot taken from the pantry. She hurried inside and fed her daughter. To kill time and to temporarily stop thinking of Paul, as it had started to give her a migraine, she engaged in one-on-one play with her daughter, whom she sat on a piece of cloth, facing her, excited. The girl laughed as she tickled her. It went on and on. Tutu realized the last ray of sunlight was beaming, and playtime should be suspended if she was to finish the last part of the menu with the rays of the sunlight.

Tutu had one wish as she picked her baby up, along with the piece of cloth she had sat on: to be the only one to cook in the backyard at the moment. She was rarely in the backyard with the rest of the women; she usually ate with her mother to avoid intimacy with them, as Maggi wanted.

Tutu maneuvered the baby along with cloth to one arm, and with her second hand, she grabbed a tub of yams from the corner of the room and dashed to the backyard.

As luck would have it, her wish was granted. The backyard was free of human beings. It seemed that the available wives were done and had gone inside with their cooking. Almost all the animals were in their cages, with the exception of two goats nestling freely at the far end of the backyard, seeming to be waiting for their owners to show them where to go.

Tutu couldn't be happier. She heaved a sigh of relief. She would be by herself without interruption, without having to answer questions that she forced herself to answer out of her own politeness. She hated mingling with the other wives.

Well, her mother's fourth rule warned that contact with them should be minimal, as faint as possible. She should never forget they were her competitors. They never had anything good to offer, but to throw dust in her face.

She bent over, dropped the piece of cloth on the floor, and at the same time, laid the tub of yams next to it. She used her free hand to spread the pieces of cloth and straighten them up. She squatted to settle her daughter down to play. Like a lamb, with well wishes, rarely disturbing Tutu, the girl dumped her left thumb into her mouth and sucked it as if her life depended on it, as if she'd been in deprivation for a long time, as if she wasn't keen on playing with her mother. She was just pretending to be nice, as her mother did in her father's house.

Seeing the thumb sucking, Tutu lost it.

"Oh no, love!" Tutu shouted in frustration, shaking her head vigorously. "You don't favor left over right. It's an abomination. I've told you that a million times—you can't be a lefty. You don't want to be left on the shelf for a stupid reason like that. Society hates it. No man wants a lefty as a wife."

Tutu pulled out the left thumb and replaced it with the right thumb. The girl looked at her with a sulking face, and immediately after Tutu straightened up, she pulled out the right and replaced it with the left, chuckling.

Tutu was dismayed.

"You think you're smarter than your mother, baby girl? Well, we'll see about that later. Right now, I've to go and get my husband's food ready. I hope you'll be okay."

Tutu looked at her daughter for an answer, even though she knew it was stupid to think that a one-year-old girl would say, "Go ahead, Mama, don't worry about me. I'll be okay."

For a second, the baby stared at her, puzzled, as if pondering over what answer to give to a mother who never stopped fussing over her—a bother. The next second, she was engulfed with her left thumb, as if to say, "Go away, leave me alone."

Tutu shook her head again and said, "Sorry to have asked. That was silly, eh? I should have understood by now, you and your left hand are perfect together, and Mama is interrupting. But, love, that has to stop. Even though you like that thumb, it is wrong. People will think that I'm indulging it, say that I'm a bad mother." Tutu's voice trembled, and she added, "Anyway, let me explain to you why using your left hand is taboo. It's because no man wants to marry a left-handed woman. And as I can see you prefer left to right, that must change. Okay, we'll talk and play later."

She knew she was repeating herself, and she started to worry again. The repetition made no difference to the little girl, who seemed to be in a world of her own. Sometimes, the habit got on Tutu's nerves. And it got on her nerves as she stood watching her in silence. All the nerves in her body cried, "*Wrong! Stop her!*" She knew they were right, but how would she stop her from the intolerable? It had been a headache. And worst of all, most of the time, her baby preferred the soiled thumb to food. She rarely cried for food. Tutu had to force it down her throat to make her stay healthy. Each time she took off her clothes to give her a bath, she got a jab of guilt. *You're not doing good work as a mother. She is still skinny and untrained.*

Tutu brooded, depressed. All of the circular thoughts in her head were dark, negative, and worried. She knew she would run crazy in the house-like-a-box if care was not taken. If she continued with Maggi rules, her daughter did as she pleased and society at her throat, she could run mad. Public opinion was stronger than the rules of nature, it sometimes seemed.

At the beginning of her marriage to Paul, Tutu would have loved to be on chatty, repartee terms with the other wives—but Maggi was against it. Tutu was frustrated about what Maggi had put in capital letters in Rule Four. In the early weeks in Paul's house, after losing the first battle with him, Tutu had questioned some of the Maggi rules because the other wives, whom she was supposed to regard as her number-one enemies, did not seem wicked. The wives in Paul's residence were not evil like those her mother shared her husband with. She had hated the fear of the unknown.

"Fear the possible evil intent of others in the house," said Maggi to Tutu. This was obviously a wrong assumption—a wrong projection that never had a way of being revealed. Communication flowed like a river between the wives, as far as she could see. As a matter of fact, the wives jointly did their best to make her comfortable on her arrival. They were full of acceptance, full of love. Tutu tried to be part of it as she saw the endeavors of the other wives, thinking that maybe some houses were different. Husbands were different. None of the wives started upheavals, as was the order of the day in her father's house. Quarrels and cruelty had been like three square meals: one in the morning, another in the afternoon, and another at dinner. Children got confused, caught in the middle. As her father's wives were enemies, so were the children at each other's throats, jealous of each other to death.

She'd wanted Maggi to hear the difference. She had explained many times in her first few months in Paul's house that she had been welcomed, helped into Paul's house with kindness beyond imagination, that harmony reigned. She had mentioned conversations with other wives. Maggi had raised her eyebrows each time and shouted, "Listen to me, Tutu. They are all devils waiting in the dark to devour you. Don't ever trust them. If you do, you'll regret it. And that will be your own fault. I've done my part as a mother should and left it for you to understand."

Yet, Tutu still wanted to be liberal, a free thinker, with a mind of her own. She never said anything to Maggi, so she wouldn't be upset. She wanted to change, to be normal, with normal thoughts. That did not last long. She was later filled with fear, filled with more bad thoughts than ever, as Maggi told of more evil the other wives could do to her. Tutu's brain was functioning most of the time as Maggi wired it: full of slyness, odiousness. Answer a question with a question. And when Tutu's baby was born, and she was concerned about her sucking her left thumb, she would have loved to ask the other wives if any of their children sucked their left thumbs in the past. And if so, what should she do? Ask about family genetics? But Maggi had said "no." She said if the conversation leaked out to Paul, it could lead to her expulsion. Paul could send her back home. She would only have herself to blame.

Maggi had said: "Sucking thumbs is a phase. It will pass, as long as you don't indulge and enable it. Instead, place your worries on your rivals in your husband's house." She explained, "Your children, only you can talk to, share thoughts with, count on. They will never betray you or use what's discussed to your disadvantage and back-stab."

"Mama, the wives are nice to me," Tutu said softly.

"Tutu, never trust them," Maggi said tightly. "A polygamous home is a hellhole, and divulging a secret about yourself could send you packing, back to your father's house. Tutu, where will you live in your father's house like a cave? A cave whose inhabitants play tug-of-war, usually on fire every minute. Besides, *Dalemosu* isn't pretty. Be warned."

Maggi had emphasized what else the other wives could do. They could kill her child with voodoo, juju, and witchcraft, on and on. That's if she allowed them to be closer to her. Tutu had shaken from head to toe, listening to Maggi's explanation of what the consequence of her mingling with other wives could be. But it was hard to be an island, to be isolated with oneself all the time. To change the subject, Tutu had asked her mother then if any of her three daughters had at least sucked their thumbs. She'd said no, and all the friends she asked had said the same thing. She had observed in Paul's house and its surroundings that no child sucked their thumb. No child was skinny like hers.

With the evil the other wives could make happen to her child, as Maggi explained, Tutu never allowed anybody around her baby and herself. Even though she knew she needed help desperately, she also knew she wouldn't be able to ask for it. There would always be that slot in her head that would stop her. That was how Maggi wanted it, had programmed it.

Tutu, in agitation, knew that Maggi's explanations were wrong. It wasn't a phase. Her daughter was one, and nothing had changed since she was born. In fact, it was getting worse as she grew. Maggi didn't live with her. If she did, she could have seen for herself that her daughter and the left thumb were like the sky and ground: inseparable. As a result, her daughter was a skeleton. And it would have taken off a pang, taken off a notch of worry if her daughter could talk, give assurance that she would be all right, that the left thumb was temporary, that she would eat to put flesh on as other babies do, as time went on.

"Tutu, rip off your clothes, run around the backyard naked, and shout your pains aloud… You'll feel better," a voice said in her head.

Tutu looked down at her daughter. The little girl was at peace with her thumb, and she shouted out. "Noooo!"

This wasn't the first time that voices had suggested she do wacky things to herself. She was helpless, concerned about how long it would take before she gave in. She knew that if care was not taken, she would do something scandalous or go crazy, since such heinousness sounded in her brain often. She could tell that in the near future, if her daughter was not talking, her ribs were still as visible as sticks, and society didn't back off, she might go insane or bite the dust. She wasn't to be blamed for the downfall. Everything was their fault.

Tutu felt like crying as the voice left her head. She wished to pay Maggi a visit, to shout out that everything she'd said was wrong—that everything about her daughter and wives was untrue, miscalculated, misjudged. She was impatient to tell Maggi this: "Mama, I've started to hear voices. Mama, I think I'm going crazy."

She'd have loved to be innocent, not aware of the evils her mother predicted—the evils she'd engraved in her mind that haunted her each day. She would have loved to avoid brainwashing, the implant of heinousness, the capabilities in polygamous homes that most of her friends never knew about. They never had the crazy lessons put in their brains as Maggi had done to her. She would have preferred to make her own observations and feed and fill her brain with realities. She knew some of her friends encountered the vile things of life, but they dealt with it, with their own wisdom, at their own pace. They were not in a wreck or in ruin emotionally. She was confused, in total Waterloo.

Abruptly, Tutu sat on the floor. "I want to change, Mama." She sobbed, ranting, "I want my own brain, Mama. Why can't I have my own brain, Mama? Why can't I rewire my brain, make it full of good thoughts? Have a mind of my own? Why can't I shed the fear and mingle as I want, as they want? Why still fear the unknown? Moji hasn't done anything bad to me. Neither has Adewumi. Neither has Rolake. Why did you put evil in me? Mama, you should've let me discover the evil in a polygamous home on my own, just like some of my friends did. And then, I'd have made my own verdict, learned from my own mistakes. Why, Mama? Why the prediction of rain that might never come? Why the prediction of a thunderbolt on a bright, sunny day? Why, Mama? Why?"

Tutu covered her face with both hands as if ashamed. She reclined her head on her hands as if her head was tired and might snap loose from the neck. Her head dangled back and forth as she accelerated the sobbing to hysterical levels. She continued ranting. "I shouldn't be blamed for my downfall. Loneliness kills. Maybe you don't know, you don't realize, Mama, you screwed me up a lot. You sow the seed of skepticism, the seed of deceit that germinates, with branches that are ruining my life, that make my life vibrate like leaves in a storm. Mama, I'm terrified of the wrath to befall me if my daughter is a lefty … afraid of society, Mama, worried sick of the other wives' intentions. I know I wouldn't have been this paranoid if you hadn't put it in me. Why would you make me believe that the other wives are evil, lying in wait for my downfall, even though they've proven the opposite? They are nice. Why, Mama? Why, Mama?"

"Mama, Mama," Tutu's baby girl babbled.

It was like waking up from a trance. Tutu removed her hands from her face and rubbed away the tears to look at her daughter. She had removed her thumb from her mouth and crawled over while she was crying.

"You can talk," she shouted and picked the infant up onto her lap. She rocked her gently and whispered. "You'll never be fed with evil. I'll make sure of that, little girl. Not by your grandmother, who I know will start as soon as you can visit her, or anybody. I…."

The little girl put her left thumb back in her mouth and laughed. Tutu's mood was gloomy again. "You know that hand must stop," she said angrily. "It must…" She hesitated and added, "Right now, I've got to get your father's dinner ready."

She placed the girl back on the piece of cloth, straightened up, and went inside the pantry.

She took out a pot, a knife, and a calabash bowl. She skinned the yam, cutting it into pieces, putting them in the bowl. And when she was done, she drew water from one of the clay gourds outside the pantry and washed the yams. She put the yams and water in the pot, carried it to the stone stove, and lit the fire.

* * *

While Tutu was going insane with her daughter's behavior, Paul showed up at John's place unannounced. John was in front of his house waiting for his dinner to be ready, cooked by Yemisi. Yemisi almost stumbled as she rushed out of the house, hearing Paul's voice. She hadn't been intimate with Paul since he'd stormed out on her.

Yemisi had been to Paul's farm on several occasions. Paul had one excuse or another to give her with a promise he would come over. The truth was that Paul was done with her. She was yesterday's news. Paul was into a young girl who had just married and probably slept a few times with her husband—everything about her was firm and fresh.

"Aba Paul, you're staying for dinner?" Yemisi said, waiting for a yes.

"No," Paul said, casually, avoiding looking at her. "I just want to borrow your husband for a couple of hours."

"And you'll be back for dinner later?"

"No," Paul said sharply. "Let's go, John."

John stood up without reading a meaning into the two conversations. They walked a few meters away from the house.

"Where are we going, anyway?" John asked.

"To Oja Oba for *ayo* competition," Paul replied. "I learned that the amateurs are going to be playing today." Paul looked happy, as if he had won already.

"I don't think that's a good idea in your present condition," John said, looking concerned. "You lost a lot to this money-drainer game already. You must—"

"That's why I want you with me. If I'm going in over my head, you jab me with an elbow, all right?"

"Paul, you know how you are; you never listen."

"Not tonight. I promise to listen to you," Paul said.

"All right, but don't blame me if you turn into your old self."

There were times John couldn't control Paul at the

game. He got into arguments afterward when Paul lost money and became miserable and erratic. It was not an evil wish on a friend, but John knew that gambling would end Paul's life.

Chapter Twenty-Five

It wasn't dark yet, and the yam was tender and ready for pounding in a twinkle of an eye. Tutu went back to the pantry, took out a reasonably sized calabash bowl, wrapping leaves, plus a pounded yam cutter. She placed the items in the bowl, setting the bowl on the ground. She dropped yams into the mortar. The pieces started receiving several blows from the pestle, and her baby cried. Tutu looked in her direction. The baby had got knocked down by a goat.

The goat had come running out of the house, gripping with its teeth a parcel in leaves that Tutu could tell must be somebody else's dinner. The animal had knocked the baby over and was chased by Rolake, who shouted at the thief, "Drop, *ole, ole!*"

Tutu ceased pounding, ran over, and picked her baby up to console her. Tutu strapped her baby on her back and went back to the business of pounding the yam. The scenario would have made her laugh, but instead, she was tensed, praying for peace.

The head of the baby girl slapped against her back as it jerked up and down with the pounding of the yams. Tutu was drenched with sweat, her back and neck in pain. Each blow of the pestle on the damn mortar was a struggle, but she wouldn't give up. Not tonight, of all nights, when everything might change for the better.

"Tutu," Adewumi said, tapping Tutu gently on the shoulder. She had come out of the house because of the noise Rolake was making as she ran after the goat. The taps temporarily stopped Tutu from giving the yams another bang in the mortar. Tutu was angry.

"What, ma," she shouted in annoyance. "What do you want?"

"I'm sorry to disturb you," Adewumi said softly. "You are supposed to keep your daughter with the other wives since you're on Paul's rota…" She trailed off. "I mean, instead of dragging her through the noise of yam pounding, Tutu, you could keep her with any of us. Come on, let me have her. Release the strap."

Instead of being overwhelmed by the gesture, Tutu was thrown off balance, glowering at Adewumi without a word. Adewumi smiled as if to counter her frown, to show that she meant no harm. She extended her hands to take the baby off Tutu's back.

Tutu wriggled her body and moved a pace away from the woman, saying inwardly, "This is my baby, and I can do whatever I want with her." Hatred, doubt, angst, and mistrust—take your pick—stationed in her head as she looked at the benevolent woman.

She knew that "lucky" was supposed to be in her brain, and why not? Why did she hate Adewumi and her help right now? A pain swept around Tutu's neck. She tried to rotate her head slowly.

"Tutu, that's what pounding yam with a baby on your back does. Come on. Let me have her."

Adewumi moved up to her.

She knew Adewumi's statement was correct, but despite this, she didn't feel the urge to throw in the towel. She felt pain; she felt fear. She wanted help, but couldn't bring herself to accept it. Tutu was confused. How would she cross the bridge of fear to the bridge of faith if she kept pushing everybody away? She felt she should accept the offer. It felt right to do it, yet she didn't want to. Her brain was alert, on guard—*What if she pinches, bites, or poisons her?* Tutu wanted to snap and say, "No, I can't trust you." But she decided to rely on the saying, "actions speak louder than words." Tutu refused to release the strap.

"Pounding is rigorous, and strapping a baby to one's back while doing it, is insane. Moreover, Tutu, jerking a baby's head up and down could damage the baby's brain… Come on! Let me have her."

Tutu's brain was wrestling with thoughts.

"Tutu, the yam will be cold and lose its texture if you just stand there." Adewumi stretched both hands again to take the baby from her back. "Come on. Let me have your baby so you can continue with your cooking."

Tutu ignored her.

"Tutu, I don't know what you've learned or what you've heard that makes you this resentful of people and help, but I can assure you of this, Tutu, nobody can be an island. Besides, I'm of the age group of your mother. You are like a child to me; I won't hurt your baby. Trust me."

Tutu glanced at Adewumi's face, and she could see the sincerity and peace. She knew Adewumi could walk away and never be bothered. She knew she needed the help the woman wanted to provide. And right there, she knew the woman was right—she couldn't be an island forever. She would go crazy. She couldn't be Maggi; she wasn't that strong. Maybe not everybody could be Maggi. Maybe not everybody could have a certificate, a higher diploma, like her mother had in what others lacked: manipulation, slyness, sometimes wrapped in wit. Maggi's sense of humor had always been bogus, with ulterior motives. When Maggi laughed with you, she was actually laughing at you.

Tutu knew she had to lower her guard and trust. The woman probably meant no harm. She had to rewire her brain, ask for help when needed, install new attitudes, and forget the screw-ups in her father's house, where sometimes wives on cooking rota would find all their morning's labor sabotaged. The soup would have too much salt in it; stew would be running like a tap. Sometimes, food would be laced with something inedible, and her father would cry out in pain as he tried to swallow. And that would start another pandemonium.

Tutu sighed, muttering in her head. "This could be the start of joy, happiness. Maggi doesn't have to know about it."

Tutu released the straps. Adewumi gently removed the baby from her back.

"Thanks, ma," Tutu said. "I'll come and pick her up immediately after I'm done."

"Take your time tonight...." Adewumi stopped and changed the subject. "She could eat dinner with us, if that's okay with you?"

"It's okay, ma...." Tutu trailed off as a result of Maggi's warnings. What if she gave the baby poison or juju?" Forcefully, she suppressed the worry and smiled. "Yes, she can have dinner with you, and I'll come around as soon as I'm done."

"Good, see you later."

Tutu watched her daughter settle on Adewumi's shoulder without a fuss, and both walked back inside the house.

She had to change. Suddenly, Maggi's voice played in her head. "Polygamous homes, same proclivity, same grooves, never trust anyone–all women want attention, want to be the only one."

"Too soon," rapped in her head. She needed more time. Maggi could be right. She went back to treat the yams to make them fluffy. She forced herself to concentrate on things before Paul's arrival.

The yams became fluffy. Tutu removed the pestle. She moved the calabash bowl near the mortar and took out the pounded yam cutter. She bent to dish out the food.

"I'm sorry that beast knocked your daughter over," Rolake apologized, panting, with a half-eaten pounded yam in her hand, standing next to Tutu. Tutu straightened up to listen to her, and Rolake continued, "That goat ran inside my room and got hold of Omotola's dinner. And this is not the first time he's been that bad. He didn't even bother as I shouted, "Drop, drop, thief, thief!" Instead, he ran out of the room, and I had to give him the chase of his life. You should have seen him at the far end of the backyard—he's old and fat, in bad shape, panting. I thought he might give up the ghost. But I got the food back!" Rolake raised the half-eaten food up like a trophy. "I know Omotola won't be able to eat it, and I've got to give her something else to eat, but the incorrigible beast has to learn that after dinner from his owner, he shouldn't raid others for more."

Who is panting like an idiot now? No, you have to be good, echoed in her brain. *Start a friendship. Forget about the past.* Tutu smiled at Rolake and said, "I could give Omotola a cut if you want."

"No." Rolake smiled back. "Don't bother. She isn't a fan of pounded yam anyway. I should have let the goat have it instead of running after him, but I was just pissed off since he does it all the time. He nuzzled the door open and went straight for Omotola's food. Omotola went on an errand to a friend's house."

"But it's just too strange he went inside without my knowledge," Tutu said, looking confused. "A few minutes ago, he was resting with his mate over there." She pointed to the far end of the backyard. "And in the next few minutes, you and him…" Tutu stopped before she said something that might insult her senior in Paul's house. She knew that type of thing could cause a quarrel in her father's house. The temperament of the women within her father's house was wired like bombs, with a *tick, tick*— ready to explode at the slightest chance.

"Get this, Tutu; those two beasts are cunning, rapid, and can cause a lot of damage if paid little attention to. The two untamed beasts belong to the first wife. I'd like to have a strong discussion with her as soon as she comes back. At least, she should've caged her animals before going out. Anyway, if you want, I could hold your baby for you, so you can get on with Aba's food. Just to let you know, you can take your time; he won't be back until very late. Our husband is a night owl, especially on the last Saturday of the month. There's usually a grand ayo game competition at Oja-Oba.'

"So, today is an ayo game at Oja-Oba? Why didn't

he tell me that? He just said he had to have a discussion with Aba John briefly and would come back as dusk sets in." Tutu looked dismayed.

Quickly, Rolake said, "I'm sorry; I might have made a mistake. I'm sure if Aba said he'd be back soon, he'll be. Where is your baby, anyway?"

Rolake said the last part in a hurry to get out of the face of the girl paralyzed by the bad news. Tutu didn't reply, seeming lost.

Rolake looked around, puzzled. "Don't tell me the second beast has your daughter, and we have to look for her?"

Tutu seemed to stir. She blinked and said, "What? No, our senior wife took her in. I'm just lost, thinking about a lot of things."

"Well, we all do when it's time to sleep with Paul. And as time goes on, you'll get used to possibilities and surprises when on Paul's rota," Rolake murmured.

"What did you say?" Tutu's face was intense with worries.

"'Never mind what I just said," Rolake said, scratching a cheek. "But Tutu, I won't be surprised if those two goats steal a baby to eat one day. They're bandits, hijackers that need to be caged outside the human domain. They need to be committed to an animal asylum. And a piece of advice." Rolake's face was dead serious. "Be careful when you see those two around and you're getting Aba's dinner ready. They could steal it or ruin it and get you into a lot of trouble. Tutu, no amount of complaining about them to Aba will get you off the hook of scolding that night if…" Rolake glanced at Tutu, hesitating as her perfect face showed a sulking hangover of worries. Rolake added in haste, "I'm sure everything will work out fine tonight. Don't let me disturb you. See you later."

"Thanks," Tutu said, muddled, staring after Rolake.

"Why did I talk about Aba? She has to discover his ways on her own," Rolake said, walking away.

Tutu heard everything. She would have loved to know what Rolake's hesitations were, apart from the fact it was the last Saturday of the month and their husband was a night owl, but she had to get back to dinner before it got cold. It came to her suddenly that all that Rolake had said might be meant to fluster and demoralize her, since tonight was her night. It might have been out of jealousy. Maggi said so, and she should know; her father's wives had invented misleading and confusing others. Tutu promised herself she would wait as long as it took. The thought of what was about to happen, even if it was going to be late, jumped into her head, overpowering Rolake's bad news.

Tutu cut a portion for Paul, one for herself, and wrapped both in the leaves. As she was doing the cutting, she realized she was filled to the brim with butterflies again. She knew there was no way her stomach could take in her portion. Maybe later, after she was done with the excitement of the night, and back in her room before daybreak, as it had to be in Paul's rules.

She rushed through the washing up and walked back inside the house. She placed both parcels in one of the five *oke* baskets arranged at the end of her room, hauling piles of clothes on top of both to keep them warm. Those five *okes* used to be her bride price item containers. Paul had filled them to the brim with bride price goodies, as was the custom, and they were brought to her father's house before she was handed over to Paul's family. That night was epic. She pushed the thoughts of the past away faster because it usually brought two feelings out of her: the best and the worst. All she needed tonight was the best. She didn't want to search for the best of the past and end up with the worst, making her feel paranoid and vulnerable. She needed to be positive.

As she was putting the food away, wanting positive energy, she decided she needed a long bath. She picked a basket containing a bath kit from another corner of her room. She took out a small calabash with a lid and rubbed the contents on her body—a body softener made of black soap in droplets of lime. In a few minutes, she was in the bamboo bathroom taking a bath. Soon she had new skin, soft and silky as a baby's bottom. She liked that. She felt it as she rubbed oil over her body. She smiled, her confidence rushing back.

She changed her *buba* and *iro*—the top and wrapper—to clean ones. She picked up her makeup kit, arranged in a calabash from the same corner of her room, and moved toward an open window. She placed the calabash on the window frame, took out a mirror, and began to beautify herself, powdering her face with *papamilolo,* a brown powder that fitted a face like a second layer of skin. She proceeded to apply *tiro,* a glossy black eye shadow, below her eyebrow. Moving away from the window, she rambled through another *oke* basket until she found what she was looking for: a sequence of *bebe,* strings of beads in a straw bag. She removed her wrapper and added more layers of bebe to complement the existing ones. She replaced her wrapper and went back to look at herself in the mirror.

"Mama will be proud of me; my glams sparkle, as she had taught me," Tutu muttered as she checked her reflection in the mirror. Everything was perfection, as her mother would have wanted it to be. She was glamorous. She had to try hard to resist the urge to keep on admiring the perfection she had created on her body, for time was running out. She knew that a teeny crumb out of place during Paul's dinner could set him off, could aggravate his mood. She had seen that happen before, and it was not pleasant—everything must be superlative. And the special touches, they should be done now. She replaced the mirror along with the makeup in the calabash and returned it to its place.

Tutu took a matchbox from another straw bag lying on the floor next to the oke baskets to light up the two *oguso* candle stands in the corridor—one near the entrance door and the other near the backyard door. These must be lit, along with those in Paul's parlor, even though he might not set foot in there before entering his bedroom, even though the rays of sunshine might still be left, so as to find a copper coin on a tan stand when he came back. This was an unforgettable task, and any mistake was punishable.

She got the candles in Paul's parlor and those two at the corners where they were placed on the corridor lit up. She went to check on Paul in his bedroom. Silence greeted her. She stood in the door frame, recalling and playing for a few seconds some of the nights she had the opportunity to spend with Paul. She was dazed. Maggi was right—she had to be selfish and stop bloody caring about others. The game should be one-on-one, she concluded as she moved back to her room.

She spread a mat at one section of the floor. She arranged sheets for her daughter's bed. When she put the finishing touches to everything, she gave her reflection a last glance. She was satisfied everything was intact. She had it—everything that would make Paul beg.… She sat down at the edge of the mat, convinced she was up to the task, sure that by the time she finished with Paul that night, he would beg and succumb to her wishes, as had happened to powerful men of the past. He would beg for more as she ravished him with everything in the encyclopedia of romance. She knew a lot now. Maggi had updated her.

For once, Tutu was aware that she was at an advantage; she certainly looked better than all the wives in Paul's house. She had the beauty and youthful body to dominate Paul's life. She should not be included in the retinue of dull, mournful faces of Paul's other wives, women who made no attempt to woo, to give him the "hots." They just accepted what Paul threw at them in good faith.

That would end now, she resolved. She would dictate everything, especially the sleeping rotation. She would steer him toward other wives when she was tired of him. She would tell him when it was okay to sleep with other wives. The one he could sleep with would have to have her approval. The one he could be permitted to sleep with, out of the sad, dull faces in the house, had to show merit, with good behavior toward her. No more wives, and certainly not a single concubine, should be allowed, eventually. Maggi had done it. She could do it.

She looked through the window. It was getting dim outside. She had to get her daughter from Adewumi's room. She knew the woman would be asleep since she had to wake up early, even on days when none of the others ventured out of the house to work. She had to at least gather two loads of firewood to sell, to support herself and the children, especially Kola. "She has to, if she must live," Moji had explained to her with glee in her eyes. "As far as Paul is concerned, Adewumi and her son are withered beings."

She had been in shock that day. She couldn't understand why Adewumi, the drop-dead, black ebony with embedded amazing grace, couldn't flaunt what she had to get Paul to crawl on his knees, begging for her love. As she watched her, day after day, it seemed that the bad things Paul did to her, making her wander for food on her own, did her body good rather than evil. She was as trim and elegant as a princess. Just as she could never understand Adewumi, so she could never understand what a woman as plain as Moji, the first wife of Paul, was doing in his house, and to the extent of having six children with him. Rolake was lovely, seemingly more intelligent than the rest, but she could tell from early banters with these three, Tutu was unique, not into Paul as the others were; her mind was just somewhere else.

Tutu walked toward Adewumi's bedroom. With caution, she opened the door. As she had thought, Adewumi was already sleeping on the mat with Tutu's baby and her own daughter. Adewumi looked divine and peaceful. Tutu recalled Moji's description of the pain that Paul had meted out for Adewumi. She stood pondering, marveling at what made Adewumi resilient despite being in a pool of sorrow. She knew Paul was an insane man not to have seen what she saw, and what other people saw and talked about. Many people talked to Tutu about Adewumi when she was engaged to Paul.

"I learned your parents engaged you to Paul Olorunfemi instead of me," one of her suitors had said. "Well, best of luck because you'll need it."

"Why?" Tutu glared.

"You're going to be a junior wife to Adewumi, and I wish you all the best."

"You're just jealous."

"Me? No. If that woman didn't have a chance with Paul, no woman could, because she is just transcendent in all things."

"I'll thrive where others failed," Tutu had shouted. "Paul is a man you'll never be to me."

She had walked away from him. Had she succeeded where others failed? She knew the man was right about Paul so far. Tutu sighed, tiptoeing around the legs of the sleepers. She kneeled down to pick her baby up. Adewumi opened her eyes slightly as if to ascertain who it was.

"It's me. Thanks," Tutu whispered as she lifted the baby off the mat.

An audible "You are welcome" came from Adewumi. She closed her eyes as soon as Tutu opened the door to leave.

The baby woke up on the way back to her room. Tutu sat back on the mat and started rocking her back to sleep. Adewumi's beauty and suffering had prompted a foul mood in Tutu. She seethed about Paul, fighting back a tear and wondering "if" her plan didn't work as she wanted and she got pregnant again whether she would face the old music played by Paul. She knew this beauty of a woman, Adewumi, hadn't been on Paul's sex rota in ages, and if she had to satisfy her urges, she was at risk. How was she doing it? Tutu could relate. She was a withered being to Paul too. She knew the suffering from abandonment, loneliness, helplessness, and frustration … that there was nothing she could do about it. She'd been taught about a lot of expectations in marriage, but never did she envision being brushed aside as the newest wife. Her mother had not taught her how to endure the pain, the waiting for him to come around. Probably Maggi had forgotten or intentionally omitted the worst part: the craving and the longing in the early moments of marriage.

Tutu was in so much pain, as much confusion. She sat there with thoughts … and thoughts … and thoughts. Deep down, one feeling dominated them all: *make love 'til spent*. She knew the feeling was crazy. She knew she was supposed to forgo tonight—tell Paul to screw himself and then go to blazes. Let Paul be in the wilderness for a change. Strange that she felt resentment toward Paul and still wanted him. She wanted him tonight. She had planned to use tonight to ensnare Paul forever … to make him want her forever. To make her relevant to him even if he knocked her up again. To make him shake off being so standoffish. She had felt immediately after the honeymoon that Paul wasn't a communicator. Later she realized that Paul was not a female baby lover. She had sensed hatred as Paul first came to meet his daughter. He had stood with a frown in the doorway, as if something was her fault; as if he hated something. He had left without a word, after minutes of standing there, silent. She had felt a pang of guilt, but for what? She could tell later that Paul hated girls, because he never came around to see the baby.

Paul was a strange man. It was sometimes like living with an estranged husband, but that had to stop now. She would make her demands during the lovemaking, during the sure time, when she had his balls glued to her. She prayed solemnly that tonight would close the deal. He had to communicate as clearly as he had yesterday, each word from his mouth sending cool waves down her spine, even though it should be otherwise. He should make her brain swim, ravished by him. As a matter of fact, her brain vibrated with pleasure in minutes; probably, Paul was back and waiting. That second part could be bad. Paul hated waiting. She forgot the pain done to herself and to others.

Hurriedly, she laid her baby, whose lips enclosed a left thumb, on the mat. And without much struggle or a cry, the girl went back to sleep, sucking her left thumb in urgency. And everything went quiet, as if the baby was saying, *"Go on, Mom, you need a time out … you need 'me' time."*

Tutu snapped to her feet like a woman on a mission. She lit two candles, placing one at the far end of the room nearer to the entrance, to guide her steps, to illuminate her path as she would be staggering back into her room in total satisfaction, she hoped. The second candle, she placed on a bamboo tray fished out from the corner of the room along with two calabash bowls—one filled with water for Paul to wash his hands, and a second for the stew. She dished out the stew and fetched one pounded yam from its warmer. As they were all on one bamboo tray, she cast a last glance at her daughter. She was an angel. Gently, Tutu sneaked out of the room carrying her husband's dinner.

She opened Paul's bedroom with a foot, but silence

greeted her. She felt slightly disappointed that Paul wasn't back. She knew she should be happy that he didn't get to his room before her; Paul could go crazy when kept waiting. She had been a witness to that in her first month as his bride. He had battered Moji for complaining that Paul changed the sleeping rota, and she had refused to prepare his food on time. That was the last thing Tutu wanted. Let him go crazy like in rough sex, instead, as he had done once. Paul had been loaded with alcohol. That night was nostalgic for her. That night she knew she would always love Paul and care for what he did to her in the silence of the night, in his room. Even though he was twice her age and more, she loved him.

What was not to love in Paul? The man was strikingly handsome, with a firm body. He knew what women wanted. For the few times she had been in his custody, she could never complain as her other friends did, the ones who had to put up with the trunk of tree they were married to. Intimacy was three blows in, puffing like a cat, and *ta-da,* they were done, not giving a damn about the satisfaction of the woman beside them. Paul was a man who knew what he was doing and when he was doing it. She knew that was the reason she was almost dying of frustration. That would be rectified soon: tell him brink of night means brink of night, not middle of the night or anytime he wanted.

She set the bamboo tray down. She was proud of herself—the stage was set without a hitch. She settled on Paul's mattress to wait for him, her head crowned with thoughts. What should be her first move on Paul, the second he finished his meal? Slip her hand inside his trousers, she concluded. She was full of erotic thoughts as she lay on the old mattress, exposing her legs as a first seduction to attract her husband. She dozed off.

Tutu was woken by a furious opening of the bedroom door, accompanied by a sharp voice.

"What the hell are you still doing here?"

The voice she knew right away as she stirred in disarray. A kick of the bamboo tray into a corner indicated that her plans had been futile. She rubbed her eyes to see well. Gloomily, she could make out Paul's figure, as sharp raps of reproach coming from his mouth like a madman made her understand fast that trouble had arrived. She managed to come to a sitting position.

"Get out. I'm not in the mood." Paul pointed to the exit door.

Tutu tried to tie her *iro* around her waist.

"Are you deaf?" Paul roared. "I said get out, or otherwise…"

Swiftly, she gathered herself and stood up with only her *buba* as a dress. From stomach to toe, she was nude, only tiny beads on display, above her hips. She bent, trying to pick up her wrapper.

"Get out now." Paul sounded like a thunderbolt.

Tutu jolted up, abandoning the robe, and raced away before he got angry enough to reproach her physically. She knew he was almost there.

Tutu nearly had her eardrum blown off as Paul slammed the door after her with a force that rocked the foundations of the house. She remained in the corridor, howling like a dog, and begged Paul to reconsider. She didn't bother that she might wake anybody up, even his male children or the other wives, or that she might look ridiculous. All she wanted was him.

As Tutu wailed, Paul shouted back from his bedroom.

"Go to bed, Tutu, or I'll give you more things to cry about!"

Tutu stopped wailing as each word came out, signaling the danger of being beaten to fluff like a pounded yam. There was no way he would reconsider, and she knew it. As she heard Paul's hand on the door, she ran inside her room and collapsed on the mat, sobbing. Why couldn't she be like Maggi? Why couldn't she be like Mama? When would it be her turn again? She knew Paul's craziness would persist for days. She could tell.

Tutu hollered, "When is it going to be my turn again, Paul?"

She knew she was overdoing it. She called her husband "Paul" instead of Aba, "Daddy." She would be in the soup. Tutu was startled to death as her daughter woke up with a loud cry. She rubbed the tears from her face as she recovered from the shock. She picked the baby up from the mat, cuddling and rocking her back and forth.

The baby went back to sleep. Gently, she placed her back on the mat. Tutu sat staring at the wall, too afraid to cry or do something stupid, not only because it could wake the baby, but afraid it could bring Paul on the run, fuming as if he was about to explode, like a volcano. And that would never be good. Tutu was lost in despair. *Bitches lived lives better than this*, she concluded.

Chapter Twenty-Six

P aul sent Tutu out because he was too disturbed to have sex. Gambling had prompted the foul mood. He had lost everything he had just collected from the sales of his cocoa and more at the ayo competition. It was half of what he made in a year, plus half of the generational farm! He had been foolish enough to challenge Tunji, a well-known ayo wizard around the Itan neighborhood. Paul was running crazy.

He paced up and down in his bedroom, racking his brain for a solution to his idiocy of the night. Paul, though drunk, was conscious of his actions. In his golden days, when his intraparietal sulcus nerves functioned like a whistle, Paul *was* Tunji. He was the best in the game, in his twenties. He enlisted in all the competitions and made others cry like a baby. That was then, and now it seemed that his indulgence in heavy drinking to a stupor meant that the intoxication probably numbed and damaged the electric batteries that activated the cranial nerves, not leaving a flicker.

Paul probably had not realized the flame had gone out with the years of drinking. Or he was just in denial because he lost all the time. It showed that the acumen parts of his brain that involved calculation, that involved profound self-discipline, that involved sharp intellect and decision-making, which had worked like a charm in years gone by, were gone. The batteries were dead, just sediment remaining—too wet or too dry to make him the man he used to be.

He had lost so much recently that it was enough to make him quit gambling, to make him go away and look for another avenue to regulate his money problems, but Paul was addicted. And as all gamblers believe, it could still be good. He still could have the chance to double his money. He was especially desperate to double whatever he had, and keep it, in case Omotola never married Jacob.

Jacob had threatened to rain war. Paul had been in a panic, and since then, he had been trying to double his money. Each time he had lost everything he had on him and had even bet money he didn't have. Sometimes the sharks had to give him three months to pay up. This was the reason the generational farm of the family—in Paul's possession as olori-ebi, his clan's leader—was decreasing, the proceeds had drastically declined, and the family had been complaining. Paul always came up with excuses, but this time around, Paul bet more than he could pay—about half of the property owned by his family. The downsizing of the ancestral farm was going to be noticed soon as the new occupant, Tunji, claimed what belonged to him.

Paul was agitated to the point of being willing to do anything for money. He knew if the ember, the dispute that was between him and Jacob, fanned to become a real fire, none from his extended family would lift a finger to help. In fact, they were fed up with him. They hated him so much that they would be willing to give a helping hand to Jacob. His four sons, whom he could count on, were too few in number to combat the multitude in Jacob's clan. The guy had an edge, as his family could wipe out a small town.

He ran over the night's scene in his mind again. He didn't know how much John had put on the line for him.

The market was full to the brim with competitors and spectators, as it always was at the end of every month when Paul and John got there. It wasn't long before Paul sat at the ayo *table and lost his head. John played his part, but Paul wouldn't listen. He knew Paul was in trouble when he whispered in Tunji's ear, and Tunji shook his head and said, "No, Paul. I'm not interested in another wife. Keep your daughter, but you can use your farmland as a bet or stand up and let another player sit."*

John tapped Paul on the shoulder and said, "Paul, it's time to go."

Instead of standing up, Paul shoved John's hand away and whispered in Tunji's ear again.

Tunji said aloud to everybody. "Paul is betting half of his family's cocoa plantation."

The others nodded in agreement.

This time, John didn't tap; he hit Paul hard on the back. Paul turned towards him like a wounded animal, and with a strangled voice, said, "If you hit me that hard again, I'll kill you."

John stepped aside to watch Paul digging his own grave. John knew his limits when it came to Paul. Few matched his strength in the town. And unfortunately, he, John, wasn't among the few. Paul had that puissance of a lion, flash of a wind that sometimes went into his head, thinking he could do and undo at will. Once, on John's behalf, he had played truant from school, lying in the bushes near the farm, waiting, and pounced on the two grown-up boys that had bullied John several times on his way to the farm. Since that day, he had known Paul's strength, as he knew in seconds after making the bet that Paul was gasping for breath—that he was in pain and losing.

As he watched Paul shaking both legs vigorously, he knew he was about to launch his anger. John decided to walk away.

John could hear Paul's voice turn harsh. Paul was a bad loser; he knew this. Once, at the same ayo *table, he had become aggressive and turned the table over, almost killing his opponent (not Tunji). Since then, emissaries from the palace and thugs had kept watch over the game. Still, John was sure Paul was going to do something like that tonight. He heard his voice changing from clear diction to a stammer, and some were laughing at him. Paul hated being laughed at. He could kill when someone made jest of him.*

As John had predicted, Paul lashed out like a bomb the next minute. John heard many voices saying, "Paul, you're going to pay tonight."

He knew he was supposed to keep walking or just break into a run and block his ears to those threatening Paul. He wanted to, but he couldn't. His legs were stiff, like piles of steel, and each pace dragged him backward. He couldn't ever walk away from Paul, who had been his pillar as a boy. He had always been there for him when other boys wanted to take advantage of him. John had known Paul since they were little. They had lived next to each other until they each got married to their first wife and moved to form their own nests. The past had been full of memories, and they would not relinquish their hold on John.

Now John got scared. He knew Paul would be damaged for life if he didn't do something soon. For old time's sake, he turned and paved his way back inside the circle. The other contestants and spectators had had enough, and wanted to rush Paul as a battalion rushes their helpless enemies at war. Paul was on his knees. John had to plead, and eventually become Paul's guarantor, even though he knew he was at risk of losing all he had. He would probably become a pauper if Paul's family renounced his friend as the head of the family. But he had to do what he had to do, for old time's sake.

John dragged Paul away from the scene. He loaded him with ogogoro from their drinking cafe until Paul calmed down. He had brought him home. The rest was his family's problem.

Chapter Twenty-Seven

"Is that a cock crowing? What the hell? Is that a rap on the door?" Paul asked aloud, waking up from a dreadful dream he was having. He sat up, disoriented. After sending Tutu to her room and spending considerable time pacing up and down in his bedroom, with dust starting to emanate from the bare floor, Paul had retired to the mattress with a hurricane of a headache. And being awakened by the cock crowing and what seemed like a knock on the door wasn't good for Paul.

He knew he would end up like his father. All the indications were there. Toward the end of his life, Gbadamosi was a broke, depressed man who ranted and cursed people from dawn to dusk, without eating. He cursed anybody around, and even people far away—especially Sarah and Simon. Gbadamosi had lost his mind when Simon took everything he owned, and he wanted more.

It was in the verdict of the palace for Gbadamosi to pay back all the extravagant *idana*, the obscene bride price, the random gifts for the family. And more: a slam of a fine, since Sarah had written, calling Simon a stark illiterate. Before the incident, before Sarah did what she did,

Gbadamosi was the envy of his friends, not only because of all he'd received, but the fact that he had a daughter catching the eye of most of the gentry, and the suitor himself, who was rich to a fault.

Simon was waiting, as if waiting to taste Gbadamosi's blood. He knew there was no way Gbadamosi could pay everything back, yet he still waited, and one morning Gbadamosi fell into something like a convulsion. All the family ran helter-skelter to save his life, and that morning, he gave up the ghost.

Paul knew the same end was awaiting him. He could feel it as he remembered the just-flashed vision, a dream, or whatever it was called, as vividly as his failure of yesterday at the ayo competition. He knew the dream was pointing an arrow at his future. He sat up without any choice, listening to the only noise, the only disturbance of the night, the crickets. In his anger, he felt like dashing out of his bedroom, fishing out the culprit crickets, and killing them one by one. He knew, though, that it was like wanting to kill all the fish in the sea by hand, one by one. As many and as annoying as the crickets were, he couldn't kill them all.

As angry as he was, he forced his concentration on the recently featured catastrophe in his subconsciousness. He was at the corner of a church, in his underwear, humiliated, facing the people who came to early mass. He was about to be ordered out of the church by the priest when a sound like a rap woke him up. He didn't know if he should be thankful for the knock or hate it, because the feeling of being all alone in the dark, with the disturbing thoughts and disturbing noises of the night, was driving him nuts.

It was as clear as crystal that he'd just had a premonition of his future—the doom to come. Paul couldn't help but wonder why his consciousness and subconsciousness interlocked and were interwoven with ills. He wondered why his humiliations took place in more than one setting. At least, he could escape to another setting. If real life was hell, then sleep should be a relief. Why were the upheavals in real life prolonged to taunt him in his dreams? Was it the end? What was next now?

He hated the idea of losing his mind like Gbadamosi, who was an embarrassment in his last days. Paul hated to be laughed at, to be humiliated. Worst of all, there was nothing he could do about it. He would be even more humiliated in a few days' time, when half of his family's farm was seized by Tunji. And what excuses would he give this time around? There was little a man could take. He was frustrated. If he ended up like Gbadamosi, he would always blame Simon, as he would blame the missionaries. Alive or dead, both would be his enemy too; they'd put him in the shit. Paul might also have Rolake punished severely and take away everything, as he'd done to Adewumi—or, he would, if he didn't assume that Rolake could still give him male children. Her two stillbirths before Omotola had been male.

He was stupid not to have listened to John, whom he'd begged to come with him, to jab him with an elbow if he lost control at the competition. He felt like hitting somebody. Tutu would have been ideal had she resisted his orders, remained adamant in his room or outside. *Wise girl! Well, maybe next time she wouldn't be lucky. She would witness his punches on her body as a welcome to his den,* Paul thought.

A cock crowed again. Paul looked through the window and could see it was four in the morning. Paul hated brooding any longer, and he was scared to go back to sleep. He sat and felt sorry for his life. He rested his left cheek on his left hand in contemplation. Raps! He looked wearily around. Since the knocking had stopped, he wondered if it was his imagination. Was it the rapping that had brought him to this present resentful world from just walking out of a weird dream?

Raps! But this time around, he heard the raps clear-cut. That was what had woke him up, and certainly, his imagination wasn't playing pranks on him. It was a knock, all right.

"What? At this hour of the morning?" He jumped to his feet at once, like an acrobatic master, to answer the door. "My hopes have been answered; somebody out there needs a dent. The owner of that knock will wish he had never been born. Whoever is at the front door at this unholy hour needs to be beaten to the extent of hospitalization!" Paul swore.

This was not unusual. Paul had been sad a lot as a kid, right after he left school. The only way he was able to suppress his anger and frustration was to fight and beat someone into a trance. That someone included family members. His grandmother was always worried about him.

With both hands, he yanked the front door open. And instantly, he folded them into knuckles, like a boxer. Paul was ready to punch, until he moved closer to the doorstep and could see his visitors. The anger inside him subdued like a fire quenched with gallons of water simultaneously. This confirmed his grandmother's saying from when she was alive and Paul was regularly engaging in all sorts of fights.

She would say, "Paul! Even a mad dog sometimes knows when to retreat without a hunter's whistle. It retreats instantly in front of a fire, in front of the lord of the jungle."

Her wisdom was accurate; he now stood in front of lions, the lords of the jungle. He was so startled that the knuckles flattened and dropped to his side in a hurry as well-known faces fixed on his, confused.

8&

Chapter Twenty-Eight

On the same night, Omotola and Rolake slept on the mat in Rolake's bedroom. Unexpectedly, Omotola placed a leg on Rolake as she turned towards her. Rolake sat up feebly and removed the leg. And immediately, Omotola turned her face away as if angry.

"Sunshine, I know this mat is getting smaller for both us, but we need to make use of what we have 'til I can save enough to buy a new one," Rolake whispered.

Lately, sleep had eluded Rolake at night. That had made her listen to unwanted noises, like the showdown between Paul and Tutu.

Rolake reclaimed her sleeping position. "Sunshine," Rolake whispered again, "I'm sorry to scare you…." Her voice went dead, and her blood ran cold. There wasn't a nerve in her entire body that wasn't gripped by fear upon hearing her husband open the front door to some people. She started to sob gently.

"This is it. This is the end," she muttered.

She never knew what Jacob was up to or what her husband was up to. Even though the missionary had promised to protect Omotola, Rolake had been truly worried about the two-month holiday—anything was a possibility. She wondered when the ill marriage was going to be, so she could seek help, but from whom? The school was on two months holiday! Rolake lay in fear, afraid to breathe.

She tried to strain her ears to understand the crew's "mission," but it proved abortive. As she stared at her daughter's back, her face came vividly to her. She could see the innocence, the beauty. She knew it was a matter of time until Omotola would become one of those women— the ones with a sad, weary face that rarely smiled—a woman like her, without a choice. Back in her teens, she was in love with a boy called Dapo, and the boy loved her. She had barely claimed puberty when her father called her into his living room and told her she would marry Paul. She had raged, refusing to eat. She wished to die instead of marrying a man almost her father's age. Dapo and his family had tried to come up with her bride price money, but they couldn't raise it. It was too soon. And immediately after her father knew she had started her period, she was shipped to Paul's house, after a lousy marriage ceremony that resembled one between a male dog and female dog.

The only happy moment Rolake could recollect in Paul's house was the day she gave birth to Omotola. The moment she held her gorgeous daughter in her hands, she prayed in her heart for her, *May she always have options in her life, a fulfilling life full of joy and happiness.*

Before Rolake finally gave birth to Omotola, she had had two stillbirths and miscarriages. And both stillbirths were boys. After the birth of Omotola, she was sterile again. Everything had been done traditionally for her to conceive, but nothing worked. Rolake hated her existence in Paul's house. She might have learned to love him, but she hated his lifestyle. She knew that Paul was a troubled man with a trio of problems—a poor man barely capable of feeding himself, with a wagon of wives and children; a womanizer who went after every beautiful woman available; and a gambler ready to gamble anything away, to suit his purpose. Rolake's miscarriages had a lot to do with her husband's violence toward his household and the unhappiness in marrying a man she had never loved, who treated her like dirt.

Dapo, whom she'd wanted to marry, had recently wed her best friend, and both of them were happy together. A day never passed without her thinking about what her life would have been if she'd had an option of choosing for herself, if she had lived in a normal world.

When Kola told Rolake that Omotola was extremely bright and had been admitted into primary school, she quietly thanked God for making her happy. Even though Rolake knew that Omotola's schooling must be kept secret until Paul couldn't stop her and was fearful of having to hide it, God had answered her prayers. Not only would her daughter have a formal education, but the freedom of choice that it brought. She thought like Kola: by the time Paul discovered Omotola was going to school, she would be advanced in study and unstoppable. Eventually, if Paul discovered, Rolake would beg him to realize the importance of education and make her daughter's case for schooling exceptional, not force her into a brutal marriage with an old man like him.

Should he refuse to comply, Kola promised reinforcement would come from the school officials. The school would do everything possible to help Omotola finish her studies. As a result, Rolake was happy, and extremely careful to send her daughter to school after the whole household had gone to the farm. Rolake would bathe her daughter and send her to school under the supervision of Kola, her co-conspirator. And before the household arrived back at dusk, all school materials were hidden, including slate and chalks. She had composed a lie that she had sent Omotola on an errand, in case somebody was inquisitive about the girl's whereabouts. How Paul found out about her going to school after only two weeks was still a mystery.

Kola had told Rolake he was thrilled to have someone to relate to in the rundown home. And he had also told Rolake she had to be strong, like his mother. Yes, she knew she had to be strong. She had witnessed Kola's and his mother's pain since Kola had started school. Apart from the fact that Paul had taken everything from Adewumi, he also waited for her to make mistakes, especially to satisfy her urges from outside the home. Committing what was called adultery was punishable by stoning to death by able men, ordered by the king.

Rolake was sure that death was an end that Paul would celebrate if Adewumi committed such an error. She knew Paul would particularly demand such a death penalty as punishment for her, to punish her son, Kola, whom he hated so much. Paul never forgot or forgave. He always lurked in the corner, waiting for revenge. He never forgave Kola for being bold enough to challenge his hegemony, his refusal to yield to his order to stop school. Kola had tarnished Paul's credibility and autonomy, and he would pay for it. Paul had sworn this countless times.

At the onset of Adewumi's mistreatment, Rolake didn't know it could be her turn next. But she'd wanted all three wives to collaborate, to gang up on Paul and bring him to his knees. She was sure he couldn't kill them all. Moji, the first wife, wouldn't cooperate, as she was full of jealous venom. "I won't lift a finger to help you destroy our husband because of Adewumi. She got what she deserved," she had said happily, adding, "as wives, we should be submissive, cultured, and do what our husband wants."

She had walked away, and Rolake knew that Moji went and told their husband about the plan. Rolake hated Moji and everything about her. She was a hypocrite who preached morals, who lived a sinister life that society condemned, calling people like her *asewo,* the tramps. Society treated these women like lepers, outcasts who were only visited in the dead of night by men who never wanted to be publicly seen with them. They were left on the shelf not by their own choice or making, but by the will of society. As life offered them lemons, they made lemonade. They were asewo, prostitutes, the trees anybody could climb. That was life.

Moji was among the asewo even though she pretended not to be, fooling society that she was among the ideal wives. Rolake had known this since her first week of marriage to Paul. How many times had she seen Moji in close contact with Jacob, her daughter's supposed husband-to-be, and looked another away? Stupid Jacob would look guilty as he rubbed his dirty hands on his frog face, with the string of his *sooro,* trousers loose, dangling on the floor, and full of excuses that he had come to see Paul.

"Since I couldn't find Paul around, I just went in to say a quick hello to Moji. You know we go back a long way," Jacob said each time, despite knowing that Paul would be at the farm or palm wine salon, and any discussion with him could be settled there.

"Back a long way? My ass!" Rolake wanted to shout at them one day when she accidentally walked in on them just finishing "doing it."

Really, Rolake didn't care if the wives amused themselves, because Paul was doing the same. She just hated being called a fool. Paul was a stallion and a sadist—a stallion with fine bones, with a fine horse—whom she knew many of her friends would love to bed. She saw it in their eyes when they came to visit, with the exception of one friend who was the reason she knew Paul was a sadist.

Paul almost married her best friend the same month Rolake became his wife. On what was supposed to be their honeymoon day, she had noticed Paul was keen on her friend. Paul's eyeballs tailed her around as she was installing her items in her bedroom. She had watched in bewilderment, giving his attraction serious thought. Eventually, after a few days, she concluded that her imagination was playing a prank—that it was stupid jealousy. But the truth came out a few weeks later. Her friend rushed in and told her to warn Paul to stop insisting to her father that the two wed. If he refused to back off, she would pierce his heart with a bullet.

And yes, she could. She wanted that for Paul. Her best friend was a straight shooter, an inheritance from her father, who was a hunter. When they were growing up, she would sharpen the edge of a stick to a point and throw it to catch fish. Fish rarely escaped her javelins.

Paul insisted and would not back off until, finally, her friend's father had a serious talk with him. She was lucky to have a father who loved her dearly, who refused Paul's bride price, and told him point-blank that marrying his daughter would be wrong, since he considered Rolake as close as a daughter. He was among the few responsible fathers who believed in choice, among the few decent people who had seen what polygamous marriages did to their mothers and wanted out. Rolake knew this. Her friend's father was among the few believing that one wife was ideal, two maximum, and after that number, a crowd.

Her friend's father never ventured to marry more than two wives, and he loved both women. Unfortunately, there were few like him, who rarely yielded to bullying from friends, who rarely danced to the tune of the society. The man had never failed to rebuke her father for taking wife after wife.

Rolake's father was a pervert, a sadist like Paul, who walked with a staff and who, even at his age and with a house full of women, still hid in the bush to watch little girls take their baths in the river at dusk. Once, he was caught and taken to the palace, but he used the excuse that he had gone to pluck herbs for medicine, as if he were an herbalist. Despite being warned and being obliged to pluck his herbs during the daytime, they still found him lurking in the bushes from time to time. Even Omotola, at a tender age, knew her grandfather was evil.

Young Omotola *had* said, "Mama, your father has dark eyeballs, and it's scary."

And a black soul, too, that you'll notice as you grow, Rolake added in her head.

But she warned Omotola to keep it to herself.

Omotola hated the man and would not visit him unless forced.

And still, the decent men, men of integrity like her friend's father, were not many. Unfortunately, you just had to make do with what you had, if fortunate, and not wind up on the shelf—because that stunk more than being dead for a week.

Chapter Twenty-Nine

P aul was startled as he looked at his guests. He counted in his head; there were six of them. One of them had a carton on his shoulder. They were from the family that owned the town and all the local regions. Well, Simon was the mighty. He could order him for breakfast, lunch, and dinner, as he could anybody from the four protectorates of the British South, East, West, and North.

"*Kaaro,* Paul."

Paul stood and stared at the speaker, whom he knew like the back of his hand. It was Simon Akindele's eldest, the leader of the Akindele clan. As a matter of fact, he occupied the same post as him in Akindele's family, *olori-ebi,* the leader of his clan. He was respected and well-to-do, unlike his wretched self, who sold the monuments of his family for the thrill of a game.

Paul felt ashamed and scared to death. Whatever brought them here this early in the morning? It must be because Simon wanted him to pick up where Gbadamosi had left off. Maybe he didn't know Paul was in more debt than his father.

As per the culture, Paul was aware that, even though

you never inherit anything from your father's genes, you could inherit his wealth, his titles, prestige, and on and on. You could also inherit his debt, his humiliation, and pain. Paul was apprehensive, and lots of debates were going on in his head. He was lost. *He was more in debt than Gbadamosi, ruining his family...*

"*Kaaro,* Paul. Would you be kind enough to host us in your house this morning?" said the spokesman with a smile.

Paul had seen Simon on several occasions as a special guest at the annual festival, on the high horse on which the king had placed him in the palace, even though he wasn't a chief. That had annoyed Paul to death. Furthermore, not once did he get down from his high horse to present his condolences on behalf of Gbadamosi, despite the fact that he had killed the man. Paul saw him with that air of hubris, disdainful.

Once, out of fear, as Simon looked directly at him in the crowd, Paul had whispered to John, who was standing next to him, to please assess Simon's countenance.

"Wow, Paul, he hates your guts." John's face was anxious as he asked how Paul had managed to get near him and piss him off.

Fear breeds contempt, and Paul had replied, "I don't know, but I know that the feeling is mutual. I hate his guts too."

Paul had stayed away from the palace for consecutive years until he finally learned that, even with all the money, with all the power Simon had, he got dumped. Simon had got burned by his first wife and cried like a baby. What man does that? And that time was epic in Paul's life.

For a long while, he had not set eyes on Simon in the

palace, and certainly had avoided anybody closer to him who might remind him of what was in the culture. That was until last year when he saw Simon and two of his children, a boy and a girl from his first marriage; whereupon he had decided that this year's annual festival was a no-go area if he didn't want to burn up his life.

Paul didn't hear the *olori-ebi;* his mind reeled with true-or-false questions. The only truth glaring in his head was that their arrival was a manifestation of the dreams— their coming was a foreboding of what was to happen. Since he knew why they were there, the question was, why more complication in his life? Where was the way out of all this? Paul stood still like a statue.

"Paul, we will be happy if we can come in and discuss things with you instead of standing on your doorstep."

Paul was unresponsive.

The spokesman added, "Paul, we've brought good news."

It was like talking to a wall. The speaker touched Paul lightly on one arm. Slowly, Paul came around and removed his bulk from the doorframe, so his visitors could come in.

"Good morning, and welcome," Paul said with a shaking voice.

He ushered them into his parlor, where dozens of tree trunks shaped like stools were visible. While the crew scouted for seats, Paul remained standing, scratching his head, followed by running both hands over his face to conceal his nervousness.

Finally, they arranged their seats to form a semi-circle, and the spokesman said, "We thank you for welcoming us into your house."

"It's a pleasure having you around," Paul said faintly. "Please let me wake up one of my wives to bring water."

He wanted some time out from his guests to think.

"Not yet," the spokesman smiled. "But thanks for your hospitality." He paused and added, "We will drink later, Paul, of course, after our discussion. Please take a seat."

Paul dragged a seat to face them and saw politeness. He stared without a word, but softened a bit.

"Paul, we need your permission to talk."

It occurred to him that if Simon wanted his head off, he wouldn't have sent his household headhunter along with crews that waited for the go-ahead. He would have sent his troopers to create the fear of God in him to pay up.

"Please, go ahead and talk," Paul said with a polite smile.

"You must be wondering why we are here this morning. Well, Simon sent us to you on a special mission. But, first of all, he sends his apologies. He needs your pardon." He paused again, continuing. "Simon wants the bad blood between our families to clear off and to start afresh. He is sorry for what happened. Paul, Simon sends his sincere apologies."

He stopped to wait for Paul's signal to continue.

Paul sighed and felt greatly relieved for the first time since they had arrived. For once, probably just once in a lifetime, he knew he had the edge over Simon, had him in the palm of his hand. He could do what he wanted. Simon wouldn't have sent the big shots in his family to beg for mercy if he wasn't a desperate man with a desperate wish.

What could that be? Paul smiled inwardly. Still, as

much as he would love to reject and treat Simon with hatred, and hurt him without mercy as he had done to his father, he would have loved to show him that little people have power too. It still came down to "beggars can't be choosers."

He knew his case was like that of a man punished by God who got angry. What court would he charge God to? He could rant, swear … and that amounted to what? Craziness? Depression? He knew he had to suck up his pride and believe in the Yoruba adage that says, "A man that runs away from a fight can fight another day." His life in balance, he needed all the friends he could find, especially the loaded ones. It was a chance of a lifetime. He wanted his money. He wanted the pain gone.

Paul shrugged and said, "What happened years ago is water under the bridge. With pleasure, I accept Simon's apology. Yes, let's bury the ashes of the past. I like that. Start a new beginning. You're welcome to state the reason for your coming."

"Thank you, Paul. We're grateful, and the second part of our mission, Paul, is that our brother Simon sends us to you." Smiling, he went on, "Well, he found a beautiful fruit, a beautiful flower in your vineyard, and he'd like to pluck it, with your permission."

"Pluck a beautiful flower?" The question sounded bizarre to him, because Paul had assumed the only "special mission" that could interest Simon must be a piece of land. But, *Pluck a beautiful flower?* It was like saying, *Paul, you've won the lottery; we came to tell you that you've hit the jackpot.*

That couldn't be right. It should be land. Simon wanted to buy land from him, as he did with other farmers. Simon owned almost half of Itan-land. He had just bought acres from a friend for his son, and the son had turned it into a recreation center. The friend and his clan were swimming in money. Probably, he was still dreaming. Paul was obviously confused. The statement was untrue. Besides, there was nobody as gorgeous in his family as the foreign women Simon imported and married, whom other men gasped to look at. Paul was lost in thought again.

Simon's father was familiar to people as he rode his horse around the town, but Simon? No. He'd never seen him on horse or on foot. In the past, people lined up on the roads to look out for his car during his annual visit to the palace. Sometimes people crashed into his compound as a convoy of cars brought those in his inner circle to parties. Once, Paul himself had seen the secretary-general of the protectorates in full uniform, and other dignitaries. But since Simon had gagged up his compound with a fortress fence and armed it with uniformed men, everything about him was a rumor, a fairy tale, or a myth.

"Come again?" Paul said after a while.

"Paul, our brother wants to pluck a flower from your backyard, with your permission."

The spokesman emphasized the last bit.

Paul refused to accept the statement or ask questions like an idiot either. He sat, face blank, to analyze the situation before talking. Certainly, he had misheard the speaker. It had to do with his wondering from time to time what his life would have turned out to be if his junior sister had married the money magnate called Simon. Simon was known in all the newspapers as the nouveau riche of the time. He'd just moved to Ibata-Itan when he came to demand Sarah's hand in marriage, which lasted until Sarah ran off.

Wait a minute. Paul looked up and sighed as he found the answer. Simon had found Sarah!

"Simon and Sarah are back together again?"

"Not Sarah, Paul. It's a new flower, a new fruit that, with your full permission, Simon wants to pluck from your vineyard," the spokesman repeated with a smile.

That he heard clearly, and he studied the group. They were as quiet as the grave. He realized they were holding their breath. He had been keeping them in suspense. Yes, it was true: a bride's father was a king in Yoruba land until the groom married the damn bride. The power reverted to the groom as he married the bride and did his duty as an in-law to his father-in-law each year. Customarily, the woman became your wife, and practically your maid. The beauty of the culture was that no woman dared ask for a divorce. Besides, being *"dalemosu"* was degrading, shameful, and worse; where would the cast-off live in her father's house, which was bound to be as crowded as a sardine can?

Fresh, new! That's better. Paul knew this and liked it. He sensed now that he was the king of the room. He could do and undo—he owned Simon.

"That won't be a problem," he said, smiling, *"Olori-ebi,* Simon is welcome to marry from my end." Paul refrained from adding, "As many as he wants." Simon could take two for the price of one, and the culture would allow it. He would, too. Instead, he said out loud, "May I ask which one of my daughters caught his eye?" Paul felt like dancing to an invisible Bata drum as he imagined which of his young adult daughters Simon wanted.

Paul had three qualified teenagers, though one was engaged. She was Kola's immediate sister, the last daughter of Adewumi. Paul would be more than willing to refund her bride price, with interest, if it had to be her. And as for the two other daughters, to Paul, it was like flushing out his accumulated debt. He had been thinking of dashing them out as gifts to his friends, since it seemed that no man wanted them. None came to pay a dime. He had wanted to use their bride price as a bet at the ayo game, if Tunji would have accepted. They cost him nothing to dash out, and it saved him the pain of them becoming a nuisance on his shelf.

"Thanks for your cooperation, Paul. Simon wants to marry Omotola." The spokesman replied.

Joy drained from Paul's face. It was the third time he'd been startled in one night. He hated it. He never saw this particular one coming. He must be in a dream again. He was tense and confused. The emotion was so transparent in his face that all the wrinkles that could possibly live on it piled up on his forehead. Simon and Sarah as a couple, even though they had attended elementary together, was still surprising to everyone, especially Paul. He didn't realize that the jet-set, *beau monde* aristocrat had noticed his little sister in school. If Simon asking Sarah for her hand in marriage was a mystery, what could he call this now?

The spokesman cleared his throat, which brought Paul around from sitting stiffly. He glared. "Is that a joke?" he asked. "If it is, it's not funny at all. What the hell does Simon want Omotola for, when he could have one of the grown-up, instantly marriageable girls in my house? Omotola is not ripe enough to get married. Simon must he crazy then. And may I ask where the hell he found Omotola, and why he now wants her as a wife?"

Paul was scared and had to lie. He had seen Omotola at the peak of puberty—she was becoming a woman. That was one of the worries he had to gamble, to make more money to pay Jacob back before he grabbed Omotola on the road and the missionaries came to him with daggers. Paul was scared that the clerics would be all over him as ants are all over sugar. He had read in the paper what they had done to fathers like him. It was never pretty at all.

"Sorry to have misled you, Paul. Simon wants to marry Omotola to his son." Quickly the spokesman rectified what he had said and added, "As a matter of fact, the young boy found the beautiful flower himself. He loves the flower and wants the flower at all costs. Simon was thrilled at his decision, and he is willing to pay all Omotola's expenses and take her future financial burdens from your shoulders."

"Omotola isn't for Simon, but his son?"

"Not for Simon, Paul. And the beauty of it: the age difference is minimal. This is love, and—"

"There is a problem. Omotola is engaged," Paul cut in, looking sad. He hated this beautiful thing to be impossible.

"We know that, Paul; we did our research. And as for the young man she is engaged to marry, Simon has reached out to him. Omotola is now at liberty."

Paul guffawed. The others joined in. They had reasons to. There was nothing "young" about Jacob. He had been hit by triple-threat sag, despite being a few years younger than Paul, and he was as ugly as sin. Paul had agreed for him to marry Omotola because he was beggared, and Jacob was ready to buy a pig in a poke.

"Sorry for the laughter. Jacob, considered a young man? That's hilarious." Paul apologized and asked, "Simon has reached an accord with Jacob, my daughter's fiancé?"

"Yes. Paul, he has agreed to release Omotola to Akinrinola Akindele. Simon has reached out abundantly to Jacob, more generously than you can imagine," the spokesman said with pride.

Paul was stunned. "Simon reached an accord with Omotola's suitor, Jacob, right?" he asked, to ascertain if he had heard correctly.

"Yes, Paul. You have nothing to worry about from Jacob. He paid him generously, as he demanded. Paul, Jacob is a happy man."

Son of a bitch, snapped in Paul's head, since Jacob had now taken away all the fun. Paul had one wish as he gambled: to make a lot of money and throw the money Jacob spent on Omotola back in his face and call him ugly. Paul was angry. *The ugly one now settled behind his back? He is now rich at his expense? He reached an accord without his knowledge? How much did he get for his daughter?* Paul's head was hot and heavy. *His happiness will not last for long. I'll kill him if he made more than he paid.* But he had other matters at hand; Jacob's case was an issue to revisit later.

Paul smiled. "May I ask which of Simon's sons wanted Omotola as a wife?"

"His first son, Akinrinola Akindele. You must have seen him around. He is a son every father would wish for. Paul, my nephew loves your daughter to death. When the boy first told his father, Simon panicked, since he had chosen a fiancée for the boy already. He came rushing to me, and I asked my nephew if he is sure he is in love with your daughter. You know what he told me?"

Paul shook his head no.

"My nephew said he is as sure as after a night, no matter what, there's daybreak. That was his reply."

Paul staggered back a bit, almost falling from his stool. The shock was voluminous.

"How on earth did they meet?"

"School, I presume. Paul, selecting a wife by father to son will soon diminish. I remember my first wife, who was abased, belittled." The spokesman shivered. "But I was afraid. I was an idiot not to say, "No thanks, father.""

"We all did that," two of the crew members added at the same time.

Paul concurred. "They're wrong. In my own observation, only one percent of hand-over wives please their husbands."

"A young man making his own choice shows life is changing. And it makes me happy as I see that joy and fulfillment in my nephew's eye, the joy that flew away since his mother did what she did and ran off. Anyway, I'm happy he is happy, and that he found it in your daughter. Paul, rest assured that even though he is madly in love with your daughter, he'll abide by the custom. Nothing will jeopardize her schooling. I promise you that. Please, Paul, we need your answer."

Paul was fully trained on the past. It was like the old drama staged again, only the actors were different: Simon and Sarah then; Omotola and Akin now. Paul was overwhelmed. "My answer is yes," he said with pride. "I'm happy my daughter is going to marry into your family."

"If that is the case, Paul, I'll boldly say you'll never

regret this. And for the onset of a good relationship, Simon sends his starting presents to thank you for your kindness in accepting him into your home. He prays for good relationships between our families."

The spokesman brought the six bottles of assorted gins forward from the carrier's side and set them in front of Paul.

"This is for you, Paul." He removed from the pocket of his *agbada* a wallet with wads of pounds in it and placed them on Paul's lap. He then whispered in Paul's right ear, "This is an additional gift—a hundred pounds for welcoming Simon into your home."

The speaker retreated to his seat. Paul opened his mouth, and not a word came out. The stack of money on his lap was more than he had made in four years. He stood up quickly. "Please excuse me. I'll be right back with a cup to sample the drinks."

In a hurry, he went into his bedroom. And before he fetched the calabash cups for the drinks as he had promised, he went straight to hide the money under the clay gourd of water in his bedroom. Later, he fetched seven cups from one of the oke baskets in the corner of his room.

He came back to the parlor, still in a daze. He opened one of the bottles of gin and served it, both hands shaking like an old man's. The spokesman offered a prayer to cement the relationship between the two families. They all said "Amen" and drank to it. The entourage left shortly afterward.

Paul's mind was running crazy with everything. He was a dead man yesterday, raised to life today. The Jacob issue was gone, he was escaping a missionary garrote, and Omotola was marrying a boy around her own age. It was a relief, because he always saw Sarah in Omotola, and that was scary.

She won't marry just any boy, but an elite. Akin was a blue blood who would eventually take over his father's business. This was one of the rumors circulated about Simon. Paul had seen Akin and Simon at the king's palace. Paul couldn't help but wonder, how on earth did Akin find Omotola? How did a wretched man like him have a daughter who caught the eyes of an extraordinary boy like Akin? Incredible!

Paul concluded it was like his sister and the boy's father, but this time around, it was happening. "God, I'm rich, and rich, and richer. I hit the jackpot, a gold mine!" Paul sat in his thoughts, indulging in the drinks long after the men had gone.

* * *

Rolake tensed, trying harder to eavesdrop on what was going on in Paul's parlor. But she could only hear her heart at a rate that scared her to death. It was like beating a drum, *bum, bum.* It seemed about to rip her chest out at any minute. She couldn't avoid lying down. She managed to get to a sitting position, as if that would help the eavesdropping, but that didn't work either. She waited for Paul's visitors to leave.

Paul's parlor opened. The happy talk that buzzed down the corridor with Paul and his visitors pierced Rolake's heart and sank it to its lowest ebb, even though it might have nothing to do with Omotola. It might have been about the other girls in the house. She couldn't help but be worried. She knew decisions had been made, but over what? She needed to know their mission, their wants, every single detail. She had decided a few minutes earlier as the strangers entered that she wouldn't give up Omotola in a silly marriage without a fight. She would move heaven and earth. She would protect her as a mother hen protects her chicks, until she took her last breath.

Rolake had decided that only over her dead body would Omotola be dragged to a crazy wedding, especially when she had climbed another ladder in education. It meant the world to her. Omotola was happily going to secondary. She had said that she couldn't wait for school to open in September.

She heard Paul close the parlor door, and everything went quiet. The silence took its toll on Rolake. She couldn't bear it any longer. She scrambled to her feet and headed for Paul's parlor, even though she knew it was wrong. Normally, she couldn't do that; she had to be called upon. Paul might get very angry with her. She didn't care. She must know everything, especially if it was about the marriage. She needed to prepare all she could to sabotage the ill day.

Rolake took in a breath and knocked. "Aba, it is me. Can I talk to you, please?"

"Come right in, my dear wife."

Rolake was confused about what had brought the sudden affection. *Dear wife?*

She opened the door with caution and entered. Right away, she could see Paul's source of joy: one bottle of Gordon's was lying dead on the floor, and the second bottle was halfway gone.

Paul continued as she entered, "It's like you read my mind that I wanted to see you. I was just waiting for the day to break."

"I came in since I heard your visitors had left," Rolake said carefully.

"Yes, they left, and they brought these gins. Would you like a sip?"

"No, Aba. Is their coming about Omotola?"

"Yes," Paul's voice bubbled. "Omotola is going to marry the most gracious boy on earth. She'll be marrying into the Akindele family."

"If I get you right, Omotola isn't going to marry Aba Jacob?"

"Yes, my dear wife. The rough face is gone forever from my daughter's life. She'll marry into the Akindele family, not a sick one like Jacob's." Paul smiled buoyantly and continued. "One thing that still baffles me, still throws me off balance, is how Omotola got noticed by the boy. Rolake, you must have seen this boy at the palace last year. Words can't describe everything about him—his aura of glamor and gentleness was the talk of the town after the festival, and now he wishes to marry Omotola. It's just incredible; I'm the luckiest man in the world!"

Rolake could see Paul was over the moon about the new man he had just sold her daughter to. Now Jacob was sick? And Omotola's ownership just changed like that. What crazy was she engaged to this time around? Rolake felt like crying. She felt dizziness as she stood looking at Paul. She hated the new deal, because the devil she'd met may have been better than the angel she was about to meet.

Jacob, she could tell much about, but who was this new guy in the pool? And for crying out loud, the Akindele's were a vast and rich clan. Just like in every family, this boy might be one of their psychopaths. She knew Paul could sell any of his girls to the lame or the blind, as long as they were rich and ready to give Paul something to satisfy his needs. She needed to know. It was the right time to probe. Paul was overdoing himself with ogogoro; he seemed drunk, in another world.

"It's joyful, Aba," Rolake said with a wry smile. She added, "The Akindele family is big. Which one of them, Aba?" Rolake was pensive.

"You could never believe it, my dear wife," Paul said in more like a whisper. "Omotola is going to marry a young boy with glory—Akinrinola Akindele. Do you have a clue who he is?"

"No, Aba."

"Your daughter is going to marry the heir to the empire of Simon Akindele. The boy is his firstborn.'

Rolake gasped. She knew the boy, as she'd seen him at the palace once. She didn't know whether to be happy or sad, because she knew her daughter wouldn't forgo school for marriage. Watching Paul, it might be the case.

"Does he want to marry Omotola now?" Her voice trembled, waiting impatiently for Paul's response.

"No." Paul's voice fluctuated. "They're both young and still students. In fact, the boy met and fell in love with our Omotola and wants her as a wife. He promised to wait until Omotola is ready, but that's nonsense. I would prefer the wedding anytime soon, to move the marriage to now. What is Omotola going to do with education anyway? It's going to be useless."

"But, Aba, I think it should be their decision, not ours," Rolake said, holding her breath.

"Listen to me, woman!" Paul sounded angry. "They didn't come to you for approval. I'll talk to Simon to fix a date. Rolake, don't you know that fish like the son of Simon could swim to another ocean at any time? And where does that leave Omotola? Go and call her for me. I need to talk to her."

"No, where does that leave you?" Rolake said to herself as she stared at Paul.

"Go and get Omotola, I said," Paul snapped.

Rolake left.

* * *

Rolake entered her room with exultant joy, and she refused to be bothered by the moving forward of the wedding. The force of joy was intoxicating enough to make a swimmer jump into an ocean without a swimming belt or a beginner pilot jump out of a plane without a parachute. For once, since her marriage, Rolake got the verve to look at the future and smile. Certain things from Paul's explanation suited her: the new man would be around Omotola's age. And that was good! He was still in school, which meant Omotola could convince him that the wedding should wait.

"God has answered my prayers. My daughter will never fall into a dungeon. She'll never marry a stark, illiterate farmer with a cramped lifestyle like that of Paul. She'll never be a purchased item for old cargo. He would do 'til Omotola had her own voice to refuse the engagement, if she so chose. Peace is guaranteed at last," she told herself as she stood in her room, looking at her sleeping daughter on the mat. She was at peace.

Rolake sat next to Omotola on the mat to wake her up. She watched her breathing softly with occasional snores, and tears escaped from their banks again, but this time, they were tears of joy. She wiped them off with the back of her hand. Gently, she tapped Omotola on a shoulder to wake her.

"Good morning, Sunshine," she said. "Your father would like to see you right away in his parlor."

Rolake watched Omotola sit up straight, as if she had been given a dirty slap on the face. She had every right to be terrified, not to trust her maniac father. He had put fear and hatred in her since she was little. Rolake knew Omotola hated Paul.

She rubbed her eyes for a second. "Mama, why do I've to go and see Papa?"

"He'll tell you himself."

"Have I done something wrong? Is it about school, or Papa Jacob?" Omotola asked, despair in her voice.

Rolake would have been happy to be the first one to tell her daughter the good tidings, but that might make Paul swell up with rage, and that had never been a good thing. Omotola had to find out the reason from Paul, she decided.

"You just have to go and see him right away," Rolake said. "It's okay. He'll explain."

Rolake stood up. She expected Omotola to follow suit. To her surprise, Omotola stared at the door as if waiting for somebody to come in.

"Come on," Rolake said. "Don't keep him waiting…"

Chapter Thirty

Omotola was wild with dread. If Paul tried to do his thing on her body, she would be perfectly tattooed when she came out afterward. She broke down emotionally as she stepped out of her mother's room into the corridor. She flicked her eyes to check if there a way out. To her disadvantage, the main entrance and backyard door were securely locked. It was a lock-up, all right. She gave up looking for a way out.

Since nothing came to her head as it throbbed, she lamented internally: Never having the right to choose the family or household being born into was a hindrance, a handicap that rocked babies before coming into this world of violence, poverty, and deprivation. A simple glimpse, a simple peep, and a simple look—many babies would have stayed put in the baby's world forever. Certainly, she would never have chosen her father's household, where he tried out a new *koboko* whip on wives and children while his counterparts around the globe invented new technologies or did memorable things. She'd have chosen a family far away from this unstable father. Then she remembered what might be the cause of the summons— possibly her behavior at the Lion Club recruitment.

Remorse filled her. She should never have ventured to join the Lion Club or waggle her tongue and lash Wole the way she had at the waterfall. Big mistake!

Slowly, Omotola walked towards Paul's parlor. Then she saw Tutu standing at the entrance of her room. Her face was full of accusation, as if Omotola had robbed her of getting laid yesterday, as if she was the one who made her howl like a dog. She was without shame: *a youthful moron.*

Omotola stood in front of her and gave her a drop-dead look. Tutu retaliated by sticking her tongue out like a child.

"My label on you is correct," Omotola said with hatred. "You're a moron with an empty brain."

A creaking sound, footsteps, and voices were heard coming from somewhere down the corridor, from one of the rooms. Omotola looked down the hallway to see what was going on. Appearing and looming like ghosts were Moji and her two daughters. The usual *yentas* of the house were on their feet, and on a talking spree! Omotola knew that was not good at all. She shifted her eyes from their lot, trembling, more salt being added to injury as she heard more pushing and shoving somewhere else. She could hear, *"Let me see"*—probably to have a good look at her body before it was tattooed from head to toe like a zebra.

There were a lot more peeping eyes, including that of her other half-brothers from Moji. *Grown-up men! They were never any good. Out of their lineage, only their younger brother was fairer. Five out of their lineage were a pack of scumbags.*

She didn't see Kola or her sister, nor his mother,

Adewumi, since it seemed that every room had sent their delegates as witnesses. Most doorways were packed like jail cells. Omotola turned back to Tutu. "There will be plenty of time for you later. At least, I could vest my anger in you when your husband is done with the tattooing. Keep hanging in there; I'll see you on my way back," she said, peeling away from her slowly.

Yes, it is Paul's lock-up, all right. Even though "prison" isn't written on the entrance of the house, we are all his prisoners. More eyes appeared at doorframes, including that of Kola's sister.

Finally, each sends their representative. Sure, they're all waiting to find out what Miss Smarty Pants did. She shook her head at the loafers, who had nothing better to do on a holy morning but to amuse themselves with others' calamities. It probably wasn't their fault; Paul had designed his house as a lock-up to suit his purpose, for each to know what he could do to any of them if they disobeyed him. She hated polygamous homes, where privacy was always as pricey as a diamond.

Slowly, she walked through the half-open door to the parlor that was illuminated with *oguso* candles. Deliberately, she left the door open, in case a helper or a rescuer might come to her aid to get her out of her predicament—possibly Kola, whom she knew would take a bullet for her. Then she saw her father and panicked. She rooted herself to a spot near the entrance.

"Close the door, my daughter," Paul said, projecting a cheerful smile and looking straight at her.

Reluctantly, she closed the door with one hand and held tight to her wrapper with the second hand, her last hope of surviving eluding her. She was all alone in a hole with a deranged man claiming to be her father. She watched Paul like a hawk. Paul pointed a finger to stools. She sat down on the first available one, wondering, *What next?*

Paul brought a stool next to her and sat inches from her.

Omotola's eyes wandered, looking for a concealed whip, and at that moment, she actually noticed some features that she had never seen before, since she had never been in close range. Paul was a hunk, with small facial marks, like that of a cheetah. His eyes were bright, almost irresistible, like Kola's. For the first time, she saw a close resemblance between the two. She was expecting Paul's visage to be sullen and his tummy swollen with the gallons of *ogogoro* gin he consumed day and night. But he looked agile, like an athlete. She forgot her problems for a while, wondering what Paul was like in his youth. Was he like Kola, who sprinted like a cheetah? Was he mean since he was a boy?

She had once read in one of the elementary books that the sports team the Yankees hated the Red Sox, despite the fact that they played the same game. Just like Paul and Kola, they hated each other. Still, Yankees and Red Sox would always be baseball players from the same clan, the one called "the American League." The same with Paul and Kola—they would always be father and son from the same clan called Olorunfemi.

No doubt about it, her father's features gave him the upper hand to be wayward without consequences. Apart from his wives, she knew some of his concubines around the town, plus she had heard her mother and friends chatting on the subject when they thought she was sleeping. None of his wives could complain.

Unfortunately, she would always be lost when it came to knowing about Paul's past. There wasn't anybody she could ask about how he was as a boy. All she knew was that Paul was the eldest of the Gbadamosi children, a man who had had six wives in his lifetime on earth, before he died of depression. Paul was the first of the four children of his mother's lineage. Her Auntie Sarah was their only girl, and a runaway bride who might be the only sane one out of Gbadamosi's children. The rest of the male Gbadamosi children were scattered all over Ibata-Itan town and lived in clay brick houses, like Paul, with the same manners as Paul. Their women were tucked away in their husbands' houses, chosen by Gbadamosi, frustrated. At family gatherings, weddings, and other events, they behaved like pigs, and even snorted like pigs.

Paul cleared his throat. Omotola suddenly remembered that it would be her whipping time now, time to pay for her sin at the Esa waterfall. That was the only wrongdoing she could recall. To her total surprise, Paul smiled instead of taking out his weapon of mass destruction that would make her wish for death. She had seen its damage on her mother's body as each mark oozed blood and took days to heal. It took months for the marks to finally disappear.

"My daughter," Paul said evenly, "The Akindele household elders came to ask for your hand in marriage, and I accepted."

Whatever, she thought in her head, but she replied with sarcasm, "You did? That's great, Papa."

She had to wonder: why change her ownership? What had happened to Jacob? Was he dead? Who was the new highest bidder? For God's sake! Who the heck was he in the Akindele family? Maybe it was another of her father's aged buddies, the perverted ones who rough-handled cradles. She would have loved to hiss aloud, to show he couldn't harm her. She had her own plan, but she decided against it.

"Yes, my daughter, it's great. I always foresaw that you would liberate this family from poverty, especially when you decided to go to school and I allowed it."

God! What a lie. Quickly, Omotola drew her lower lip inside her mouth and stapled it shut with upper teeth so as not to scream, "Liar! It took two nun sisters and a reverend father to undo your grip."

Countless times, Omotola had been honored in the school. The headmistress had sent invitations through teachers to Paul to witness the honors, but he always bailed out.

On the last Prize Giving Day, Omotola would have wanted Paul to be there to see how the teachers appreciated her, to hear her guiding angel, Sister Teresa, as she beamed boldly with tears in her eyes, wishing her all the best in secondary school. She'd said, "You're one of a kind, Omotola. You have to believe that, and that will help you believe in yourself. Don't let people bring you down."

Paul didn't bother to show up, even though the invitation was personally delivered to him and Rolake by the headmistress, Miss Anne. Only her mother was present that day. Since she'd started school, every time she came across Paul, he treated her with disdain, or mockery, or a crazy expression—or all of the three together on his face that said, "I'll wait and see." And now she was a heroine? Besides, Paul had never forgiven Kola for enrolling her in school. *So, does that mean he is going to forgive him now, or what?*

Omotola sat like a statue as Paul continued. "Well, my endurance has paid off. And now I'm about to reap the fruits of my labor."

She released her lips, staring at Paul with disbelief in her eyes. *What on earth is he talking about?*

Omotola's school expenses, from uniform to books, were taken care of by the missionaries—apart from the food that her mother gave her, her fate hung around a missionary's neck. She decided to let Paul carry on with his garbage, as long as it didn't involve a beating weapon. She nodded to tell Paul that she was in agreement with his decisions, and he should go ahead with his formulated rubbish.

"I'm happy you agreed. And so, as from today onwards, you're not to run any errands. All you've to do is to study and make yourself beautiful. Your father-in-law is a mighty man to be reckoned with in all the regions, and his daughter in-law must always be presentable."

Interested now, she asked, "Papa, you mean I shouldn't run any errands in the house, especially fetching water?"

Every child had to fetch water in the evening, to fill the all-purpose jars in the backyard plus the one in Paul's room.

"Yes," Paul said. "You're exempt from all errands and house chores as from now on. Let the loser, good-for-nothing, set of remaining children of this house exercise that."

Paul stood up and opened the parlor door. "You can

go," he said. "But ask your mother to come and see me immediately. She has a lot of work to do in order to start grooming you to be suitable for your husband."

Omotola snapped to her feet, happy that she'd escaped scolding and flogging, but she was certain that a new, aged pig was waiting for her imminently.

* * *

She hurriedly skidded into the corridor in case Paul decided to call her back.

Kola shouted, "Way to go, Sis. I'm filled with joy!"

"So am I, Brother, so am I!" Omotola glanced at Kola, who leaned his back on the front door of Rolake and Omotola's room, facing her mom, talking.

She was impressed. She knew Kola would come out to help. He was probably waiting for the right time to barge in. Her mother was waiting too, probably to offer a shoulder for her to cry on. Omotola marched to their spot, still in her wrapper and far from the earshot of the peepers. Omotola whispered, "Kola, I've just been to the lion's den and came out without a scratch. I'm floating in joy."

Omotola flashed her beams around to hurt the *yentas* standing in front of their room, conversing. One of them hissed and disappeared inside. The rest of the peepers started to enter their rooms. She knew that they had gone in, disappointed the show was over without her crying. Perhaps they were afraid the ray of sunshine on her face might turn their stomachs inside out to reveal their evil thoughts. That's what Omotola would have wanted. She hated polygamous homes.

"So, am I, Sis. It is joyful indeed."

Omotola turned her face back to Kola and her

mother. "Kola, I was so scared, and—"

"Why would you be scared?" Kola cut in. "I'm sure joy has been leapfrogging in papa's stomach since his visitors left, and as we're speaking. Really, Sis, it's a big deal, and I'm proud of you. Your mother woke me up and asked about the résumés of your suitor in the Akindele family, since Aba told her he goes to school. She assumed we might know each other. And as soon as she mentioned Papa Simon's firstborn, who's called Akinrinola Akindele, I knew it was Akin. I was in a trance but did my best to explain who Akin Akindele really is."

"Omotola," Rolake said. "Kola told me he is a very good boy. I've never been this happy in my life."

Rolake smiled. Omotola was at a loss, thinking, *could it be true?* Because she hadn't seen her mother's smile touch her eyes in a long time. And it wasn't the fake grin she plastered on her face to make her look happy. She stared at each mouth as it spoke. But everything that came out sounded like Greek and way beyond her scope.

"No, ma," Kola said, "more than that. Akin is a divine boy who has it all. He is a nonpareil in everything. As you get to know him, you'll thank God he came into our lives."

Kola turned excitedly to Omotola. "Omotola, since I was told, I couldn't go back to sleep. *Wow,* snaps in my head with each breath I take. And I had to come out of my room before I ran crazy with thoughts. And of course, to congratulate you, my darling sister. You know, I would've heard the commotion that was in the passage when the visitors left if that wife of Papa's hadn't kicked up such a disturbance, howling like a dog. What's her problem, anyway?" He turned face to Rolake.

Rolake was embarrassed and dropped her eyes to watch her feet instead of answering Kola's question.

Meanwhile, Omotola was still at sea.

Kola asked again. "Did Papa beat her or what?"

"No, Kola, she was emotional. She is a new…" Rolake trailed off.

"Her behavior was gross. Somebody needs to tell her that people need to sleep around here. Whatever the problem she has with her husband, it should be rectified in broad daylight." Kola grunted.

Kola had played football with some friends from the neighborhood until very late. When he went to bed, he'd slept like a log—until Paul had closed his bedroom door with a bang and Tutu had lost it, crying at the top of her lungs. Almost all the people in the house heard everything that took place.

"I'll talk to her," Rolake promised. She wanted Kola to drop the subject before it got nasty. All the wives before her knew when to throw in the towel and go back to their rooms, even though they had a rendezvous with Paul on his rota. Especially when Paul didn't come back before ten o'clock in the evening and it was the last Saturday of the month. Tutu would learn. They had all had to. "I'm so glad you found a young boy around your age, Omotola. It's a relief. The world is getting much better, and…" Rolake stopped as she started to babble, and tears streamed down her face.

"Jesus, Sis," Kola said, touching Omotola's arm as she clamped both hands around her wrapper. "You just got engaged to the best boy on the planet."

"I did?" Omotola asked as she finally came around to reality.

"Yes, didn't you hear what we've been talking about? The household elders of Akindele came to ask your hand in marriage for Akin? Sis, you're marrying the greatest guy on the planet."

Kola spoke slowly for Omotola to understand. He embraced her. Omotola detangled herself fast from him. He had to hold on to Omotola's door handle for support, or else he'd have been flat on his ass.

"What are you talking about, Akin Akindele? Yeah, right. The joke of the year, right?" She frowned.

Kola said, "Not a joke, Sis. He wants to marry you. Please, ma, explain to her."

"Yes, Sunshine."

"Don't listen to him, Mama; he is just kidding. Played too much football with him yesterday and probably in his dream last night, right?"

Omotola removed her wrapper, folding it. Meanwhile, she searched desperately for confirmation from Kola's face. His nose usually wiggled when he was lying. To her surprise, that didn't happen. Only his eyeballs glinted, as if he was happy.

"No, Omotola, I didn't play ball with him last night, because he is out of the country. He will be in England throughout the month of July."

"This is not hilarious," Omotola said, frustrated. "It's not April first. The prank is foolish since it's the beginning of July. Kola, get a grip. April is long gone. His Royal Excellency, Akin Akindele, would not stoop so low to marry a girl like me. Besides, and for your information, he's been engaged to marry one of his kind from his circle. It's the daughter of a timber mogul in Ajoni-Itan. Everybody in my primary knows that."

"No, Omotola, you're wrong." Kola shook his head. "It's not April Fool's. I'm serious; you're marrying him. And everything makes perfect sense now."

"Nothing makes sense, Brother."

"It does, Omotola. At our football game last time, Akin was on a high, demanding to know about your likes and dislikes. A lot of his questions circled around you. I thought it was part of the club formality. Well, to tell the truth, I was uneasy, baffled, but I did my best to convince him of the gem you are, even though you're a 'she.' And I told him he'd never regret letting you into the club, in case he was having second thoughts, or others tried to convince him otherwise." Kola was still shaking once in a while about Bayo's statements. He didn't want to go into the length and breadth of the discussion he'd had with Bayo, so he added, "Now I realize it wasn't a second thought. All the information was for him, and I'm glad I helped. I furnished Akin with information about you—more than necessary to convince him to allow you into the club."

He stopped for Omotola's response, but she didn't reply. Kola shrugged and continued. "Sis, imagine what your engagement to Akin Akindele will fetch you at home and in school. The guy that just asked for your hand in marriage is a god with power. You should be shouting a rejoicing song with a high pitch that can be heard at the Esa waterfall, the source of your happiness. You will never be bullied in life again. Not by Papa, if he doesn't want to die in poverty, or by any student, if they want to stay in my secondary school. Omotola, going to Papa's parlor wasn't about flogging or scolding—it was about telling you that you're the most fortunate girl on earth. No more worry about that old cargo, Jacob, or worry about those inconsiderate brats in school. And as for me, a bosom friend of Akin and a bro to the most fortunate girl in the world, my future, as yours, is secure."

"You're lying," Omotola shouted. "Why didn't you tell me about the discussion with Akin until now?"

"Because I didn't want to give you a throbbing head over it," Kola grinned. "Never mind, Omotola. I'm not lying. I'm damn serious. You are going to marry Akin Akindele. Words are not enough to explain what you're about to experience."

How is that possible?

She knew, like every pupil in her primary school, that Akin's presumed fiancée, Solape, had everything in excess. One time she had visited Omotola's school, and she had emerged from a car like a goddess. She was softly spoken, elegant, with impeccable silk stockings. She was a student of a Methodist girls' grammar school in Ladden, one of the best-rated girls' secondary schools in the British provinces. If Omotola had not wanted to be nearer home, she herself would have chosen this school, since she'd been given a full scholarship to any secondary school in Nigeria. The school and the girl's background had everything to offer. And those would give her an upper hand eventually, even if it was true that Akin had missed the road for once, choosing her. Not to mention that both sets of parents would never let it happen.

She shook her head. "Think Kola, what will Akin want with a girl like me when he is engaged to a goddess? And if he's not pleased, with a snap of his fingers, she can be replaced by another goddess of his choice from his circle. Thanks for the heads up, but give it a rest!"

"That is where you are wrong, Sis. Akin is—"

"Hold your breath, Brother!" Omotola interrupted him sharply. "I'm optimistic, but not that much." Her patience finally worn off, she added, "Mama, your husband wants you for…" She failed to grasp the purpose and concluded, "Whatever he wants you for."

"That's okay, Sunshine," Rolake said softly, leaving for Paul's parlor.

Tutu appeared in front of her room as if she'd been called. Her eyes followed Rolake's retreat. Omotola watched her in silence. As soon as Rolake entered the parlor, Tutu turned towards Omotola and Kola. Omotola shot a dark eye at her, and Tutu shot her own back, then watched the entrance to Paul's parlor intensely.

She'll learn, like the rest of us, Omotola thought, turning her back on the woman. She faced Kola. "And as for you, my delusional dreamer brother, Akin is way out of my league. I'm pretty sure he'll be more comfortable within his own society."

Without waiting for Kola to reply, she entered her mother's room to resume her ruptured sleep.

જી

Chapter Thirty-One

Rolake walked in as Paul bent to blow out the candles because daylight had arrived. She could see the beauty and the mystique of his form. Paul straightened up and gave his full attention to her, with a stunning smile that could open up any woman's legs in the world. Rolake just stood fascinated, trying to curb the enthusiasm to touch him and ask him for sex right away. Finally, she sent out a weak smile. "Omotola said you want to see me."

"Yes, I've things to go over with you pertaining to the engagement of our daughter. Shall we go into the other room to discuss them?"

Paul's voice was smooth, seductive, anger-free, a departure from their discussions earlier on.

Rolake was touched. She knew what going to the other room meant, and perhaps the other room wouldn't be necessary since she felt the same way he did. They could just do it right away, where they were. She could walk up to him as a woman; she had her needs, even though she knew Paul was a rake, a devourer of women.

She had been blown off by Paul more than three times in the previous month, and the preceding months had not been good, either. Paul had been stressed lately, driven by mood swings. But for some reason, she knew his sudden invitation was wrong. She pushed the feelings away. And it was easy, because when you've been in the desert for a long time, you know how to survive.

She knew better than to succumb to temptation, to make love to Paul in broad daylight and revel in the physical aspect that attracted women as sugar attracts ants. She also knew better than to be swept away with charm used deliberately to seduce, to conquer. What excitement and happy mood produced by the sudden serotonin in his body could be drowned in a second. Paul was a man of the moment. He lived in the moment and, as in any moment, a teeny thing could sour it, could rise and overcome the adrenaline in his body, and he would start throwing a fit of rage.

"Your bedroom!" Rolake demanded sharply. "Why not here, Aba?"

"Yes. There is better." Paul said, turning towards the parlor exit. Rolake had no choice but to follow.

He entered his bedroom without giving a second glance to the girl, Tutu, who flattened her body against her bedroom doorframe like a lizard does to a wall, and who was on the brink of crying. Rolake hesitated; she wanted to say something to her.

Maggi Rule Five (the last rule). Be ready to defend your position from all the competitors with all your might. Use whatever is available, and that includes insults and combat. That will bring fear and respect, since you never know how long you're going to live in the hole.

"*Agba iya aje*. My mother was right; you're all old wicked and witches!" Tutu said, crying. She ran inside her room and slammed her door shut.

Rolake felt bad, and she knew right away why Paul's charm couldn't work on her in his parlor or bedroom. With strong determination to resist any advances, reluctantly, she followed Paul into his bedroom. She waited near the door and made no effort to close it as Paul always insisted.

"Close the door and come here," Paul ordered.

He patted a space for her on the mattress he was sitting on. Rolake declined the offer by shaking her head.

"Paul," she said abruptly. Paul's eyeballs were cold. She couldn't believe she'd just called him by his name. Probably the adrenaline level in her gut was so high that she wanted to provoke him. And after a moment of hesitation, she added. "I'm fine here. Tell me what you want."

"I don't want much, Rolake. All I want from the mother of my glorious daughter is to sit with me on this mattress, and that we share the moment."

Paul flashed a smile full of charm, full of seduction. He made no reference or angry remark for being called by his name. Normally, in the past, that could have earned Rolake a lot of suffering, but she was not flattered, not blown away with cajolery. As far as Rolake was concerned, she felt she had to be bold and resist his sexual advances.

Rolake shook her head again. "When a young girl prepares all day long," Rolake frowned, "she becomes inflamed, head to toe—her body says, 'Ready for action tonight.' When she waits with eagerness for her husband to come and gets treated like a doormat … it's evil, Paul."

Saying "Paul" the first time may have been a simple mental lapse, in response to Tutu's pain, despite the provocation it entailed. But this second time around, she had said "Paul" intentionally. She didn't care about his reaction. She waited for Paul's anger to strike. He had withdrawn his smile and seemed sad and maybe angry as he sat stiffly, looking straight at her. Rolake knew she had provoked a sleeping tiger, and she waited for the attack … but the opposite happened. His face softened into a grin.

"Paul—you said that twice," he murmured softly. "I like it. But that familiarity must be strictly between us. Rolake, I know you're talking about Tutu, but she has to wait until I want her. I've the prerogative to choose the woman I desire to be with, and it is you now."

"No, Paul." She smiled. "I'll pass this morning."

There was an interlude of silence. Paul smiled back.

"All right then, if that is what you want, I'm okay with it. You know, Rolake, that you're the boldest out of all my wives, and don't think I didn't know that. Call Tutu for me, would you?"

"Yes."

Rolake was at the exit.

"Tomorrow night is our night, then."

Rolake turned from the door post and said, "I'll be all yours." Silently she added, *Paul.*

He smiled, and Rolake was gone.

* * *

On her way to Tutu's room, Rolake couldn't be happier that she was bold enough to refuse Paul sex. Still, a nagging, banging voice in her head told her how stupid it was to have walked away from probably a once-in-a-lifetime opportunity to see Paul naked in the brightness of daylight. And to use the opportunity to impose some rules on him, since Paul would do anything to make her support him in getting Omotola married to the newest bidder. Paul was as excited as a puppy, and it was an ideal moment—but at what cost and for how long could she hold his focus on her? She could never do that to Tutu or jeopardize the happiness of her daughter for her own selfish ends. Walking away was the right thing to do. She tried to believe it.

Rolake knocked at Tutu's door. No answer. She tried again. *Has she stepped out?* She stood, wondering: *if she had, and with Paul waiting, in the mood for sex, she could be in a lot of trouble when she gets back.* Concerned, she rapped the door again, to no answer. She got fed up with knocking, and she opened the door. Her eyes zoomed around the room until they finally settled on the corner Tutu had crawled to. She held her sleeping baby close to her chest, as a little girl holds her doll for comfort, as if to say, "*It's me and you against the world.*"

Tutu looked tense and seemed lost in her own world. Rolake pitied her—a young girl with her first child, abandoned in a corner like the rest of them. She could still remember her first years in Paul's house. She had been tossed aside as well. Paul went after her best friend. She didn't feel his absence around her, though, because she hated him and would've killed him in his sleep if she'd had the opportunity. But her heart was aching for Tutu. She had just been dumped like a bag of rice in the corner. Rolake knew how painful it would be for her at that age. She needed all the affection there was, to make her into a responsible woman. Tutu's life was like a projection of what Omotola's life would have been, had she not chosen school. For the millionth time, Rolake beamed.

Everything was coming together for good.

Rolake cleared her throat to announce her arrival. Tutu looked up with hatred shooting from both eyeballs, and her baby wriggled in her arms, crying.

"I'm sorry to disturb you and the baby. It's just that Paul wants to see you."

Tutu didn't speak, but started rocking her baby back and forth. The baby stopped crying and dumped her left thumb into her mouth. And gently, she settled her head on her mother's chest.

"Oh, Omotola junior, she is on to her left thumb too!"

Tutu just sulked and seemed as if she were not going to respond.

"Tutu, don't be stupid and risk being beaten this morning," Rolake added. "Paul is waiting for you in his bedroom; he wants to see you. And I shouldn't have to remind you what happens when he gets impatient."

"I thought he was seeing you?" she croaked.

"No, I went with him to discuss Omotola. That's all."

Tutu eyed Rolake suspiciously and went back to sulking without a word.

"Nothing happened, Tutu," Rolake said reassuringly. "It's your turn, and I'm not cruel enough to take it from you. I know how much you prepared for it, and…" Rolake trailed off, not knowing what to say anymore. She stood and watched Tutu just staring into space.

"Okay, I'll go. If you change your mind," Rolake said, eventually, "You know where to find your husband … if he doesn't find you first."

Rolake turned to leave.

"Omotola sucked her left thumb too?" Tutu asked.

"Yes," Rolake confirmed as she turned to face the girl, who sounded a bit brighter. "Omotola is a lefty."

"And you let her do it?" Tutu asked sharply. "What about society? I mean, when she goes to her husband's house. I mean, when she marries Aba Jacob? Won't she be sent back home?" Tutu said, rushing everything out.

Rolake smiled. "Tutu, I don't care what society says. All I care about is my child's welfare. To hell with society! I could never go to the extent the other mothers go to. Bind their children's left hand with rope and hang it around their neck as if the arm is broken, as if they have fractures, so they won't be able to use the hand. No, she is left-handed, and that's it."

"So, what do you tell people? I mean, when they shout at you and make it your fault?"

"Nothing, I just walk away. And if they're asking nicely, I'll tell them nicely that I'm working on it. And that's it. I won't inflict pain on my daughter to please the world."

"I know it's hard to change that attitude in a child without pain. I've been talking to mine, taking out the left thumb and replacing it with the right one. She'll just wait for a few seconds before changing it to the thumb she wanted. I'm worried sick about when she grows up. I mean, of marriageable age. I know that soon your daughter is going to marry. Do you think Aba Jacob would tolerate that?"

"Oh, no; thank God for his miracle in my life! That frog face won't marry my daughter."

"She is engaged to him, right?" Tutu was confused.

"Not anymore. She is marrying the son of Aba Simon Akindele, his firstborn."

Tutu was taken aback. "Are you serious?"

"Yes, and that was what the morning commotion was all about. The elders of the Akindele family came to ask for her hand in marriage, for their boy. That is what I was discussing with our husband. And speaking of our husband, you've got to go. Or else—"

"He can screw himself," Tutu cut in. "I don't care. I'm more interested in what we're talking about, especially the welfare of my daughter, rather than a man who wanted me as an afterthought. So, Ma Moji and Pa Jacob could have each other fully then?"

Rolake busted out laughing. She had never seen Tutu so defiant. Or known that she knew about the Moji and Jacob thing. She had thought the girl was a crybaby. And she had also thought she was the only one that knew about the two. That secret she had promised to take to the grave, to avoid turmoil and tension. Rolake walked inside Tutu's room and closed the door gently. "You knew about them too?" Rolake asked.

"Yes, ever since the start of my six months in this hole. He came one afternoon when all of you had gone to the farm. He was as startled as a statue to see me at the front door and, when he finally got a grip of himself, he said he had brought medicine for our *iyale.*" (*Iyale* is the respectful name for senior wives), and Tutu continued. "Our *iyale* I had seen in the morning, before I dashed to my parent's home, hale and sound. In my own opinion, she thought I would be gone all day as usual, which is probably why she invited him over. They were together for hours in her room. Besides that day, I've walked in on them more than twice. I pray Paul walks in on them, or I might tell him myself. She is a woman full of garbage. She told me infidelity is wrong. And yet she enjoys intercourse with another man at will."

Tutu sounded upset and betrayed.

"Tutu, you just have to let it go. Our *iyale* can entertain herself the way she wants. Don't let us make it our business. And one more thing, this conversation never happened."

"Why are you so unconcerned about her or angry with her?"

"Because it doesn't matter, Tutu. Our husband is doing much worse."

"So, we just pretend and look the other way while Ma Moji and Pa Jacob enjoy themselves right in front of our noses? To me, that's wrong," Tutu complained.

"Tutu, I know it is wrong and annoying, but looking the other way is probably the best. We pretend to be ideal wives without an enmity between us because Paul is like a serpent and never ventures to wipe his mouth. He never gives a damn about any of us. Being at each other's throats is like being fools. Just look the other way, Tutu, and take care of your kid."

Tutu's face softened, full of praise, full of admiration.

"I'll always admire you for your simplicity. You're great, and I'm just so happy talking to you. You can't know how relieved I am that the left hand doesn't matter, that I shouldn't rack my brain about it—you know how much I love and respect you right now?"

"Tutu, some of the children in this house take after their father, our husband Paul. Next time Paul wants to reach for you, check which hand comes first! Our husband is a lefty, and some of his children take after him. Look at Moji's two daughters, they are not lefty, and they are still on the shelf. And look at my daughter. As lefty as she is, right from birth, she got a suitor even though I'd have killed him before letting him marry my daughter. And now there's a great suitor. So, breathe, Tutu."

"I can't believe she is marrying into the Akindele family." Tutu gasped. "I heard their women are always imported from all over the world. Well, they send their men all over the world to look for the best. And Omotola is marrying an heir of Aba Simon Akindele. I just can't comprehend it. Where do you think they met?"

"My best bet is school, although I haven't asked her yet."

"I'm happy for you. And I pray mine goes to school and meets someone special. Not the dregs from around the corner. Do you think Aba will allow other children to go to school? At least, I want my daughter to—"

"Tutu, Paul is waiting," Rolake cut in softly. "We can discuss this another time. And right now, let me take your daughter, so you can meet your husband."

"Right."

Rolake relieved her of the baby, placing her on her shoulder. The child went back to sleep immediately. Tutu stood up, straightening her wrapper.

"You're my hero. I love you."

Tutu touched Rolake gently on the arm.

"Go, Tutu! He is waiting. Take your time."

She smiled and was gone. She looked so young and innocent. She wasn't cut out for a depraved house like Paul's. But here she was, just like other innocent girls—in the prime of life, hurled into crazy marriages, at the mercy of more senior wives like the crafty, deceitful Moji. They both knew her as the worst tramp amongst decent women—a dog among the sheep. And her children were not any better.

Rolake hoped Tutu would learn fast to accept people the way they were—people who preached what they could never do, just to make themselves look forthright. She hoped the girl would not cause a rift, because it was never worth it. Paul was never worth it.

Rolake was over the moon, knowing that her Sunshine would not wind up in a hole with Jacob's wives, as well as Moji and other concubines who were old enough to be her grandmothers and great-grandmothers. If it came to the worst. Omotola would, at least, be her husband's first wife.

Chapter Thirty-Two

Omotola had left Kola with the promise of going back to sleep, but she couldn't sleep, so full of thoughts. She sat on the mat, watching the front door of the room she shared with her mother—a space they inhabited as frequently as she breathed. She wanted her mommy now. She would have stood up and yelled, "Mama, I need you now!" if she wasn't afraid that this was all a dream. Besides, Paul would go crazy if awakened by noise from an uncultured girl. Then, all hell would break loose.

The truth was, since she saw Akin on his father's balcony years before, he been in her dreams, a delicious fantasy. It was a secret she never told anybody. Now that her dream and fantasy had come to life, she felt frightened. At one point, she had checked her body for bruises to see that she wasn't thoroughly beaten, perhaps forced to take a concoction that made her hallucinate. And nope, not a scratch! She had pinched herself more than twice on each of her arms to test that she wasn't in a dream with Akin Akindele again. Finally, she pinched herself harder, and "*ouch*" came out this time. She wasn't dreaming. She was awake. No concoction and no hallucinating. Yep, all the things she had heard *must* be true.

But she needed help now, before she went crazy. In her dreams, she had been in a full romantic relationship with Akin Akindele on several occasions. She loved every minute of it—his physicality, the kissing, all that she could handle in a dream. But in reality! That, she could *not* handle. She needed motherly advice, motherly coaching, motherly everything. The sight of Rolake and a baby through the doorway surprised Omotola.

"What took you so long, Mama? And whose baby is that?' Omotola quizzed her, annoyed that someone else had caught her mother's attention.

"Don't tell me you're jealous of the baby I'm holding?" Rolake said, smiling.

"No, Mama, it is just that I've been waiting for you for a long time." She hesitated, pointing with a frown. "Whose baby is that anyway?"

"Tutu's daughter."

"Tutu's daughter!" Omotola screeched. "She allowed you to carry her princess? That is unbelievable. Do you know how many times I asked her to let me hold her baby, since you refused to give me a sister or brother?"

Rolake looked guilty. She closed the door with one heel and walked toward Omotola.

"I'm sorry, Sunshine; I didn't know you wanted to see me. I'm sorry that I haven't been able to give you another sibling. It is just…"

Sadness swept over Rolake. The lack of conception had never been her fault, as she couldn't choose a mating time with Paul. He decided. The few times she got pregnant, she either had stillbirths or miscarriages. She felt for her daughter in a house where other children had siblings. It had been a nightmare since she wanted more children to complement her Sunshine, but she just had to wait.

Omotola felt it.

"I'm sorry I said that, Mama. It's just because I'm confused about everything since this morning, and I've been waiting to talk to you. So, where is Tutu, anyway?"

"She is … busy," Rolake said unevenly.

"And left you with her precious?" Omotola's face was alarmed. "It must be life and death then. She sees everybody as a "dropper" and her baby as an egg that can be smashed into pieces. She seems to have a dark mind, never trusting anybody."

"Omotola, you have to cut her some slack. This is her first baby, and technically, she is a child herself. When I had you, I was like her, binding you to me everywhere I went. Give her a chance, Sunshine. Would you like to hold the little one now?"

"Not now, Mama. Maybe later. It's just…" Omotola stopped, her face deeply dejected.

"Talk to me, Sunshine," Rolake said, concerned.

She lowered herself with the baby onto the mat next to Omotola. She managed with one hand to spread Omotola's wrapper out like a sheet for the baby to sleep on. She did, without a fuss. Rolake touched Omotola on her lap.

"What's the problem, Sunshine?"

"Mama, please tell me the truth. Am I really engaged to Akin Akindele?"

"Yes, it is true. The elders of their house came and left."

"God!" Omotola screamed.

"Omotola, I know it's scary, as Paul dumped you in the laps of the highest bidders, but you can decide what you want for yourself in the future. You don't have to marry him. You could finish your studies and move out of town if that is what you want. Be like your Auntie Sarah. Omotola, the boy has promised that your relationship will never tamper with your studies. And I'm happy to hear that. That will give you the opportunity to finish your schooling without Paul's interference. Sunshine, this is a chance not to miss! We'll seize it. Sunshine, don't be depressed. I should get breakfast ready. You can watch the baby for me."

"Mama, I'm not hungry. It seems you don't get why I'm scared?"

"I thought it was because you didn't like him."

"No, Mama," Omotola cut in. "Do you have dreams, and the dreams come true?"

Rolake looked straight at the wall. She could see the cheap wall plaster that Paul used, and its cracks here and there. It was just a matter of time before something longer than a lizard gate-crashed the rooms. Rolake didn't have to think harder, because none of her dreams ever came true. She had wanted to be the first wife of Dapo, perhaps his only wife, have more than five children with him, and live in love. All that had been shattered. The dreams had broken. All life had offered her was a den of lions.

"No, love," Rolake said, turning back to Omotola, "all my dreams are in the past, and never came to pass. So, I live in reality. Sunshine, what are your dreams?"

Omotola sighed. Anybody could hear it. "Mama, Akin Akindele has been in my dreams."

"Oh!"

"I fell in love with him the day he treated me like nobody, when I saw him on his father's balcony and I said hello. He ignored me. He looked past me. Even though I told myself I hated him then, he has been fervently in my dreams. I never tell anyone, but I love him, Mama."

"Sunshine, you're too young to love." Rolake was astonished. "You don't know what love is."

"Mama," Omotola said strongly, "that is a lot of crap. You can fall in love anytime. Don't tell me you didn't have your mind set on a boy before being shipped to Aba's house." Omotola narrowed her eyes.

This time around, it was Rolake who let out a loud sigh. She turned her face back to the cracked wall to avoid eye contact.

Dapo never lived nearby, but he came to see his grandmother, who lived next door. He was a little boy then, and Rolake was a little girl too. They met and innocently liked each other. Even before his voice broke and before she started her menstrual cycle, Dapo had already told her that he would marry her as soon as they were grown up, because she was the girl of his dreams. Unfortunately, he couldn't come up with the bride price.

"Sunshine, you're absolutely right." Rolake agreed with her.

"So how did you fall in love, Mama? I would like to know."

There were things Rolake never wanted to talk about. Her past with Dapo was one of them. She looked sad.

"Omotola, I know as long it takes, you won't let the issue go because you're searching for answers," Rolake said. "But I'll tell you this once. I was with a neighbor one day. The neighbor was advanced in age, loved me even more than my mother ever did. We were sitting in front of the house she lived in when a boy broke free from his mother's hand and ran to the woman. As he wrapped his hands around the woman, our eyes met, and that was it. It was magical. In the next few minutes, he took me away from his grandmother and his mother, and we spent time together. Yes, Omotola, that day was always in my dreams, because I replay it in my mind daily."

"Do you still see him?"

"Not a lot. I avoid him if I can, because the past still lingers in our brains each time we accidentally meet. We both feel uncomfortable being next to each other, and it is painful for both of us, since there is nothing we can do about it. Omotola, he married one of my best friends. I would rather die than cheat on her with him." Rolake started to sob. Omotola placed one hand on her arm, gently caressing it to console her as Rolake admitted, "It's painful, Sunshine."

"I'm scared of the same thing happening to me," Omotola said, truly worried. "I love him, Mama, but it is just scary to be engaged to him. It is one thing to have him in my dreams, and it is another matter to have him in real life. Mama, between us, Akin is every girl's dream, I know that. And how am I going to cope with that? You know the worst part?"

Rolake shook her head, brushing off the tears with both hands.

"He is engaged to a rich, highborn girl, Mama. How am I going to take him away from her? What would happen? Is he going to be engaged to the two of us and choose later, or what?"

"Sunshine, you'll have to ask him, since you like him.

Had it been what I thought—that you didn't like him—I'd have just advised you to play along until you've finished your studies. But now it's different. I'm just as troubled as you are right now. Sunshine, you have to ask him."

"Mama, I can't ask him. He is in Britain for one month's holiday. Kola said that. I'm worried. I don't think the parents of the girl would allow me in just like that. Apart from that, Mama, I don't speak his language or live in his world."

"I thought he spoke Yoruba and *Ede-Geesi,* like you. And lives in Ajoni-Itan town like you?" Rolake said, smiling, trying to cheer her up.

"Mama, stop teasing. You know what I'm talking about." Omotola enumerated her worries: "I swear, I've a temper, I'm a lefty, and worst of all, I'm plain, from an indigent home. Those are the few drawbacks that I can recollect."

"Omotola, if there is one thing I know in life, it's that love has no boundaries," Rolake said, reassuring her. "Love doesn't discriminate. And one other thing—beauty is in the eye of the beholder. Pure love doesn't see blemishes, doesn't see inadequacy. Everything is beautiful. Sunshine, don't sell yourself cheap. You're the smartest, the most caring, and toughest girl in town. How many girls were ever courageous enough to commute kilometers in a day, five days in a week, come rain come sunshine, to school without giving up—especially when home and school are on fire about it? And on top of that, you're the best in your class. Even though I can't read and write, Sister Teresa shows and explains everything to me when they give you prizes at the end of the year. Akin must have fallen in love with you, head over heels in love with you, to have asked his family to come over. I'm sure he must have seen everything I see. You've nothing to fear. You're equal to any "high-cheeks" girl, and he is not going to be short of your *idana* money, as it happened to me. Sunshine, shine as you were born to."

"Thanks, Mama."

"I'm glad I could be of help. Breakfast now."

"I'll watch the baby for you." Omotola peeped at the baby. "She sleeps a lot. Maybe her mother crying yesterday night disturbed her sleep as well."

"Maybe," Rolake said, standing up, smiling. "I'll be right back."

She left in a hurry.

❧

Chapter Thirty-Three

Adewumi was dressed in *buba, iro,* and a scarf that had seen better days. On one shoulder dangled a shawl, and underneath her armpit was tucked a reasonably sized basket while the second hand gripped a machete.

"Kola, are you coming or not?" Adewumi shouted as she knocked for the third time on the door of the room Kola shared with his half-brothers.

She could hear grunts and struggles.

"Kola," Adewumi said, "if it is too early for you, you can come along tomorrow to help. I'll go. I'll see you later. There are some leftover cooked yams from yesterday in the pot in my room, which you can warm up and eat with *igba* sauce or find something else. See you."

Abruptly, Kola opened the door, dressed in jeans and a white t-shirt. Desperately, he adjusted his clothing and fastened his pants buttons. Adewumi frowned.

"Kola, those clothes are too good for where we are going," she advised. "We are going to work, not for leisure."

"It's okay, Mama."

Adewumi gave Kola's clothes another examination.

"Mama!" Kola said.

"All right, let's go." She shrugged. "It's just that I can't afford to buy new clothes now, and…" Adewumi stopped, looking depressed.

"Mama, all you've done, I appreciate," Kola said candidly. "You don't have to worry a lot about me. I'm in the Lion Club now, and I've generous friends."

"You mentioned that before. I keep forgetting." Adewumi smiled, looking at the sky, praying, "I'm thankful to God for that opportunity."

Kola could come and go in Akin Akindele's house, as he could come and go with his stuff. Since being friends with him, the pain of wanting had ceased.

Adewumi turned toward the exit of the house and Kola followed, still struggling to put his clothes in order. They walked outside to sunshine whose rays could dry a very wet cloth in five minutes.

"Look, the sun is really up the in the sky, and that means we're late and we have to hurry up."

"I'm sorry to have kept you waiting." Kola apologized as he leveled with Adewumi. "I played football with friends yesterday, and so aimed to sleep until dawn and wake you up, until that *iyawo* sabotaged it all." He was referring to Tutu, the newest wife. "She cried like a baby for a long time, and I couldn't go back to sleep. When I finally did, Omotola's mom woke me up to say that the family of Papa Simon Akindele had come to ask for Omotola's hand in marriage, for my friend Akin."

"You are a friend with Aba Simon's son?" Adewumi was puzzled. "I never knew that. And I don't think I've met him. You should probably invite him for dinner one of these days."

"True, you never met him. I've never invited him home. And I'm not going to invite him over. It would be suicide," Kola said sadly.

Who would invite an aristocrat to a vulgar home, on fire with abuse? One where uproar and brawling can erupt at any time? Paul could go into an insane tirade on purpose, not to mention others, simply to embarrass Kola in front of a friend. Adewumi processed the reasons in her head.

"I'm sorry, Kola," Adewumi said, apologizing. "I keep forgetting the world we live in."

She stopped to fold her shawl and put it on her head, then placed the basket on it and resumed walking.

"Mama, I can carry those for you," Kola said.

"You sure? I mean, you might not want your friends to see you carrying…"

"Mama, I can carry them." Kola insisted.

He took the basket and the machete from Adewumi. Adewumi unfolded her shawl and placed it back over her shoulders.

"So, a lot happened last night and this morning too?" Adewumi asked, wanting to know more.

"Mama, you didn't know any of this?" Kola was surprised.

"Kola, I woke up at five in the morning yesterday to gather two trips' worth of firewood to sell from a far-away farm, and finally managed to prepare dinner. I knew that I had to go to the farm as early as possible today since your brother-in-laws promised the same—"

"So the two are coming to the farm?" Kola interrupted.

"No, Kola, the two of them are at the farm right now," Adewumi said pointedly, throwing a disapproving look at him. "As a matter of fact, we are supposed to be at the farm by now, but no—thanks to you, my alarm clock that didn't work. Kola, the last thing that could disrupt my sleep, since you've promised to wake me up early, would be riots between husband and wife. So, why was Paul going crazy?"

"Sorry, Mama." Kola smiled. "In all honesty, I don't know what happened between her and Papa. Except Papa slammed his door shut with a noise that woke me up. The poor girl wailed in the corridor."

"Uh," Adewumi said. "It was the last Saturday of the month; Paul would have been at an ayo game. He mostly comes back in an unpredictable mood." Adewumi adjusted her shawl. "It is one of the worst days to be near your father. She'll learn."

"Because he would have gambled all his money away at the ayo pool as usual," Kola said knowingly, "and become miserable."

When Kola was little, twice the sharks had come to force Paul to pay up, only he didn't have the money. The members of the Olorunfemi clan had to rake up money from here and there to pay up. Adewumi hated her son being exposed to that as a little boy.

She changed the subject. "So, how did it go with the elders of Simon Akindele's house and Paul? Did he chase them away?" Adewumi said.

"Why would he do that if he wants to live and not die in the mucus of poverty?" Kola said. "He accepted, of course."

Adewumi stopped walking, standing rigid, remembering Paul's visit a few weeks earlier. "*You're a stupid woman. If I ever hear that you've gone to Simon*

Akindele's farm to work as a laborer, that day you'll be out of my house. That idiot you're working for killed my father! Adewumi, I'll never tolerate a traitor in my house."

"Then how do you want me to live and feed my children when you take everything from me?"

"I don't care how you live. But you set foot on that farm again; you are out of my house. You and your stupid son will be out of my house."

Adewumi had cried, devastated, for days.

"You okay, Mama?" Kola said, wondering what made her stand, rooted to the spot.

"I'm okay. It's just strange he accepted. Come on, Kola, let's keep walking."

"Why so, Mama?"

"Because early this summer, he rushed into my room and forbade me to set foot on Simon's farm for the harvest of cocoa this year. He said Simon is his number-one enemy. He killed his father. Kola, I had to cry to your sisters for help, and one of their husbands gave me the land—"

"Mama," Kola cut in, infuriated, "why didn't you tell me all this before now? I would've—"

"No, Kola, forget I mentioned it." She interrupted him with a shaky voice. "I'm sorry I mentioned it. I never wanted you to find out, since I knew you'd be mad. A day never passes when I don't remember the time you almost cut Paul's head off because of me. And each time, it sends a cold shiver down my spine. At that tender age, he would have provoked you to commit a murder. You'd have thrown your life away!" Adewumi sobbed. "I would never have forgiven myself if that had happened. And I'm sure Paul's deranged sons would've killed you. Bloodshed would have been rampant. I never prayed for that. I never wanted him to drive you crazy with frustration. All I want is to be there for all of you, to see you grow up and settled. Son, I'm tired of uproar, chaos..."

Adewumi looked helpless.

"I-i-it j-j-just..." Kola started, stammering and stopped.

Adewumi wiped her face. "I always wondered how a father could hate a carbon copy of himself. You got so much from Paul."

"Mama, he has no right to stop you from living. He took everything and still has the guts to tell you what to do? Mama, that is outrageous! If you had told me, I would have given him a piece of my mind. But if you still want to go to the Akindele farm, I'm a hundred percent behind you. He can't stop you from living."

"Son, it doesn't matter. I can't go back, even though Paul is in reconciliation with the killer of his father because of Omotola's engagement. Sometimes it is good to stay aloof, because if anything happens to the relationship, I'll be Paul's target. Son, I don't want that. All I want is to feed and be the mother of my children. And I'm happy; I'm almost there. As your last sister gets married and you finish your schooling, going abroad as you told me you'll do, I'll go back to the trade I learned from my mother."

"What trade is that, Mama?"

"Your grandmother wove shawls to carry babies until she became ill with a hand-shaking sickness. I had resolved to do that when Paul took away everything, but it takes time, and I need immediate and constant money."

Kola's face was full of pity.

"I pray I get a scholarship to study medicine, become a doctor, and give you the world," he said, feeling guilty.

"Honey, I know you'll give me the world," she said with pride.

"We should've moved to your parents' house, as I suggested, instead of staying with this control freak."

"And live where?" Adewumi asked. "On top of his wives? You see how they are packed in like sardines. Besides, *oko lade obirin.*" She recited the old saying that "a woman's crown is a man." She explained to her son, "It is a disgrace for a woman to go back to her parents' house, even if the parents allow it and can afford to pay back the bride price. *Dalemosu* women are looked down on. Their lives are never the same. Kola, my problem will be over as soon as you fulfill your wishes in life. And any day you can't come to the farm this summer because of your club, just let me know. Helping me on the farm is not do-or-die. You need to relax and be with your friends."

"Actually, Akin left with his father for Britain, so there are no activities of the club this summer. So, I'm free, except for a few days next week. I have to teach a girl some activities of the club."

"Uh—a girl," Adewumi said curiously. "Anybody I know?"

"No, she is not someone you know. She is not from here. She is just a friend."

"She is your girlfriend then?" Adewumi said, brightening up.

Adewumi was conversant with quite a lot of girls, frequently helping them, in the hopes of matching one up with Kola. She could have made a move on behalf of Kola on one, in particular, that she liked, although that was supposed to be Paul's role. Some in Kola's age group were starting to get married. However, Adewumi knew better than to lead any girl on. Kola might never want to settle for an illiterate.

"Mama, please, can we not talk about this? She is just a girl I know and am willing to … help," Kola stammered, wiggling his nose.

"Kola, why not—she is more than just any girl, isn't she? Because your face said otherwise! You have that trait, the tic on your face like that of your father when lying."

"Mama, okay, yes," Kola said, sighing. "But she is from the upper class. Her parents are around Simon Akindele's level. And I'm not sure of anything."

"Sure of anything, what do you mean?" she said, anxious for a reply.

"I don't know if she likes me. She only asked me to train her for the next club recruitment, and her parents…" Kola stopped.

"Kola, the girl would be stupid not to want you if you make your intentions known to her."

"That's easy to say. But, even if she likes me, what about her parents? Mama, it would've been easier the other way around—like Akin and Omotola."

Kola looked dispirited.

"Son, it is like giving birth to a child. When the head is out, the rest is easy. I'm talking from experience."

Kola was disgusted, and he exploded. "Mama, what type of explanation is that? What do I know about a baby being born?"

"Sorry, I should have used a more familiar example. When you hold a snake by the head, you conquer the whole body. Better now."

"No, Mama. They are gentry. And their marriages orbit around their circles."

"If Akin Akindele, your friend, is to marry from our family, it says a lot," Adewumi said with conviction. "Omotola is a wonderful girl who, I'm sure, will fit in anywhere, just like you. My only prayer is for Paul not to spoil the relationship. So, when can I meet her?"

"Are you hearing what I'm saying, Mama?" Kola said, nonplussed at Adewumi's adamant beliefs. "Apart from the class, other things … my speech … I can't…"

"Yes, son, I hear you correctly. And I know you're worried about stammering. And since I'm sure you take everything from Paul, that part won't be a problem. Paul is as smooth as a baby's butt when it comes to the act of wooing. For a long time, he had me fooled. The only thing that brings out that defect is anger. Wooing comes naturally. He is a fox, and … forget I said that." Adewumi fidgeted, quickly adding, "I mean, your father has qualities."

Kola smiled. "Mama, please stop the cover-up. I know what you're talking about. I know some of his you-know-what's around here. And all he ever does is chase them and go crazy."

"It's because he is frustrated," Adewumi said.

"I can't believe you're defending him after all he's done," Kola said, astounded.

"I know it sounds that way, but your father was a complete gentleman in the beginning. He was among the best in Ijakadi then. And the best ayo game player until…" Adewumi's voice cut off.

"Until what, Mama?"

"Until his sister left. He got deep into gambling, and

when his father died, then he lost it. Your grandfather, on the other hand, I'll say was strange—not Paul."

"But my grandmother told me he started to be erratic after he dropped out of school. She warned me not to be like him."

"That I never knew. All I know is that he has changed and has been in more tempestuous seas since your auntie ran away. Kola, you should've seen her. She was a beauty during her lifetime. She was engaged to your friend's father, Aba Simon. Did you know that?"

"Yes, Papa mentioned her name and circumstances a couple of times when he was trying to lure me out of school. Why do you assume she is dead? She might still be alive, but hiding."

"I don't think so, Kola." Adewumi shook her head, looking gloomy. "For a long time, Aba Simon wasted resources and manpower looking everywhere for her, but she was never found." Adewumi whispered, "She was a replica of Omotola in everything—beautiful, determined, and very smart. Kola, I know it is hard to believe that your father was a good man with great acumen, and that he was well respected back then, but it's the truth. All of a sudden, he changed. The man I loved and married—he was just gone. It is sad."

"So, how did you marry him?"

"You want to know how I met your father?" Adewumi's face cheered a bit. "And I'll tell you. We were in the palace, and your father was invited by the king as *ogbufo* for the new district officer, an Oyinbo man, to translate the new rules from the colonial master to the Yoruba language. Your father spoke the Oyinbo man's language perfectly and translated as the man wanted.

Right there, I fell in love with him, and since that day, I had him in the back of my mind. When old enough to marry and suitors came from left and right, I hated them all, including the one chosen by my father. At one glance of your father in our house, I was happy. I never realized it was going to be this way."

Adewumi's face went dark again.

"Mama, he was married then. Why?"

"Being married has nothing to do with anything. In fact, I'll say I was among the few who had the opportunity to marry the man they loved. Marriage was a mess. A young girl could be thrown into any man's lap, as long as the bride price was right and she was available. I loved your father, Kola. And I was over the moon when he came to ask for my hand in marriage, or else I would've probably married the man my father had chosen, who already had two wives."

"Do you still love him? I mean, you must hate him now."

"Not necessarily. And that's the problem. I think I'll always love him. As long as he allows me to be the mother of my children in peace and doesn't run me crazy, I'll always be the happiest woman on earth," she said lightly.

For an hour, they walked in silence, each in their own thoughts. Adewumi couldn't take it anymore.

"You see, since we have been walking," she said, as a joke to break the silence, "we didn't see anybody. The courageous have gone to the farm early, and they are not lazy, like us!" Adewumi smiled.

"I'm sorry, Mama, is it still far away?"

"There." Adewumi pointed. More seriously, she said, "Kola, promise me that you'll never lose hope—that no matter what life brings to your shore, you won't give frustration a chance. Because disappointments will come, but the way you handle them will make you whoever you become in life."

"Mama, I won't be depressed or go nuts like Papa, if that is what you're worried about."

Kola smiled, shifting both basket and machete to one hand, wrapping his free hand around his mother's shoulder. After a few minutes of snuggle-walking, Kola could see his two brothers-in-law far away, in the middle of the plot.

As they approached, Kola's first sister's husband said, "Good morning, ma. Kola, I'm glad you could make it."

"I'm sorry we're late. It's my fault. What can I help you with?"

"That's okay." The man pointed to a shed. "Grab a hoe over there and come over."

Chapter Thirty-Four

Akin awakened, checking the side clock. It was seven a.m., British time. Although still dark, without a glimpse of sunlight, it looked like it was four a.m., Nigeria time. "Welcome to another world, Akin," he murmured to himself.

He got out of bed, crossed to the far end of the room, and opened a capacious armoire. Trends in fashion from handmade Italian suits to safari suits, pants, sweaters, shoes, and more to match any occasion were arranged perfectly before him. He couldn't help but laugh at how his father always went beyond expectations to make him comfortable. He knew he would never wear almost all of these clothes, especially when he did his own shopping.

The day before, at Kano International Airport, Akin had stood indifferent, with mixed feelings, as he boarded the airplane with his father and three of his indispensable employees: Boyede, Ojo, and Sunday, his chief butler. That was after three stopovers, in three towns, lodging with different friends of his before arriving at the northern airport, far from the southern part of Nigeria. He was intrigued with the newest machines of the time, the aircraft, but he felt weary and upset at the same time, since he knew little about the state of things with Omotola's household. He worried that Omotola might not like him. He worried that Jacob might refuse to relinquish his grip on Omotola. Then what? If the choice were up to him alone, he would have turned back home and flown on the intriguing machine another day.

"Papa, did you hear anything from the family who went to Omotola's house?" Akin had said, touching his father's suit as they finally settled next to each other on the airplane.

"Not here, Son," Simon had snapped. "We'll talk about it when we get to Britain. You understand."

"Okay, Papa." He decided to give the matter a rest until they reached the villa.

On the plane, Simon was nervous and tense, Akin had noticed. And he knew why. His father preferred the "clipper," a type of sea plane, to the uncertain jet aircraft in which he sat. He had complained about that to Mallam Abubakah, the proprietor of groundnut exports from Nigeria. He was the last friend of Simon's with whom they lodged in Tofi. The Mallam had smiled and said, "Simon, there's a first time for everything, but I'm sure you'll enjoy it. It's faster."

Akin had slept for half of the thirteen-hour flight and only awoke to eat. As they stepped out of the airplane, an entourage with a line of cars was waiting for them. In convoy, they were taken to the villa. Immediately, dinner was served.

Toward the end of the dinner, Simon had said. "Son, I know you're worried about Omotola's suitor and family, but I can assure you everything will be fine. I'll give you the details as soon as I receive them from my brothers.

Right now, I need to check and organize the schedules for tomorrow in my office. Sunday will show you to your room. And if you need anything, I'll be in the first room down the hall. And one other thing. Stanley will be here at noon tomorrow. As you know, he'll take you anywhere you want."

"Splendid and thanks, Papa. I guess I'll see you in the morning. Good night."

"Good night, Son."

It was a lie that Simon hadn't heard from his brothers, because they had sent a telegram to him at the Mallam office that everything had been done according to the tradition. Omotola was engaged to Akin. But Simon still felt reluctant about his son marrying Omotola, and that was the reason he wasn't sharing the news with him.

Akin went with Sunday to his room. Simon immediately went to his bureau, thinking that the one month in London could change Akin's mind toward Omotola. He prayed that time and space would alter the whole situation—that Akin would meet another girl and change his mind about Omotola. And then the engagement would be annulled and smoothed out with Paul, without anybody knowing. Everything usually came down to money, but if Akin was adamant, then he would get the news after his period in London. Simon had explained that to the Mallam when he got the telegram from his office. The Mallam just smiled and said, "Kids of today!"

"…Believe they know better than their fathers," Simon completed his statement.

Simon's words that "everything would be okay" had lifted Akin's morale, and he'd gone to bed relieved. At two a.m., Akin had had enough sleep. He got off the bed to see if his father was still in his office downstairs. At least he could sit on a couch and keep him company. But the light was off, and the entrance door closed. He went back upstairs. And on the last stair, he could hear Simon talking and a female voice answering at the far end of the corridor. Akin decided to turn back to his room before waking up someone accidentally. He slept until seven.

He took a long shower, dressed warmly, in case the weather was as chilly as it had been the day before when they stepped off the airplane. He would love to tour the property with his father before Stanley showed up, so they could talk over many things. But deep down, he knew that waiting for his dad was like waiting for snow in Nigeria. It would never happen, especially when a female voice shrilled in his bedroom. He had known that since he was a kid.

As Akin walked to the corridor to see if anyone was there to help with the tour, he was caught off-guard. Gleeful voices emerged from his father's bedroom. Abruptly, the door opened, and two people stopped in the doorway. Akin watched the obscene view—his father and a woman fondling each other. Both of Simon's hands were inside her blouse, and the woman's hands Akin's eyes traced downward before returning to his father's face. Their eyes met. It was like walking in on the reverend father having sex with a nun. Sharply, Simon withdrew his hands, as if suddenly beaten by the woman's nipples. The woman gasped.

"Oh, my God!" the woman shrilled. "Simon, you didn't tell me Akin was in London. What's wrong with you? I forced myself to come over, as I thought you were hiding other things from me. You know, the usual."

"The usual" was other women. The woman was Oyinkan. She'd arrived unannounced shortly after Akin went to bed. Playfully, she slapped Simon on the shoulder, like old friends do. Gently, Simon pulled away, his face sullen. Akin felt like throwing up. He felt like breaking into a run. He felt like shouting. He felt a lot of things. He just stood, stunned, depressed, the joy of his day quenched. He knew the woman, and his mind reeled, wondering what could possibly be the motive of the two together. He broke eye contact with his father. He made Akin sick. He turned his face away, but stood still as they approached.

Simon was fragrant with fear, and to cover it up, he said in an unsteady voice, "Akin decided to tag along at the last minute."

Oyinkan smiled again, and unabashed, she said, "If I had known, I'd have brought my daughter along. You know, Simon, there is no better place in the world to woo a girl and please a fiancée like London. I could have arranged their shopping, their—"

"Please, Oyinkan, there will be plenty of time for that later," Simon cut in hastily. "You've a flight to catch."

"Yes." Oyinkan smiled. "But not until I've had breakfast. I think I still have plenty of time." She checked her gold watch to confirm this, and then she nodded. "Yes, plenty of time, Simon. It's only just past eight, and my flight is at midday."

"Shall we eat then, so you can be on your way? I've got plenty of things lined up for this morning." Simon's voice was taut.

He led the way downstairs toward a room at the far

end of the corridor. A butler, an Oyinbo man Akin hadn't seen before, stood out in front and opened the door for them. The woman went in first, then Akin, and finally, Simon.

Akin couldn't stand the two. He stood apart, waiting for them to take their seats at the table set for five before choosing a seat in a gem of a dining room. The long, mahogany table was filled with bone china, crystal, and cutlery tableware and every gourmet breakfast delicacy. As the two took seats near the door, Akin walked to the far end of the dining table and sat down. Behind him was a lovely window overlooking a large, breathtaking yard, as exquisitely landscaped as a royal garden.

Akin chose cornflakes. Simon chose oatmeal. The woman dove into the pastries on the table like a greedy pig. Akin placed Omotola in his mind to allay the view of the two of them. He replayed the Lion Club recruitment day. He could see her beauty, her boldness, and for a long time, he was in contact with Omotola with his inner eye.

"Can you pour coffee here? I hate orange juice," Oyinkan said to the butler standing a few meters away, waiting for orders. He came to their table.

"Certainly, madam," the butler said with a bow. He turned to Simon. "Sir, would you like to have something else too?"

"Get on with what they want first while I finish my orange juice," Simon said, looking uncomfortable.

"Yes, sir." The butler served Oyinkan and walked over to Akin. "Would you like to drink anything else, Master Akin?"

Akin gave up his daydream and said with a set smile, "Yes. Cocoa will be fine, thanks."

As the butler served his beverages, Akin couldn't help but hear Oyinkan's satanic litany of wishes. She wanted to bring Solape to Britain next summer. And Solape and Akin would stay at the other villa with her. Simon could visit at will. She would not stop talking, and Akin's patience was going downhill. She always had something to say. Simon just listened with a thin smile. Akin wished he were still in bed, rather than having to watch the woman and his father's togetherness and hear her gibberish.

"Can I have tea, please?" Simon said, placing his empty orange juice glass on the table.

"Simon, don't tell me you've become British?" she said, laughing hysterically. "It's them who have tea as refreshment all the time."

The butler placed a cup on a saucer and served the tea.

"I just don't like coffee. It presses on my bladder and…" Simon stopped.

"Simon," she said jokingly, "are you sure that's what pressing your thing, not the other women?"

Immediately, the butler left them and took up his post at the dining room entrance again. Simon didn't answer, but he was looking embarrassed. He picked up his drink. Akin stared intensely at his bowl of cornflakes, as if studying each fragment that composed each piece of cereal.

Simon wanted to pour another cup of tea from the teapot, but Oyinkan placed her hands over his. "Love, allow me," she said softly. Simon removed his hands, staring ahead. "Did you hear from Akin's mom recently?"

Akin looked up, aghast, watching the two again.

"Oyinkan, this is not an appropriate place or the moment to ask me that," Simon said, strongly. "You have to go. I'll see you back home."

For the first time that morning, she looked sober, and her voice was unsteady.

"I'm sorry I asked. Please, darling, don't be upset with me."

"No, I'm not upset," Simon lied. "It's just that I have a lot on my mind and hate talking this morning. I'll walk you out to the car."

"That is kind of you, but I need to get my luggage from your room first."

"My guy will do that," Simon said, turning toward the butler. "Please take her luggage from the dressing table in my room to the car outside."

The butler nodded and left the room. The woman cheered up again.

"Is Akin always this quiet, or is it me who makes him this quiet? He hasn't said a word since we met."

"He is a reserved boy."

"My daughter—"

"Shall we? This way," Simon cut in. Immediately, he stood and headed toward the exit.

Reluctantly, Oyinkan rose. She addressed Akin. "Akin, your next trip to Europe will be with my daughter, you understand? Anyway, I'll see you both back at home. We'll plan everything together."

Akin was mute, as usual. The woman finally walked away from him and launched into another subject with Simon, who was standing at the door. "Just a quick reminder, Simon," she said. "Don't forget the Brait party. I'll send the material for the dress, the damask, through my driver, since you don't want me to come to any of your offices. We'll talk back home."

Simon came back shortly after the noise of the car engine faded out of the compound.

"Papa, how—how could you?" Akin was breathing fire. He slammed both palms on the table. A few of the crystal cups fell off the table and shattered.

Simon nodded to the butler to get out. As soon as the dining room door closed behind them, Simon answered with a tremulous voice, "She came to buy damask in London and decided to check on us before going home, to thank me for allowing her to use my other villa. She lodged at my former villa. Most of my friends lodge there when they come to London. You see, Son, she wasn't here when we arrived. She came…" Simon stopped. The atmosphere was tense. He looked like a kid caught stealing from the cookie jar, whilst Akin looked like a father ready to scold him.

"And how did she get into your bedroom?"

There was an awkward silence in which you could have heard a pin drop. Simon's face went dead without giving an answer. After a long moment, Akin screamed, "Papa, how could you, with that woman? My mother's best friend! And your best friend's wife! Not to mention, you picked her daughter to be my fiancée!"

"Sorry. I'm so sorry, my son. It was an accident," said Simon.

"Does she come to London every summer? Does the 'accident' happen every year?"

Simon retreated into silence.

Akin roared again, "I want to be sure about her trip— so I can avoid her and her daughter like I'll avoid hell!"

"She comes every summer, but don't worry about what she said. There won't be any arrangements unless you want it so."

"Hell, no—" Akin stopped, as the truth came to him. It wasn't an accident, as if you got drunk and ended up with the most hateful and resentful person in your life. Olu had told him about them once. They were kids then.

"Akin, is it appropriate for Papa to slap Mrs. Ogunlade on a buttock and squeeze it?" Olu had said, looking appalled. He had come from the backyard apartment unit to the hall to join Simon's party. The two brothers stood in the hall watching their father's guests stream in.

"What do you mean?" Akin asked.

"I meant that Papa slapped your mother's friend, Mrs. Ogunlade, right on her buttock and squeezed it. And both walk—" Olu stopped as Joyce arrived.

"Have you seen your father around?" Joyce demanded. "His friends have started to arrive. I checked everywhere he could be, he—"

"No!" Olu interrupted. "I got to go."

He broke into a run. Akin and his mother just stared after him. Akin had thought he was overrating the event, as he usually did, to impress. The way Olu described what he saw would have been hilarious if it had been someone else. But it wasn't funny.

Akin felt the same way now. "Papa, let me ask you some questions. How long have you been seeing her? I mean, was my mother still around when you started 'accidentally' seeing each other?"

"Son, can you drop the matter?" Simon snapped, adding, "I don't want to talk about the subject or your mother.'"

Simon's eyes dropped to look at his oatmeal.

"Just like always, Papa, sweep everything under the rug. Pretend it never happened." Akin's voice was grating through a sad smile. "Reverend Philip has been right all along about you." He shoved his chair back on the marble floor. The noise was ear-splitting. Simon looked up in surprise. "I'll be in my room until Mr. Stanley comes around, Father."

He stormed out.

✣

Chapter Thirty-Five

"I must get out of this silent, spooky house before I go crazy," Omotola said aloud, taking a cloth from the nail rack on the wall. She would bathe fast and see Yinka, whom she knew would be at home preparing for her wedding, due the first weekend in August.

When Rolake went to prepare the breakfast, Omotola sat thinking about what awaited her as Akin Akindele's fiancée. She knew the town would go crazy, especially her friends, when she became part and parcel of the Akindele family that was previously so out of reach.

The sudden engagement was like a bomb thrown, scattering thoughts in Omotola's head, but she'd managed to tumble into sleep after breakfast. That was after Tutu came to collect her baby and Rolake had left to see her friends, especially the one that had married the man she had wanted all her life. Omotola knew she would be at the center of their discussions. She could not remember ever seeing her mother so happy.

The house lay in complete silence, like a morgue, as Omotola woke up. She wandered into Kola's room, but he wasn't there, or anyplace she'd checked on the compound. The club activities and contact with other members were dead until September. Most members lived far away, and Kola had said that most of them were on holiday abroad. She knew Kola couldn't be with any of them. And neither could she count on him being with his friends around town that early. Their schedules were as tight as a nutshell. The majority were married, and the unmarried had lives far different from Kola's. He wasn't found on Sunday when she needed him! Omotola was cross. *Where is he?*

While Omotola was looking for Kola at the house, he was at the farm. Kola had helped Adewumi offload the firewood from her head. And an excited Adewumi told Kola that she'd got a piece of land! Just as excited, Kola had promised to be of help the next day. Kola went to play ball afterward and forgot to tell Omotola.

Omotola walked to the backyard. She picked a bucket from the pantry and walked to the first of the three jars full of water. She bent to draw water. Suddenly, her backside got sticky with the voices of the two she usually tried to avoid: the two daughters of Moji. She could hardly believe that they were in the house. They walked up behind her.

"How the hell did you manage to know the Akindele family so well that one of them wants you?" the eldest asked in annoyance.

She was afraid, but she kept on drawing the water, ignoring the two. One of them slapped her hard on the butt.

"Hey, what did you do that for?" Omotola shouted angrily, turning to face the two.

"Didn't you hear me talking to you? You're such a rude girl." The senior sister spat each word out with hatred, while her junior sister stared at Omotola with menace. Something had provoked them. It was Paul.

Before stepping out as the proud father of the year to boast his joy, Paul had gone into Moji's room and poked the two sisters, not with a needle this time, but with a sharp dagger. He made it quite clear that they had little time left in his house. And he decreed that, during that little time, they would have to serve Omotola by fetching water and doing other chores around the house. The two sisters had locked themselves inside their mother's bedroom, crying like the bereaved. They fell to planning some ominous act to take Omotola's life by smothering, strangling, or a simple accident. Neither of those would be a bad idea. And it would take away Paul's present joy. He had humiliated them, and they wanted revenge. They heard Omotola going to the backyard. They were happy the house was *so* quiet.

Omotola refused to answer. She turned to pick up the bucket.

"My sister wants to know what your mother did to get you a husband from the archduke's family—witchcraft, juju, or voodoo? If you tell us, we'll make your death less painful."

Omotola didn't answer. Instead, she picked up the bucket and tried to pass them, to take her bath. The senior sister held her by the blouse with her right hand while the left hand folded into a fist. The junior sister snatched away the bucket and poured the water on the ground.

"I said—"

"Why don't you leave her alone," Tutu cut in. She was walking to the backyard, holding her baby. "Look for somebody your own size."

"Shut up, dog. Are you going to holler like you did last night?" The junior sister said, shouting as Tutu approached them. "Come, dog, I've been willing to kick your gut since you reared your head in this house. Come and earn your death too." She was beckoning to Tutu with both hands. The senior lost interest in Omotola, who jumped up and gave her a sharp fist in the throat. She made a strangling noise, gasping for breath as if her thorax was blocked. She released Omotola's blouse, and her hands went to her neck. Omotola ran toward the house.

"For doing that to my sister, your death is going to be painful!" the junior sister yelled, enraged.

"You've to go through me first!" Tutu shot back. She placed her baby on the ground. The junior sister was about to run after Omotola, but changed her mind and charged for Tutu instead. They struggled. Eventually, she flung Tutu to the ground. She jumped on her, holding Tutu's throat firmly with both hands, strangling her. Tutu's eyes popped open while her hands flailed weakly in the air, trying to grab the junior sister's neck too. The senior sister followed Omotola inside the house and dragged her back out to the backyard. She hit Omotola on the nose, and blood trickled down. Omotola yelled and jumped on her, clapping both legs tightly around her waist. She raised both hands, scratching her prey on the face. The senior sister's face was bleeding as she flopped around, trying to fling Omotola off her.

"Are you out of your mind?" a man screamed, sounding like Paul. The four women froze and disengaged from each other. But it was the voice of Moji's last son, the two troublemakers' elder brother. He held a koboko whip in his hand, ready to strike.

"Omotola and Iyawo, this way!" He pointed to the left. Tutu coughed repeatedly as she moved with Omotola to the left. "And you two, this way." He pointed to the right. "What the hell is going on?"

"We were just asking Omotola questions when Tutu interrupted," the senior sister said, lying. "And that is pretty much it."

"Really?" Tutu said in a faint voice, coughing repeatedly. "It's not that the two of you ganged up on her?"

"Sorry, Iyawo, don't bother to talk again," the man said. "I heard everything. You don't have to explain further. As I walked in from outside, I could hear their voices. I'm so sorry they did what they did."

He faced his sisters and said tightly, "You should be ashamed of yourselves. You make our mother and myself sad. Instead of you two being supportive, being good sisters to her, and maybe, as a result, God would grant you husbands, you started to molest her. News flash, sisters! If our father hears about this, you know what that means? You'll both be out of this house this minute. You're walking on a tightrope here, if you don't know. You've overstayed your welcome in this house." He pointed to Tutu. "Look at Iyawo! Here is somebody younger than both of you, and she's settled down already. If you get troublesome again, I'll be the one to tell our father myself, so he can flush both of you out of the house. Get out of my sight before I change my mind and give you what you deserve."

He raised the whip as if to strike them. They ran inside the house in fear.

"Once again, I'm sorry," the man apologized. "If any

one of them intimidates you again, please tell me. Omotola, congratulations!"

"Thanks, Egbon," Omotola replied.

$\wp\ni$

Chapter Thirty-Six

There was a big board signpost announcing the location of the Lion Club between Ajoni-Itan and Ibata-Itan town, yet people missed it because of the thick forest and mountains. That might happen to Bola, who was coming from Ajoni-Itan, but Kola didn't care. He got to the Esa waterfall an hour before he was supposed to be there. The site was fantastic and well preserved. Kola was impressed. Simon Akindele had a gateman and laborers who kept the land tidy. Members needed permission to use the place if Akin wasn't around, and that permission he had just received from the gateman, who had then gone home to fetch something. He would be back later.

The weather was nippy, and the grass was still wet from the heavy rain of the night before. The sun was out doing its best to heat up the ground. Kola was wearing a shirt over a light T-shirt and shorts. He realized he was silly to have selected these goofy clothes as the cold got on his nerves within a few minutes of getting there. He regretted not bringing a pullover and not wearing trousers. He decided to run. He ran three laps around the property and got heated up. He felt better. He then went to the summit of one of the mini rocks near the waterfall, where he could see cars driving past, but the cars looked as small as tortoises. From here, he'd be able to see Bola before she could get to him. He sat down, with his shirt next to him, thinking about Bola.

He wanted to be with Bola as much as he wanted to be a doctor. He'd held that aspiration since Primary Three, when he had heard from his teacher about Andreas Vesalius, the great physician of the sixteenth century. In that class, Bola's desk was between him and Akin Akindele. Kola felt humiliated, shivering, as he remembered now what had transpired in Primary Three during their second week in class.

"Akin, I forgot my pencil at home. Can I borrow one of yours?" Bola had said.

Akin dimmed his eyes and answered, "You can't have any of my pencils." He swept up the four pencils that littered the table, put them back in his wallet, and looked straight ahead.

"You can have mine," Kola said, even though it was the only pencil he had. "I'll sharpen it for you."

"I don't want your dirty pencil." Bola had replied with a frown.

The class pupils had laughed. Kola had slumped down his seat as he was laughed at and insulted. The next minute, Bola rumbled through her school bag and hoisted out a pencil. She turned to Akin and said, "Found my pencil, Akin."

Akin didn't answer—he just looked straight ahead, as he always did most of the time. Kola couldn't breathe until their teacher finally arrived.

Since that day, he knew how far he could go, because

the others were no better—especially the girls, some of whom he didn't even really fancy, but out of politeness, wanted to help. They were the worst, drama queens who stared at him with hatred. And if that didn't say enough, they'd say things like, "Who are you talking to? Get out of my face!"

Those days were painful. So, what was different now that he thought they liked him? And why did he care so much that he wanted one of them to agree to be his steady girlfriend? Was it because Bola had shown him her white teeth and lifted one strand of her Raster? Even if she wanted him, would she want him as he wanted her? Wouldn't she look at his background, hiss, and treat him like a leper, as she and everybody else did in primary school?

He'd been nothing to these upper crusts until he made it to the Lion Club and became a friend of Akin. He knew this. And now, was he really anything to them? Was he just overrating himself? In letting these thoughts bubble up, he felt insecure. He wanted to turn back home. It was a bad idea to anticipate dating Bola. She would just laugh in his face. Maybe he'd give their dating a chance for a few months before graduating from high school, and the humiliation wouldn't last long. A car engine was turned off at the road's curbside.

Kola stood up, watching a tiny figure emerge. The body frame, he could never mistake, even if he was blindfolded. She emerged from the car in a *bonfo* gown, a mini gown that barely reached her knees, without any sports bag or anything at all. The sight evaporated Kola's worries but sent cold shivers down his spine. Something managed to dry his throat, and he started to sweat, even though his body temperature had dropped again while sitting at the summit.

He climbed down from his perch with his shirt hanging loosely in his left hand.

"Am I late?" Bola asked cheerfully as he reached her.

"N…ope, r-right … on time." Kola's tics kicked in, and he looked embarrassed. *Oh, boy, it's like old times. I wish for death right now!* He raised his shirt to his chest as if protecting it and looked away from Bola's eyes.

"I'm glad you are not mad," Bola said, touching him gently on one arm.

Kola took a deep breath and faced her. Her expression was welcoming and patient, not sly or jesting. Kola relaxed.

"I'll never be mad at you. Come on, this way." *Jeez! The tic's cured*, he said in his head as they walked to the foot of the Esa waterfall.

"I would have been here earlier, but we accidentally missed the signpost. We were almost at Ibata-Itan town when we turned back."

"It happens all the time. Would you like me to turn around, so you can remove your gown or change into gym clothes?"

The statement sounded silly to Kola because Bola didn't have a bag. Although, she might project a bag from the sky, or he could run after the car that brought her, which had made a U-turn immediately after she alighted from it and sped off. Or would she just use what she had on? He needed to ask anyway, to start a conversation.

"Actually, I want to talk to you first."

Oh! Maybe she saw me sweating over her and wants out. Who could blame her?

"We could sit around here, but let me spread my shirt on the ground so your gown won't be wet."

Kola would have proposed the summit to Bola, to avoid the wet grass. But he wasn't sure about her capability to climb, and he might sound like a pervert, suggesting that to a girl in a skimpy outfit. Nervously, he spread the shirt out and patted it for her to sit on while he sat on the grass next to her.

"I'd love to be in the club, but want to get something off my chest first." As Bola said *chest,* Kola looked at her bosom. Realizing that was stupid, he looked away—right into Bola's eyes. Kola felt as guilty as sin, but Bola smiled. "I've got something on my chest, doesn't mean…" She stopped and grinned.

"I know what you meant," Kola whispered. "I'm sorry, it's just silly. You were saying?"

Adewumi had been right. Like father, like son!

"I like you a lot," Bola explained, rolling her eyeballs seductively. "And I started to like you a long time ago. I did everything I could for you to notice that, but you never did. You were always friendly with big-boobs girls."

"What! Always friendly with whom?" Kola was dismayed. "Where is this accusation coming from, Bola?"

"Because you fancy girls like Teju, Kike—you know, big boobs… You want more?"

"No. They're wrong accusations; I've never been with any girl in the school."

"True, but you like Kike. She was kind of your girl at previous inter-class sports. I remembered you loved it when she shook her front right in your face on the last sports day."

Kola could see why Bola would be agitated at that.

He had been there, but it wasn't him the girls were trying to impress. He was with members of the Lion Club, and they were at their school's inter-class sport event, and next to him were Akin and many club members. Kike and some girls came out wearing wet, white shirts as if it was a wet T-shirt contest. Anyway, their T-shirts were wet on purpose, to make their fronts visible. And they were certainly visible. They were standing out in front of them. He had laughed his head off as Kike happened to be standing in front of him, and her friends happened to be standing in front of the others, dancing and jiggling what they had inherited from their mothers. They were loud and didn't stop until a nun came, wrote their names down, and asked them to go and change in the dormitory. They all got suspended for a week.

"Kike wasn't alone. I remember vividly, you were talking about the wet T-shirt affair. It was just hilarious."

"And you had eyeballs all over her!"

"Wait a minute, Bola. I wasn't with Kike or anybody. Anyway, I thought you and Femi were an item. So, where is the jealousy coming from?"

"Coming from the fact that you never noticed me." Bola's voice wobbled.

"Bola, if anybody should get cross, it should be me," Kola said softly.

"Why would it be you?"

"Because, Bola, I've noticed you since Primary Three. You remember the time you wanted a pencil, and I offered mine, even though that was the only one I had? But you preferred that of Akin Akindele and called mine "dirty." I was humiliated, Bola, and couldn't—"

"I don't remember that," Bola cut in. "But I'm so

sorry I said that, if it is true."

"Never mind. I shouldn't have brought that up. Bola, I noticed you a long time ago."

"I'm just glad to hear that. I've been unable to sleep well since the last time we talked, since I've been thinking about you. Kola, I like you. Would you be my steady boyfriend?"

"I'm sorry, but what about Femi?" Kola's voice trembled.

"It stopped before it even started. It's over," Bola said earnestly.

"Why was it over before it started, Bola?"

"We were never compatible," Bola said, looking tense. She started to push down the hem of her gown to cover her lap, as if suddenly finding herself exposed. "Besides, I befriended him so I could be nearer to you. And when I realized it wasn't working, I dumped him for you. You've always been on my mind."

Bola looked at Kola with empathy in her eyes.

"That's difficult to believe." Kola laughed inside. *Yes, my number-one enemy is gone!* But he maintained a straight face. He waved off a bug that flew at his face. Deep down, he wasn't convinced all the obstacles were gone. *What about the cutest, most desirable guy that almost all the girls in school were seeking?* "Bola, I don't mean to be rude, but I need to know this."

"What, Kola?" Bola said, looking nervous. "Please tell me."

"What about the fever for Akin Akindele? I know you like him. I just don't want to be a second-best, a substitute. Besides, he is my dearest friend."

"Who?" Bola asked angrily. "That snob, that self-centered, arrogant brat? Nothing could ever happen between us. Maybe, when I was stupid, I thought he could be the one. And that changed long ago. Besides, he is engaged to Solape, a friend. He is not for me, Kola. Even if he wasn't, he is just too boring—with a pompous attitude, as if he's better than everybody who lives." Bola sounded fed up.

"You know Solape?" Kola said, looking surprised.

"Yes, as a matter of fact, we were close friends until she got engaged to the arrogant one. It seems arrogance oil secreted into her brain from her fiancé. And the oil later seeped from brain to face. And if you touch her face, you can be stained."

"What?" Kola's face was blank.

"Kola, it is a metaphor. What I'm saying is, she is full of herself since she got engaged to *Lord* Akin. She became a *Lady* overnight. She attends a Methodist girls' grammar school in Ladden, and we used to jam during the holidays, but that has changed. She feels she is too much for a girl like me," Bola said briskly, with a tight face. "And for your further information, she and her fiancé are perfect for each other. Both have a condescending attitude. They are as perfect as water to a fish."

"Not anymore; things have changed." Kola smiled. "Bola, Akin isn't a bad guy—he's just reserved, that's all. If you get to know him, you'll see he is an amazing guy."

"No matter how you try to convince me," Bola said with a disgusted expression on her face, "in my head, Akin Akindele and his bride will always be arrogant snobs to me. They are just into themselves, you know. So, what changed? Akin ran into rotten?"

Bola was spunky. Kola could see it.

"What do you mean by 'ran into rotten'?"

"Don't know, Kola. It just came out." Bola shrugged, smiling.

Kola's face was alert.

"Do you hate him that much? I mean, if you want me as your boyfriend, you will have to like him. He is my best friend. You understand."

"Kola, I don't hate him per se. But I think it wouldn't kill him once in a while to smile and reply to greetings. He looks implacable most of the time, and demonstrates he thinks he is better than everybody."

"No, Akin is a cool guy. You misjudge his character. If you get to know him, you'll sing another song. I mean, a praising one. And he hasn't fallen into rotten by impregnating a girl, if that is what you meant. He asked for my sister Omotola's hand in marriage before he left for England."

Bola's eyebrows lifted. "What! When? How?" Words failed her.

"Bola, I can't help you fill in the gaps." Kola smiled. "But Akin saw my sister at the recruitment, and before he even made his intentions known to me, his family came to ask for her hand in marriage, and my father has accepted. I'm waiting impatiently for his arrival. Oh boy, he has a lot of explaining to do."

"Do Solape and her parents know this?" Bola said, remembering she was going to be a maid of honor to Banke, Solape's half-sister, in April. Banke's mother was Bola's aunt.

"How should I know, Bola? Seems you've not been listening," Kola said. "I just told you, I'm as out of the loop as my sister. The guy just threw a bomb and went away."

"You're happy, then?"

"Amazed, but happy. I just can't wait for him to come back. I love him with all my heart. Bola, I'll tell you today, he is a great guy. So is my sister. And I'm happy—they both belong together."

"I'm happy for your sister, even though I haven't met her. I hope she'll bring Akin around and that he'll descend from his lordliness and pay attention to the little people around him," Bola said. "Some people are going to be pissed off, erupt like a volcano when this leaks out. But not me, Kola. I'm happy for both of them. I wish them joy in all their future endeavors. I really do, because I like your sister already," Bola said, seriously. "Kola, what about us? Please, can you be my boyfriend? I like you a lot, and I promise Akin will never be a stumbling stone. I'll endure him even if he looks past me. I want you to be my boyfriend—you've been on my mind a long time."

"Kola, I'm back," the guard said. Kola and Bola turned their faces towards the voice. "If you need anything," he added, "I'll be over there." He pointed to the security post in front of the site.

"Thanks. I'll come over if I need anything," Kola said. The man left. He turned to Bola. "That's the guard. And, you were saying?"

Kola heard everything she'd said perfectly, but he just wanted her to express herself over and over.

Bola frowned. "You didn't hear what I said?"

Kola shook his head no.

"Okay, Kola: I love you, and have been in love with you for a long time." In a softer voice, she added, "Please, Kola, tell me you want me. Do you hear me now?"

Kola smiled. "Of course. I heard you the first time; I

just wanted to be sure."

Bola's voice dropped to a whisper. "Are you sure now? I'm in love with you." She watched Kola's face as if her existence depended on it.

Kola was still for a second, as if thinking it over, even though inside he cheered, *Hoorah!*

"Yes, of course," Kola finally said. "To be honest with you, I liked you since day one, together in Primary Three and—"

"And I was stupid not to have seen that," Bola cut in.

"I'm thrilled that—"

She kissed Kola before he could finish his statement. She wouldn't let go of his lips.

Chapter Thirty-Seven

Moji hadn't been paying attention recently. She wasn't paying any attention either to her two daughters, who were sitting with her in the shed of her farm on Friday at dusk, disgusted, complaining that life was a bitch. She sat dumbly and stared into space. Her lack of concentration had started the minute Omotola got engaged.

Of course, she'd heard about her two daughters ganging up on Omotola from her son. And duly, in tears, she'd apologize to Omotola's mom and Tutu, begging them to keep the matter away from Paul, because where would she go with her two daughters acting like brutes? They weren't brutes before, but society and Paul had soured them.

"Mama, what's wrong with you?" Her first daughter snapped. "You didn't answer my question. Are we Omotola's slaves now? She is not allowed to fetch water, run errands, and worse, she has to use the water we fetched. Mama, is it fair?"

Moji rose from her seat on the ground and said, "Go home, both of you. We'll talk later. I've a place to go."

The two exchanged glances. "What? Where are you

going?" the first one said.

"To see somebody. I'll see both of you at home," she said nervously. "I promise to be home to prepare dinner."

"Mama, we'll come with you. It's dangerous to be by yourself this late. It's better we go with you," the second said with a wan face.

If I died, I would meet my maker, arose in Moji's mind, but with a cosmetic smile, she said, "No, that won't be necessary. Go home. I insist."

And she walked away from her daughters. She could hear their rambling protests, but she was happy that they made no effort to follow.

Moji hated how Omotola's new engagement had snatched her from the jaws of a shark, from the venom of a cobra, where she would have loved the girl to be. She had done Kola and his mother much harm. Her next stop, or rather, her next victim, should have been Omotola. She was ready to compete and prepared to put in Jacob's head that he should treat her as Paul treated his women. The plan had been shattered, and worst of all, Jacob was swimming in money. Moji was off his chart.

And who was he doing now? Was it true he was doing the just-married neighbor's wife or was that just a rumor? Could the person be beautiful and young? Could it be the youthful, good-looking wife of his neighbor, whom Moji was told used Jacob as a handyman from time to time? Was it her? She had seen them together once, and there was a flash of intimacy between the two. Moji had been running around like crazy trying to find out the truth.

Moji had gone to Jacob's house under the pretense of seeing his first wife, her friend, but actually intended to ask why she hadn't been seeing him. That's when she saw

Jacob and the girl talking in the gap between their houses. As if scared, the girl had disappeared into her husband's house in a hurry. Seeing Jacob with the girl had sent a sharp knife through her heart. Moji had burst into tears after she left Jacob, who was slightly upset and did not give her much audience, dismissing her with the promise of seeing her soon at her farm. It had been several months, and Jacob had never shown up.

There were rumors upon rumors that, since Jacob had recently made a fortune from Simon, his wives barely went to the farm from the wake of Monday to the sleep of Friday, as they usually did before. Hired bodies did all the work on his farm, and that of his wives. But, this Moji knew for sure: Jacob's house had been refurbished. As a matter of fact, he'd acquired a new site to build a larger home, which Paul didn't have the common sense to do. Instead, he'd been using the money given to him to upkeep his heart's desires somewhere else rather than spend it on the house. All this, Moji knew, and only the idiots among his wives didn't know.

Her arrangement with Jacob had been on Friday evenings. After Jacob sent his wives and children home from the farm, and she sent her daughters home, Jacob would come around until they were done. They would both walk back to town and go their separate ways at the entrance to town. Sometimes, with urgency, they would just arrange their meeting anywhere, since both knew Paul's schedule, which was so predictable. Well, it was urgent now. It had been months, and Moji needed a fix. She wanted Jacob now, and the desire took control of her as she went to look for Jacob.

Moji took the path that used to be Jacob's route to

her farm, and after walking half a kilometer, she reached the back of Jacob's hut. She stopped in her tracks as she heard a woman giggling and Jacob's voice smooth as a ripe pawpaw, saying, "Thanks for that, it was incredible."

"Anytime," the woman replied. "Since I know the way now, I'll be over here as often as you want."

"No, no, no! You can't be over as often as he wants. Not now, not ever!" Moji muttered tersely under her breath as she put all her might against the hut door. It opened, revealing Jacob and the woman inside. The woman was startled as she leaned back on both hands, naked like a fully fed child. She quickly sat up straight, wrapping one hand across her breasts and dragging the second hand to cover her pubic hair. Jacob just covered his genitals with a piece of cloth that lay next to him. He waved a banana leaf, fanning himself, satisfaction written all over his face.

As a matter of fact, not only was satisfaction on his face, it seemed his rough face was getting smoother as well. What was the secret? Doing a young woman he knows in and out, or what? Moji wondered as she stared at the two in disbelief.

"What are you doing here, Yemisi?"

Yemisi said nervously, "Came here to ask Aba Jacob something. Bye!"

She jumped to her feet, fumbling with her clothes, and hurried to dress behind Moji, who was halfway inside the hut.

Yemisi was beautiful! She was on a list of women with whom Jacob could only dream of sleeping because he didn't have what Paul had. But with a shilling that came by way of Simon, he got what he wanted. Yemisi was all his.

Jacob watched her go. "She could ask you the same question."

"No, she can't. I'm here to see your first wife," Moji said.

The door of the hut slammed shut. They were alone.

"You know you're lying—" Jacob hesitated, waiting for Moji to answer his question.

Instead, Moji stared without a word.

"Okay, then, why didn't my 'see you soon' sink into your brain?"

"It's been months, Jacob, since you said that. You never came around again." Moji's voice was pitiable.

"I've been busy; I'll see you when I can," Jacob sneered.

This enraged Moji.

"Busy doing what? Doing Yemisi?"

"She is none of your business. Go, Moji. I want to get dressed."

"Now you're ashamed to stand up naked in front of me?" Moji yelled. "Tell me something. Is it true you're sleeping with your neighbor's wife too?"

"It is none of your business which women I sleep with."

"You're a bastard camping your best friend's wife."

"So was your husband. Paul was her first until he moved on!" Jacob stopped and leaned backward as Yemisi had done. "And what are you going to do about it?"

Almost in tears, Moji said, "Paul? You're lying. Who did he move on to?"

"Go home, woman. What we had was good, but that was then." Jacob said crisply. "Find someone else to arouse your plant."

"You're a real bastard." Moji's voice was taut. "I'll tell about you and them—you'll have to explain what you've cooked up to burn the whole house down."

Jacob sent out a sardonic smile. "You're not doing such a thing, because you are as guilty as them. And if you do anything stupid, I'll make sure you get the same punishment as them."

"You can't prove anything, Jacob. Nobody knows about us. You and your concubines are dead, Jacob. Wait and see what their husbands will do to you, and what the town will do to them."

"Are you threatening me?" Jacob's voice was baleful. "If that's what you're doing, Moji, don't, because you're not covered. All of Paul's other wives know about us, I can tell, and many others." Jacob said slowly, "Moji, you've nothing on them and on me. Go home and look for another swain to oil your hole. As for me, I'm done. Moji, go. I need to get dressed."

Moji stood, unmoved. Without being bothered by her stare, Jacob stood up naked, and deliberately, in no hurry, he picked up his clothes and faced Moji to dress. Moji just stared at his body, his genitals. She was rigid, in a trance. As Jacob was putting on his cap, Moji whispered, "I'm sorry, Jacob, to have said all that. It was jealousy. And please forgive me, for old time's sake."

Moji walked toward Jacob and took hold of his arm. He shoved her hand away and looked intensely at her.

"Moji, it's over. Move on! What we had was good, I'll admit it, but it's time we moved on."

"Just like that, we move on because you want to move on?"

"Sorry, that's the way it is. I've got to go."

"You know that's wicked and cold. Who do you want me to move on to?"

"I don't know—probably to a neighbor's husband, to your husband's other friends… to anybody who wants you." Jacob looked at her as if she was nothing and added, "Oh, or to your husband."

He stood, mocking her. Water dropped from Moji's eyes.

"You're a son of a bitch frog face."

Jacob's eyes clouded, and he roared, "*Oburewa alagbere odoko obinrin ita!*" He pointed to the door.

Moji refused to move, but went hysterical. "I'm an ugly, wanton harlot, an adulterous woman to you now, and *I* should get out?"

"You started name-calling. Didn't you hear, never throw a stone at somebody else's houses when you yourself live in a glass house? Go home. And if you refuse, I shall call the neighbors from other farms on you. And it will be you who has to explain what you've been cooking to make the house burn down. So, get out, Moji!" Jacob snapped.

Whether she liked it or not, she knew it was time to go. Men like Paul and Jacob were bastards. As soon as they got what they wanted and were ready for something new, they never gave a second glance backward—they crushed and stabbed whoever got in their way. Moji lived with Paul, and she was accustomed to that behavior. She wasn't a novice. She shouldn't have come to be dumped like a bag of rice. She felt low.

Moji resolved to take revenge. She turned towards the door and stopped to face Jacob, who was standing with hatred in his eyeballs. "This is not over, frog face," Moji said. "I'll make you pay."

She stepped outside and gave him a last searing look.

"Bring it on, ugly harlot!"

Jacob slammed the door of the hut in her face. Moji sobbed, walking away, eyes on the ground until an iota of rain dropped on her head. She looked at the sky, and it was gray.

"Come on, God. Not you too."

She hadn't put her head down yet when the rain gathered its strength and poured as it had never poured before. She ran toward her farm and tripped backward. Finally, she managed to get to a sitting position. She sat there in the storm, crying hysterically.

Chapter Thirty-Eight

The summer was over, and it was the beginning of the new academic session. Omotola stood frightened inside the bamboo bathroom, thinking about the day in school. She was lost, still wondering without ceasing if everything that was happening around her of late was real. Was she actually engaged to Akin Akindele? And if yes, what would happen to her in the new school as the engaged bride of Akin Akindele whom everybody worshiped? Would there be rivalries? And why had he absconded since?

Omotola hadn't seen him since that day of recruitment at the Esa waterfall. He had told Kola that he would be spending half of the summer in the UK overseeing his father's company. The second half would be spent in Nigeria. He hadn't been back. She had no clue as to where he was. Or what would happen if they finally met. She thought it would have been better if they had met over the summer and talked. Then she would know for sure if he really liked her and that he wouldn't take a look at her in school and hate her. Or worse, call off the engagement.

She felt disturbed. She really loved him. It made her

not want to start the new phase of schooling anymore. She wasn't ready to embark on secondary school. This moment in her life terrified her. And never in this world would she have believed any situation would make her want to skip school. School was her passion, a secret escape from the chaotic life around her. Its four walls were safe, and at recreation time, under its trees, she could meditate on her future with glints of joy, convinced it would be bright. Emotionally, since a few days before school had opened, she was kaput. Even the mottos she relied on to calm herself failed to remove the pangs of anxiety.

Vigorously, she scrubbed her body with the Lux fragranced soap that Paul had sent her mother to buy in Ajoni-Itan. Thoroughly, she washed her mouth with a pako stick. She couldn't stink anywhere. She had to be perfect, and she had to sparkle. But she felt weak and broke down, starting to cry.

Eventually, after obsessively scrubbing her body and mouth and feeling satisfied, she entered the room she shared with her mother. She felt uneasy again. She sat on one of the two stools, and flashbacks took over her thoughts: *"She is dirty and poor; how can she afford to come to school?" "Her mother cleans toilets to send her to school." "She buys a long uniform for herself so she cannot outgrow it easily."* The sound of the girls' laughter echoed in her head. Would secondary school be any different? She became pensive as her eyes roved around, finally resting on the small table at one corner of the room, where her mother had placed her breakfast.

She wasn't hungry, which was very unusual. It seemed that her stomach shut down along with her brain. She turned her head sideways and stared at her new uniform for a change: a white blouse with a navy-blue skirt, in impeccable condition. And underneath, on the floor, was a pair of Cortina shoes and a leather school bag from the Bata store. Paul had paid for everything with the incentives received from Simon. She'd arranged her passed-down books from Kola in the bag. Now, like her dress, shoes, and her bag, everything around her must be impeccable. She must have good grades, must have good behavior, and must dress well. She quaked at the responsibility.

What if she didn't make good grades? What if she failed her year? What if she ran her mouth? Would everybody still like her? What were the teachers and other pupils like in secondary school? She wasn't liked in primary school by her peers. Students hated her for being a smarty pants. She got bullied throughout. Only the teachers were fond of her and encouraged her. Would that happen in secondary school? Would her only consolation be good grades that smoked her out like a healthy chimney? Would her academic performance be as unbeatable as it was in elementary school? Would she make headway in education? Most of all, would her life be the same again?

She had been searching for answers, and since none were forthcoming, she felt alone. Practically, throughout her five years in primary school, she had had no friends. Dupe and her friends had actually killed her social life. She was now engaged to Dupe's brother. What if Dupe said ugly things about her? What if Akin changed his mind? Definitely, there would be girls like Dupe and her gang in the new school. She couldn't go wild. She had to behave well at all times.

Omotola started to sob again. Then she heard people conversing in the corridor. Her mother's voice was one of them. She might come in. Omotola wiped her face, stood up, and started to put on her uniform. She was zipping up her skirt when Rolake entered, walked toward her daughter, and gently pulled her into her arms, chanting *oriki*, the family praise poetry. Omotola felt uncomfortable. She wriggled to break free, but it didn't work.

"Stop, Mama," she said. "I'm going to be late. I've got to finish getting dressed. And you need to get ready for the farm before your husband crashes in."

Rolake released her from the embrace. "You are right, Sunshine," she said, beaming. "I'm so proud of you, and the whole community is as well."

More fear swept over Omotola's body as she heard "the community." She watched Rolake wipe a tear from her face with the loose part of her wrapper, and she dashed out. She felt sorry for her.

"Bye, Mama!" she called after her.

"Thanks, Sunshine."

The community and the townspeople were her other ordeal. They now saw her as a heroine, a God-sent martyr. Akin's impromptu engagement to her made others, especially mothers, look up to her as a savior of the time. It seemed that the story of her life started to jog the neurons in the brains of the men in Ibata-Itan, and all of a sudden, it seemed that fathers were aware that something good could come out of going to school. After all, Omotola sailed through. And thanks to school, Omotola was enlightened and was going to marry the son-in-law everybody wished for. Where else would they have met?

Fathers just stood and looked at her with affection. And with two weeks left to go of the holiday, a lot of people had crawled into her life without warning. People she hardly knew came to her house to wish her the best of luck. And the talk in town was all about her. Omotola's eardrums beat with "too good to be true," exaggerated, and paradoxical stories that kept coming out of nowhere about her. All eyes were on her, especially those of hopeful mothers telling her she must not fail them.

Girls younger and older than her had been registered in primary school. Many fathers had cut off their daughters' engagements and enrolled them in school. Yinka's father was one of them. He called off the wedding and registered her in school, though the feud was still fresh and unfinished with her suitor's family. Omotola was overwhelmed as she went to say goodbye to her primary school teachers, and Sister Anne said there had been a massive registration of male and female pupils. The poor sister was happy but lamented the inadequacy of classrooms in the school to cope with the demand. She added that they just had to be creative. They couldn't afford to turn parents away and ruin their children's chances of schooling.

Omotola hated the attention. She would have preferred to be invisible. She had to blame Sister Anne, Sister Teresa, and Reverend Mathew a little bit. It was their fault; they shouldn't have speeded things up. For another year, she could have avoided the crowd. She sat down, thinking again. Abruptly, Paul entered, startling her. She gasped.

"I'm sorry to have scared you," Paul said. "I just want to ask if you need any help on your first day in secondary school, and to give you this as pocket money."

Paul held one shilling in his hand.

Lunch money! Since when did Paul ever do that? Probably he wanted the golden child to be solid, Omotola thought. Hesitantly, she stood up and took the money.

She knew Paul wanted closeness, but she wasn't ready to let him into her good graces, and certainly not that morning, of all mornings. Paul seemed to have changed positively. But the changes scared Omotola more than when he was an awful man. Paul had never set foot in their room that she could remember until she was engaged. She had seen the soft side of him, and that was weird. He appeared to have transformed into a loving father overnight. Overnight! Lately, he put forward a refined appearance of a devoted father and husband, and pretended as if he cared. Worst of all, he came in almost every night to ask how her day was and other stuff that was irritating. She didn't want to talk about it. Each time, he tried to groom her like a horse, as if her mother wasn't doing enough of the grooming already. Her language, including body language, must be regal and noble at any given time of the day. And more, she got constant reminders that she was a golden child—the pillar of the Olorunfemi glory lay on her shoulders. She was the child that would liberate the Olorunfemi family from poverty. It was a lot to process, and she hated it.

As the initial startled feeling wore off, she was desperate to get rid of Paul, because the last thing she needed was the image of him in her head all day long. She picked up her school bag, rearranging the books as if she was the only person in the room. Omotola was going about her business, and Paul stood next to her, scratching his head. He gazed wearily around as if looking for something. Omotola watched from the corner of her eye. She could see that he seemed lost and confused.

"Okay, if you need anything, please let me know," Paul said finally.

"All right, Papa, I will let you know," she said with a weak smile. Paul headed to the door. She sighed. A minute later, she could hear him urging the rest of the family out to the farm. She left the bag to take a small mirror from the basket in a corner, checking her appearance. A glowing face stared back at her. A lot had changed from her old look—the long, shapeless gown of the past had been replaced with a tailored white blouse and a short, navy-blue skirt, which highlighted her figure. The uniform was thoroughly coal ironed for almost half a day by her mother. She had white socks and Cortina sandals! All these came from the Bata shop, courtesy of Simon. Omotola looked stunning. Her mood elevated a bit. And for the first time since the morning, she smiled, feeling happy. She hoped the mood would continue and that she would make it through the day without sinking into fear and drowning in a panic attack. She checked her appearance again.

"Omotola, have you a comb I can borrow?" Kola asked at her door.

"Yes," Omotola said, placing the mirror on the small table and taking a comb from the basket.

"Kola, do you think I can cope in secondary school?" she asked, walking up to him to give him the comb.

"Omotola, yes," Kola said with confidence. "Since you started primary school, you got all the prizes on all the subjects without breaking a nail. You finished the syllabus for the whole year before the second month of school. Then, bored, you wanted a new challenge. Last prize day, Sister Anne said that in Great Britain, you would have been in a special school with special attention. Omotola, you'll do fine in secondary school. Trust me; I have faith in you. But now I have to go and get my things ready for school."

"Thanks, Kola, but hurry up. I don't want to be late."

"You are welcome. I promise you won't be late."

Kola left.

Thirty minutes later, without a sign of Kola, Omotola walked to the corridor, agitated. She waited in the hallway for Kola to open his bedroom door, ready for school, hoping he'd continue his pep talk. But Kola was still buried in his room.

"Kola, c'mon…. We have to go," she said impatiently, pointing out the obvious. "The sun is rising on top of the odan tree. It means it's six o'clock, and we need to walk one hour and thirty minutes to get to school. And morning devotion is at eight o'clock. If you don't come out now, we're going to be late and miss it!"

"A few minutes, please."

"C'mon, Kola, we're going to be late."

She hated to be late to school, especially on the first day. First impressions counted most to her. Her first impression should be something to write home about— not a naughty one that would brand her as a problem child.

"A minute more, please, Omotola," Kola said. "I'm arranging my books."

"I'm leaving now, without you. See you in school," she said.

She hissed like a cobra. She had her own problems; lateness should not be part of it. She knew Kola had been playing football again, and spending valuable time running around without arranging or preparing for the beginning of school. Luckily, he was brilliant, and that was what gave him the strength to play around; otherwise, he would have been a failure like some of his lazy friends or back on the farm he hated.

"Wait for me, please! We will take a shortcut," Kola said.

Omotola blocked her ears to Kola's pleading by jamming both hands on them, even though the load of books on her left shoulder hurt. She knew they would be late if she took Kola's pleading into account, and the only way she could make him hurry up was to pretend she was leaving without him.

She advanced toward the front door, and she stopped in her tracks by a strange noise that resembled a car engine. Quickly, she unblocked her hands from her ears, to be sure.

Yes, it was a car engine, all right. *Who brought a car?* She quickly unbolted the entrance door and jumped over the ill-fitting, unstable mud steps constructed by Paul for easy access to the ground.

She almost tumbled with the load of books on her shoulder. Parked under the odan tree was a white Mercedes-Benz. Only one family dared to own expensive cars like that in Ibata-Itan town: Simon Akindele's family. Well, the king technically owned one. And it was supposedly bought by Simon for the king.

A tall, bald man alighted from the car, dressed in a suit, leaving a girl sitting in the front and a young man in the back. Briskly, he approached Omotola to introduce himself as the driver, and his name was Leye. Politely, he took Omotola's bag from her arm. She followed, even though she was afraid of the time machine in front of her, and of the people waiting in the car. As he was putting her bag into the trunk of the car, Akin emerged. She was dazed and almost fainted. And far away, she heard Kola shouting, "Wait for me, Omotola!"

As if in slow motion, she watched the darling paragon of a boy walking towards her. He opened the car door for her. Obediently, she got in. Immediately, he closed the door and traced his way back to his seat from the other side, sitting next to her. It was like a dream.

"Good morning, Omotola. I'm Akin Akindele; it is a pleasure riding with you this morning," he said, smiling, taking her right hand in his.

The nerves in Omotola's right hand seemed to be paralyzed, but she nodded her head to acknowledge that she knew him.

"You look terrific." Akin smiled again.

Omotola opened her mouth to talk, but nothing came out.

Akin started to talk. He said a lot of things, but Omotola failed to register anything. She was used to seeing him as an introvert, a snob. So, where did the gushing talk, like the Esa waterfall, come from? She did her best; she nodded at everything, even though she didn't understand what he said about his holiday in the UK.

Akin was telling Omotola he was sorry to have traveled and never had the chance to meet before school opened. He was supposed to go for only a month, but the plans changed. He wanted to write letters, but his father laughed, and said, "Waste of time, son. The letter will probably arrive at the same time as you get back to Ibata-Itan."

He had come back from Ladden to Ibata-Itan the night before, having arrived in Ladden only the previous day. On getting to Ibata-Itan, he would have come over, but his father objected because it was too late. However, Akin had promised himself that he would see her first thing in the morning and go to school together so that they could chat and get to know each other.

Leye asked Kola to bunk up with Dupe in the front seat. Dupe hissed, angrily moving to give him some space. The car sped off. Bile rose in Omotola's mouth. She wanted to vomit, just as her mother had wanted to on her way to Ajoni-Itan, on her first ride in a time machine, in the company of five other passengers. In fact, Rolake said their driver had to stop twice for three of his passengers to empty their stomachs in the bushes. So, Omotola swallowed hard to suppress the urge of vomiting. She felt better. *Poof*, the urge disappeared. And that raised another problem—she couldn't breathe properly. She battled breathlessness for twenty minutes, like a person about to drown. She gasped as she nodded along, listening to Akin. She could swear that she only gulped air once or twice, like a fish, during the ten-minute drive to school.

Soon the car ground to a halt. Omotola opened the door without waiting for anybody to do it. All the other passengers did the same, except Dupe, who was going to another school. She was moody and hissed constantly at the slightest bump of the car. The driver opened the trunk and handed Omotola her bag and that of Akin.

She took her bag from Leye and hovered near the car, not sure of what to do as a crowd of boys gathered. Some were club members wanting to welcome back their president on his first day back in school. A boy took Akin's school bag. The whole ambiance was too strange for Omotola. She looked away.

Akin touched her gently on the shoulder, and she jumped. He grinned.

"Sorry to startle you. I just want to introduce you to everybody." He said, "Everybody, meet my girlfriend, Omotola. She is starting in our school today. I want you all to know her and be nice to her."

Omotola was mortified. But the guys she'd seen on her recruitment day, including Wole, said, "Welcome to our school, Omotola." All with smiles.

She murmured, "Thank you," compulsorily, wishing to escape, struggling with her school bag, which was slipping down from her shoulder, as if it, too, wanted to escape.

"Would you like to come with us?" Akin paused and added, "If you want, I can carry your bag for you."

Walk with you and let you carry my bag! Side by side, like king and queen? Omotola alone in a pool of boys and the royal person carrying her bag? No, thanks. Not on her first day in school. In Omotola's head, that was showing off—*Cock-a-doodle-doo!*—not cool at all.

Still, Omotola was surprised and touched by the gesture, even though she knew one of the boys would take the bag from Akin before hanging it on his shoulder. But Akin had asked publicly, in front of his boys who worshipped and respected him. That was one side of Akin that was strange to her.

"Thanks, but no," Omotola said swiftly. "I would like to walk around the school compound first."

"Okay, see you later," Akin said, smiling. "And good luck on your first day."

The ground trembled and spun around in her head. Omotola held fast to the luggage on her left shoulder for stability.

"Me, too," Kola said. "Knock them dead!"

"Okay," she managed to say.

* * *

Omotola waited until Akin, Kola, and the troop of boys walked away. Once they were out of sight, she ran breathlessly across the field. She stopped near an oak tree, dropping her bag on the ground. She held her chest with both hands, breathing deeply and continuously, mouth open, until she felt better.

She leaned her back against the tree and spoke to herself aloud. "Twice today, I was almost startled to death. Probably a third time wouldn't be pretty—I'd probably slump on the ground, banging my head on something and winding up with an ugly bump somewhere."

What's scarier: father, fiancé, first time in the damn machine called a car, or the crowd? Omotola thought this over. Come to think of it, she believed Akin was the scariest—in a good way, though! Everything about meeting Akin electrified her!

She was happy she didn't embarrass herself with silly vomiting or passing out for lack of air in the face of her suitor. It might have made him hate her and vanish from her life. She knew she couldn't breathe in the car because she was captured by his love. And she knew she had to work on stabilizing her breath fast. If not, she could pass out sometime soon.

She probably had to ask her mother about tips to deal with the anxiety of love, desire, and of wanting when crazy about someone. She was sure those things might trigger a panic attack. Then she remembered that there wasn't any chemistry between Paul and Rolake, because it had been a marriage without the incense of love. She was bought by Paul—the way Omotola would have been bought by Jacob if she had not been rescued by Akin. Well, so she had to look for alternatives.

The assembly bell rang. She straightened her dress, picked up her school bag, and walked in the direction from which the bell had rung. The open space she'd run across was the assembly field. She queued on the line marked for first-year students. When the field was almost full to the brim with pupils, she saw Akin and his entourage, including Kola, giggling, talking, and walking toward her. They stopped a few meters away. Omotola stood watching him, even though the space between them was congested with students. Their eyes met, and he smiled with an intense stare. Both of Omotola's legs betrayed her. They quaked as if they were about to snap off. She liked Akin a lot—more than she had imagined. The staring was a repeat of what had happened at Esa waterfall. But this time around, she controlled her posture and legs, and she refused to avert her eyes. For reasons not known to her, she didn't want to be the weakest link. It might be a game. No, she realized it was because she wanted to look at him forever. She continued with the game of admiring the love of her life. Just like at Esa waterfall, she wondered what he was thinking. She maintained a steady look to deduce what was on his mind.

"Hi, you must be Omotola," A girl that smelt rich

with a broad smile said, standing next to her.

She turned, baffled. *How on earth did she know my name?* To Omotola's knowledge, she hadn't caused any harm since her few minutes at school, so what was up? "Yes. Can I help you with something?"

"My name is Lanke. I'm in Form Two. And I heard so much about you. Can we be friends?"

Omotola was speechless.

"Us, too," a girl said. "We'd like to be your friend." She and three more girls joined the other two.

Omotola assessed their lot; they were above her caliber. They looked sophisticated, with faint makeup and perfume. She was skeptical of their sincerity. The last time she'd encountered a rich girl, she got dumped. That was Dupe Akindele.

"Okay, that will be nice," she replied finally.

"We'll pick you up for lunch," Lanke said with a giggle, "so we can get to know each other better. So, see you later then. Bye!"

"Okay." Omotola shrugged.

The five left together.

As soon as the girls went to line up in the rows for their classes, she glanced at Akin, but he had turned his eyes away. Omotola absorbed, charmed by his attractiveness.

Chapter Thirty-Nine

At first recess, Akin walked down the corridor of Form Four, looking for Kola. He was flanked at right and left with his disciples and others that just wanted to be seen with him, while the rest of the students lined one side of the corridor, watching. All that Akin needed to do was wave like a king to them, as though they were his subjects, but he hated the whole exhibition. That was why he only promenaded when necessary.

Akin couldn't wish for a better day. The morning had been perfect—he'd sat and spoken to the only girl he'd ever wanted. He would like to talk to Kola about Omotola. He wanted details on Omotola's feelings toward him, and also to tell him about the ride to school arrangement he struck with his father that morning. That arrangement, he'd strongly forced on his father. The two had had a small row the evening before over it.

"Son," Simon had said. *"I know you are excited to see Omotola this night, but let it wait 'til tomorrow. Your driver will pick her up so you can talk to her."*

"That's thoughtful, Dad; it means a lot to me. And it means I've got to wake up earlier, so I won't be late to her house."

"Son, I mean this once she can ride with you," Simon said pointedly. "And the rest, you'll see her in school."

"Why is that, Dad? I've promised to be circumspect around her. I'll never lead her to anything that will jeopardize our future."

"It's not me; it's the culture," Simon said promptly. "There should be distance between suitor and bride before getting married. I'm just going to allow this one time."

"Then the culture won't prevent me from walking to school, would it? I won't need a driver anymore. I'll find my way like my fiancée does." He gave his father a hard look.

Simon softened. "You're stubborn, Akin. I'll see what I can do."

"That's not good enough, Dad. Did you know she got bitten by a snake once? She almost died."

Kola had missed a match with Akin one of those days. The next day in school, Kola looked upset. He said his sister, with whom he walked to school, had got bitten by a snake. While in London, it occurred to Akin that Kola had been talking about Omotola. He had determined that both of them walking to school would stop. He had blamed himself for not once asking Kola how he got to school. And when he finally did before he left for London, Kola confirmed that he traveled to school on foot. Akin had felt bad because, if he wanted to, he could ride ten cars at a time whilst some had to wander through the bush for hours to get to school.

"People walking in the forest get bitten by all sort of things, all the time," Simon had said, hesitantly. "You know what, I think she can ride to school with Dupe in another car. I'll arrange that as of this afternoon, Akin. And I think it's time I meet the girl. But I'll let her and her parents know when."

"Splendid, Dad," Akin said, looking relieved, thinking the arrangement was better than nothing. "Thanks, I really appreciate it."

Akin could have sent an errand boy to Kola like before, asking to meet him downstairs near his car or somewhere else, to avoid the spectators. He just wanted to maintain the special bond between a brother-in-law and suitor. He wanted to show respect because, if memory served him well, as his father and Leye had explained the culture, the bride's family was to be treated like royalty. They needed to be pampered and accorded the utmost respect until the marriage, because the slightest error could call off the engagement. And that was one thing in the world that could run him crazy—he knew that.

Kola's class was empty. Akin changed his mind and decided to search for Omotola instead. He looked down from the balcony of the third flight of stairs to check the lawn. He couldn't be happier when he saw Omotola alone, wandering away from her mates, going toward an oak tree at the far end of the field. He discarded his entourage and went after her.

Omotola sat down facing the school gate.

"Hi, Omotola. You got a minute?" Akin said.

Omotola looked up, blushing, but managed to control her voice. "What are you doing here?"

"I should ask you the same. What makes you as far as North to South with your classmates?" Akin sat next to her, and both faced the street.

"Got sick of their radiant attitudes, giving me more credit than I deserve. I wanted to be by myself."

"Should I go, then," Akin said softly, "even though you've been on my mind all day?"

"Not you, Akin." Omotola blushed. "I have?"

"You bet." Akin's voice was smoky. "So, how is your first day in my school?" Akin took her hand.

"Stupid and annoying, as all are treating me like a queen. I can't stand them anymore. It's probably because I'm used to being invisible … alone." Omotola's voice slowed down. "As a result, I meditate under the trees. You know, it brings fresh air and just gives you peace."

"I wasn't far from your predicament in primary school—I was lonely too."

"Lonely?" Omotola said, looking surprised. "You have boys that will die for you."

"That's not friendship, Omotola. I want a real friend that will like me for me, not for other things. Olu was my best friend and…" Akin hesitated. "What I'm trying is that I was just like you until I started the Lion Club and accepted your brother Kola into the club. He was one hell of a straight arrow. If he hadn't refused my coming to your house many times, I would have met you long ago, my dearest fiancée."

"Kola wouldn't let you come to our house? I thought you…" Omotola stopped short of adding what was in her head—she'd thought him a snob, an arrogant boy.

He must have read her mind. "You thought I was an arrogant, self-centered jerk… I'm not," Akin said, looking bugged. "I warm up to people that have dignity and decency, who believe in making their own destiny, like your brother. He is one upstanding man. I'm happy that befriending him led me to the girl I will love for the rest of my life. Omotola, you mean the world to me. I'll be sitting under the trees from now on, since I'm sure you'll be doing the same, somewhere, looking for peace. And if you want, we will both sit under the trees together."

"Thanks," Omotola said, wondering what had happened to the Akin she used to know.

"Hey, I should be the one to thank you. Good advice is priceless," Akin said, laughing. "Omotola, I forgot to tell you in the morning that another driver will be driving you and Dupe to and from school. And that starts this afternoon; my father made the arrangement. I hope you're okay with it?"

"Really? I'll be going to school in a car?" Omotola turned, and their eyes met.

"Yes," he said, loving the way they were gazing at each other. Memorizing each other… He loved every moment of it. He knew it would be one of their games.

"You have to thank him."

"You can thank him yourself when you see him; he wants to meet you officially. And my best guess is Christmas time. He promised to let your parents know in advance."

"Your father wants to meet me—you mean Mr. Simon Akindele wants to meet me in his house?" Omotola said, turning her face away fast. She stared at her shoe instead.

"Yes, Miss Omotola," he said softly, touching her on the cheek. "He wants to meet his future daughter-in-law."

Omotola was quiet, but her face showed consternation.

"Omotola, you don't have to worry; my father is nice."

The school bell rang to announce that recess was over and all should be back in class. Akin snapped to his feet and helped Omotola up, as she seemed lost. "You okay?"

"Yes, it's just too soon," she said, unevenly. "What about the gatemen, the gate…"

Akin smiled. He knew exactly what Omotola worried about—the gatemen were bitches. Akin winked. "Omotola, trust me, all will be fine."

Chapter Forty

Omotola had never been this happy. Even though Dupe could still be a pain, and Simon might have reservations about his son's choice of a girl, and Paul might still misbehave or be an embarrassment, Jacob was out of her life. And Akin felt the same way as she did—that was all that mattered, all that counted.

Bola dragged Kola to the back of the school immediately after the bell rang to dismiss the students. They both escaped through the hole the students had cut in the barbed wire that protected the school so they could make out during school hours. Bola had never been this happy in her life. Her mother might have a heart attack if she realized who she was in love with. The most important families in Itan Land (Akindele and Ogunlade) would be at war, and all the Itan Land aristocrat families in confusion, but she didn't care.

Well, love is crazy, unexplainable. My mother and the wars are in the future. I live to enjoy now, she told herself. She sighed, enslaving Kola's lips.

Author Biography

Folasade Fasoranti grew up in Nigeria, where she witnessed the pitfalls of polygamous homes and the jealousy and strife created through one man marrying multiple wives. To escape such a fate, she earned a bachelor of arts in education from the Adeyemi Federal University of Education. Eventually, she left Nigeria for a new life with her husband in Brussels, Belgium, where she still resides and is a member of the Brussels Writers' Circle. When not parenting, she can be found hard at work writing novels and poetry.